THE COMPLETE IDIOT'S GUIDE TO

Dehydrating Foods

by Jeanette Hurt

ALPHA

A member of Penguin Group (USA) Inc.

This book is dedicated to Yvonne Miller, Jim Scotton, Richard Leonard, Marie Starsiak, Elsie Stiffler, Sheila Webb, and all the writing and journalism mentors who told me I could write. It's also dedicated to Mr. Bill Picha, super math teacher.

ALPHA BOOKS

Published by Penguin Group (USA) Inc.

Penguin Group (USA) Inc., 375 Hudson Street, New York, New York 10014, USA • Penguin Group (Canada), 90 Eglinton Avenue East, Suite 700, Toronto, Ontario M4P 2Y3, Canada (a division of Pearson Penguin Canada Inc.) • Penguin Books Ltd., 80 Strand, London WC2R 0RL, England • Penguin Ireland, 25 St. Stephen's Green, Dublin 2, Ireland (a division of Penguin Books Ltd.) • Penguin Group (Australia), 250 Camberwell Road, Camberwell, Victoria 3124, Australia (a division of Pearson Australia Group Pty. Ltd.) • Penguin Books India Pvt. Ltd., 11 Community Centre, Panchsheel Park, New Delhi—110 017, India • Penguin Group (NZ), 67 Apollo Drive, Rosedale, North Shore, Auckland 1311, New Zealand (a division of Pearson New Zealand Ltd.) • Penguin Books (South Africa) (Pty.) Ltd., 24 Sturdee Avenue, Rosebank, Johannesburg 2196, South Africa • Penguin Books Ltd., Registered Offices: 80 Strand, London WC2R 0RL, England

Copyright © 2013 by Penguin Group (USA) Inc.

International Standard Book Number: 978-1-61564-226-7

Library of Congress Catalog Card Number: 2012951746

15 14 13   8 7 6 5 4 3 2 1

Interpretation of the printing code: The rightmost number of the first series of numbers is the year of the book's printing; the rightmost number of the second series of numbers is the number of the book's printing. For example, a printing code of 13-1 shows that the first printing occurred in 2013.

Printed in the United States of America

Note: This publication contains the opinions and ideas of its author. It is intended to provide helpful and informative material on the subject matter covered. It is sold with the understanding that the author and publisher are not engaged in rendering professional services in the book. If the reader requires personal assistance or advice, a competent professional should be consulted.

The author and publisher specifically disclaim any responsibility for any liability, loss, or risk, personal or otherwise, which is incurred as a consequence, directly or indirectly, of the use and application of any of the contents of this book.

Most Alpha books are available at special quantity discounts for bulk purchases for sales promotions, premiums, fund-raising, or educational use. Special books, or book excerpts, can also be created to fit specific needs. For details, write: Special Markets, Alpha Books, 375 Hudson Street, New York, NY 10014.

Publisher: *Mike Sanders*

Executive Managing Editor: *Billy Fields*

Acquisitions Editor: *Brook Farling*

Senior Development Editor: *Christy Wagner*

Senior Production Editor: *Janette Lynn*

Cover Designer: *Kurt Owens*

Book Designers: *William Thomas, Rebecca Batchelor*

Indexer: *Johnna VanHoose Dinse*

Layout: *Ayanna Lacey*

Proofreader: *Virginia Vought*

Contents

Introduction

An ancient art. A traditional method. A trendy practice. Dehydrating foods encompasses all three, but for me, drying foods is simply a delicious culinary technique for both cooking and preserving foods.

As a food writer and recipe developer, I've always been open to trying and using new techniques. But I got into food dehydration almost accidentally. Two of my neighbors have been drying enthusiasts for years, but I wasn't initially interested. Why dry food yourself when you can buy it dried? Although I preserved my own salsa, made my own soup stocks, and hadn't purchased a boxed cake recipe in more than a decade, I didn't understand what the dehydrating fuss was all about. That is, until I was gifted with a secondhand dehydrator.

The boyfriend of a dear friend left his food dehydrator at her house after they broke up. Several months later, my friend discovered the dehydrator, and because he didn't want it, she offered it to me. So I said, why not?

After cleaning the dehydrator, I began to tentatively experiment, first drying dill from my garden and savory from my neighbor's garden and then drying mushrooms from the mushroom farmer at a local farmers' market. Slowly, apple by apple, berry by berry, I began branching out into homemade raisins, fruit leathers, and more.

Home-dehydrated pineapple sealed the deal for me. Succulent and tart, my home-dried treats tasted so much fresher and sweeter than the sugar-coated store-bought versions, and my son and I finished the whole batch the morning they came out of the dehydrator. I learned that home-dried foods taste so much better than anything you can get from a grocery store, and I've also found that drying foods myself not only saves me money, but also helps me prevent kitchen waste.

Home food dehydration is exciting, and for me, it's opened a whole new culinary avenue to explore, from crafting my own fruit leathers to making fresh yogurt to experimenting with raw food recipes. There's something so satisfying about doing it myself, using my own palate, to make snacks, crackers, and even soup mixes. Each bite just tastes more perfect than the last.

I hope you'll discover the same sense of excitement and enjoyment as you learn to make dehydrated foods. *The Complete Idiot's Guide to Dehydrating Foods* will have you drying your own strawberries, making your own fruit leathers, and even marinating your own beef jerkies. By the end of this book, you'll be drying like a pro. Happy dehydrating!

How This Book Is Organized

I've organized this book into three parts:

Part 1, The Basics of Dehydrating Foods, introduces you to the history and economic benefits of drying foods and also shows you how to equip your kitchen, shop for ingredients, and stay safe during food prep. It also teaches you some proper techniques to make drying foods a breeze, and it gives you the tools to make all the recipes in this book.

In **Part 2, Simple and Easy Dehydrated Foods,** I share all the basic recipes you need to make dried fruits, vegetables, and herbs, as well as dried dairy products and meat jerkies.

Part 3, Delicious Dried Food Recipes, shows you how to make fruit leathers, fruit and vegetable powders, soups, backpacking recipes, and so much more. It also explains how to incorporate dried foods into recipes, offers recipes for dehydrated pet treats, and even shows you how to make dehydrated gifts for your family and friends.

At the back of the book I've included a glossary of terms, further resources you can use on your dehydrating path, and a list of frequently asked troubleshooting questions.

Extras

I have to admit—I'm a food geek, and I love to share my knowledge and enthusiasm about dried foods. To that end, I've added some interesting tidbits and facts throughout each chapter. Here's what to look for:

CHEF'S CHOICE

In these sidebars, you learn some fun information along with substitutions and variations to recipes.

DEFINITION

Check these sidebars for words that might be unfamiliar to you but are frequently used in dehydrated foods and culinary circles.

DEHYDRATING DON'T

These warning sidebars tell you how to identify snafus and especially how to avoid them.

DRYING TIP

These sidebars share little bits of interesting information.

Acknowledgments

This book could not have been written without the loving support of my husband, Kyle (who is also my photographer); my parents, Tom and Mary Hurt; my sisters, Julie Hurt (and Joe) and Karen Mahan (and Jim); my parents-in-law, Craig Edwards and Sarah Dowhower and Jeanne and Ed Potter; my sister-in-law, Marcie Hutton (and Eric and Ryan); and of course, my son, Quinn. Extra-special thanks goes out to my crew of dehydrating experts who shared their time and knowledge with me: Meagan Bradley and Excalibur Dehydrators, Durham Herzog; Dr. Patricia Kendall of Colorado State University; Barbara Ingham of the University of Wisconsin-Extension; Chef Jeff King of The Sausage Guys; Chef Jimmy MacMillan, executive pastry chef of the University Club of Chicago and JMPurePastry, LLC; Nielsen-Massey Vanillas; and my friends and neighbors: Barb Koenig, Terese Peterson, and Juli Hacker.

Special also thanks goes out to Quinn's babysitters, my nephew Eric Hutton, and Drake Hacker; Bec Loss, my web designer; Damon Brown, my writing goal buddy; Marilyn Allen, my simply fabulous agent; and my wonderful editing staff: senior acquisitions editor Brook Farling, technical editors Steve and Tammy Gangloff, senior development editor Christy Wagner, senior production editor Janette Lynn, and the other talented people at Alpha Books. Lastly, thanks to Doug S.: I never would have gotten into dehydrating if you hadn't broken up with my friend, leaving behind your dehydrator.

Special Thanks to the Technical Reviewers

The Complete Idiot's Guide to Dehydrating Foods was reviewed by experts who double-checked the accuracy of what you'll learn here, to help us ensure that this book gives you everything you need to know about making your own dehydrated foods at home. Special thanks are extended to Steve and Tammy Gangloff of Dehydrate2Store.

Tammy began dehydrating to dry cake fondant for her decorative cakes quicker. From there, she began to explore and experiment more with dehydrating. Soon she was making instructional online videos with the help of her children, Steve, Scott, and September, and her late husband, Jim. Her free informational website for fellow dehydration enthusiasts, Dehydrate2Store.com, is an eclectic source of food dehydration tips, instructional videos, and more.

Trademarks

All terms mentioned in this book that are known to be or are suspected of being trademarks or service marks have been appropriately capitalized. Alpha Books and Penguin Group (USA) Inc. cannot attest to the accuracy of this information. Use of a term in this book should not be regarded as affecting the validity of any trademark or service mark.

The Basics of Dehydrating Foods

Part 1 starts by laying out the steps you need to follow to dehydrate foods deliciously and safely. In these first few chapters, I detail all the techniques, equipment, and safety practices you need to know to successfully dehydrate foods. I also discuss the various methods of dehydration and how to choose a dehydrator to meet your needs.

Part 1 also provides a solid foundation for making all the recipes in this book, and it's important to read it before moving on to the recipes. Learning the techniques and safety practices helps you more easily create the recipes in the later sections. These chapters give you a proper introduction to dehydrating foods, but they also explain the economic benefits of drying foods yourself, and even a bit of the history of drying foods.

All About Dehydrating

In This Chapter

- Why dry your food?
- Economic reasons for drying food
- A brief history of food dehydration
- Ways to dry your food

Sun-dried tomatoes add zip to a bland pasta sauce. A sprinkling of dried chives and dill on top of a baked potato tastes of spring—in the middle of winter. Dried pineapple bits turn a basic trail mix into a bit of backpacking nirvana.

The versatility of dried foods is practically endless, and you probably already use dehydrated foods when you cook. But there's a big flavor difference between commercially prepared dried foods and foods you've dried yourself in your own dehydrator. Simply put, a homemade raisin is juicier and tastier than anything you can find in a box on the grocery store shelf. Not to mention, there's a certain satisfaction you get when you or your loved ones eat food you dehydrated yourself.

When you begin to dry the mint from your garden, make homemade fruit leather, or experiment with homemade beef jerky, you join the legions of home bread bakers, canning enthusiasts, and other home chefs who are rediscovering the joys of doing it yourself. But make no mistake—today's home dehydration methods are not like your grandma's, and it's easier than ever to dry foods yourself.

In this chapter, we explore some of the main reasons why you'll want to start dehydrating food, and I also share some of the economic and other benefits I've discovered. Because food dehydration is an ancient method of food preparation, I share some of its rich history, too.

Why Dehydrate?

When my neighbors Terese and Barb first told me they were into food *dehydration*, I gave them a quizzical look. Why dehydrate apples if you can go around the corner to the grocery store and buy a bag of *dried* apples? With the plethora of dried foods available, even organic varieties, why would someone go to the trouble of doing it at home?

I didn't understand—until another friend offered me her ex-boyfriend's *dehydrator*. He had broken up with her, but he had forgotten to take his dehydrator with him when he left, and she wanted nothing to do with the memories it brought up, so I said I'd take it. Terese saw me carrying in the dehydrator from my garage and promptly handed me a big bunch of savory from her garden to get started. Soon, the aroma of that tangy, minty herb filled my house, and when I crumbled a few of the dried stalks into my breakfast casserole the next morning, I was hooked.

> **DEFINITION**
>
> In this book, I use the terms **dehydrate** and **dry** interchangeably. Both foods have had the moisture removed after heat is applied via evaporation. A **dehydrator** is an appliance that produces heat to dry foods. It's similar to an oven, but produces a lower-temperature heat. There's a big difference between dehydrated or dried and *freeze-dried* foods. Freeze-drying is a completely different method of removing water from food. The food is quickly frozen and then placed in a strong vacuum that sucks out the moisture.

Dehydrating Is Easy

One of the big reasons to dehydrate your own foods is because it's easy. Unlike other methods of food preservation, such as canning, you don't have to sterilize a bunch of jars and boil them for hours. You prep the food, put it in the dehydrator, turn on the dehydrator, and you're good to go. And except for periodically checking your foods to see that they're drying evenly, you can basically set the dehydrator and forget about it until the machine turns off or you turn it off. The dehydrator does all the work for you, and you don't have to babysit it.

What's more, all you need to get started is a home food dehydrator and perhaps some sheets of parchment paper if you'd like to make fruit or vegetable leathers. Dehydrating doesn't require a lot of equipment, nor is the equipment difficult to use.

Dehydrated Food Tastes Better

There's nothing wrong with commercially dried raisins or apples, but when you make your own dehydrated foods, starting with the freshest foods available, the results simply taste better. Even with expiration dates on the packages, you have no real idea when the food was harvested or dried. But when you dry the apples you picked in your Aunt Gabby's orchard last weekend, you know how fresh they are. Nothing beats the flavor of freshly dried foods.

What's more, many fruits that are processed in factories are "juiced" first. The juice is sold, and the nutrient-deprived food casings are dried and sold as "dehydrated fruits." That doesn't sound appetizing!

When dehydrating foods yourself, you can use the best-tasting foods you can find, and whenever you start with a higher-quality product, the end result packs in so much more flavor.

You Control the Sugar and Additives

Most commercially dried fruits are laden with sugars—high-fructose corn syrup, sugar, sucralose, … you name it, they're most often packed with sugar, in all its various forms. And if you're like me, you might think fruits taste sweet enough without being coated in sugar. When you dehydrate your own food, you can use as little or as much sugar as you want. You, and your taste buds, control the sweetness.

You also control whether you add sulfur or not. Manufacturers often add *sulfur* to commercially dried fruits that have a tendency to darken in color. The sulfur prevents *oxidation* and spoilage. If you're allergic to sulfur, you don't have to add it when you dry the foods yourself.

DEFINITION

Some fruits and vegetables darken or turn brown when the flesh is exposed to oxygen, especially during dehydration. This process is called **oxidation. Sulfur** is a chemical you can add to fruits to prevent oxidation and spoilage. The chemical compound of sulfur used to prevent oxidation in commercially produced dried fruits is sulfur dioxide, which is a toxic gas. Sulfur bisulfide is the recommended chemical compound for home-drying methods.

Dehydrating Saves You Money

Dried cherries, often packed with sugar, can cost as much as $16 a pound. If you purchased the same cherries in bulk at a farmers' market, the cost could be half as much, and unlike with canning and other food-preservation methods, you don't have to labor over your end product when you dehydrate them.

Plus, some commercially dried foods are quite expensive. Commercially prepared fruit leathers, which mostly are apple-based, can cost about $2 per small snack. When you make your own fruit leathers from applesauce you made yourself, it costs much, much less—and it tastes so much better! The same can be said for homemade beef jerkies, dried soup mixes, and many other foods.

But the economic benefits don't stop there. Dehydrating can also prevent waste and save you money at the same time. The average American wastes more than $400 worth of produce every year, simply because the food goes bad in the refrigerator. If you have a dehydrator, you don't have to contribute to this waste.

Made a tuna salad and have a bunch of celery leftover? Chop it up and dehydrate it. Leftover onion from onion soup? Dehydrate it. Extra bushel of apples on sale at the farmers' market? Dehydrate it. I'm a big fan of dehydrating celery because I've almost never used an entire bunch of celery before it's gone bad in my refrigerator. Durham Herzog, a well-known home-dehydrating enthusiast from Wisconsin, uses her dehydrator anytime she has leftover ripe fruits and veggies she can't eat before they'd start to rot. "It's saved me a lot of money over the years," Herzog says.

 DRYING TIP

Leftover frozen and canned vegetables and fruits are just as easy to dehydrate as fresh produce.

Dehydrating leftover produce can save you a last-minute trip to the grocery store if your recipe calls for onions, celery, or carrots, for example, and you don't have any in your refrigerator. Having a dehydrated stash in your pantry saves you both gas and food money.

You don't need a large amount of vegetables, fruits, or meats to dehydrate them. What to do with those bits of dried leftover produce? Grind them into powdered fruits and vegetables, and add them to soups and smoothies for a flavor and nutritional punch. (For more about making your own produce powders, turn to Chapter 12.) Gena Hamshaw, a clinical nutritionist and author of the Choosing Raw blog (choosingraw. com), takes this one step further and suggests using nuts left over when making nut milks and pulp left over when making fresh fruit and vegetable juices to make raw food breads and crackers in her dehydrator.

I've also found that when my garden has a surplus of dill, rhubarb, or zucchini, drying the foods actually helps me use them. Otherwise, I end up giving away my fresh produce—or in the case of my mint that tends to grow wild every year, I end up pulling it out and throwing it on compost pile. With my dehydrator, the problem of too much mint is solved!

You Can Eat Locally—All Year Long

There are many advantages to eating locally, from expending less energy and money to transport the food, to benefiting the local economy, but one of the biggest reasons to eat locally is that locally grown food contains more nutrients. Fresh food loses more nutrients the longer it has to travel to get to your kitchen. When you eat locally, your food doesn't have to travel as far to get to you, so it retains more of its vitamins and minerals. Drying your own fruits and vegetables allows you to be a locavore and eat locally grown produce year-round, even if you live somewhere that has long, cold winters.

When winter comes, I often long for a taste of summer, wishing I had that rhubarb or zucchini that had overtaken my garden the previous summer. Before I had my dehydrator, I would give into my longing and buy produce grown and trucked in from South America. However, since I've had my dehydrator, I have that dried summer goodness at my fingertips, no matter the month on the calendar.

Dehydrating Throughout History

Food drying goes back to ancient times. In fact, food drying—along with freezing—was one of the earliest forms of food preservation. Evidence suggests dried foods were common in the Middle East and Asia as early as 12000 B.C.E.

According to Dr. Brian A. Nummer, of the National Center for Home Food Preservation, "The astonishing fact about food preservation is that it permeated every culture at nearly every moment in time. To survive, ancient man had to harness nature. In frozen climates, he froze seal meat on the ice. In tropical climates, he dried foods in the sun." Early methods of food preservation, Nummer says, enabled humans to stay in one place and develop communities, without having to travel around to find fresh food.

The earliest methods of drying foods were pretty simple. Fruits and vegetables were dried by the sun—some right out on the vines, others picked before drying. Grains were also dried, and some of the earliest recorded instances of drying grains were found in Egypt. Archaeologists also recently discovered the earliest grain silos in Dhra, Jordan. Those silos, which date back 11,000 years, contained remnants of barley and wheat.

One of the earliest recorded mentions of dried fruit was found on clay tablets dating to 1700 B.C.E. The slabs, which were found in ancient Babylonia, were written in Akkadian and held recipes for drying dates, figs, apples, and grapes along with recipes for adding dried fruit to bread.

Grape cultivation—and raisins—started in the fourth century B.C.E., and the Phoenicians and the Egyptians spread their cultivation, sun-drying them and then storing them in jars and baking them in breads with honey and sometimes eggs.

The Romans were big on all sorts of dried foods, but they were especially sweet on dried fruits, including raisins and figs. Raisins were a common component to meals, and figs were often rubbed with spices like cumin, anise, and fennel seeds. Ancient instructions for housekeepers in 100 B.C.E. detailed "She must keep a supply of cooked food on hand for you and the servants … she must have a large store of dried pears, figs, and raisins."

The Romans not only dried their foods out in the sun, but they also combined drying with salting. The ancient Phoenicians, from at least 1250 B.C.E., also preserved fish by laying gutted, dried fish in layers of salt.

CHEF'S CHOICE

Salt was so important that Roman soldiers received a *salarium* of salt as payment. That's where our word *salary* comes from.

Smoking was another method often combined with drying for food preservation for fish and meats, especially sausages and hams. Fermentation also was sometimes combined with dehydration. Grains were dried and fermented in silos, but other foods were fermented as well, often through the process of burial in the ground. For example, in Iceland, poisonous shark meat was buried, which not only dried it out but also removed the toxins. Cheeses, fruits, and vegetables also were buried and aged in this manner.

Over time, food dehydration became more complex. In the Middle Ages, special buildings called *still houses* were built to dry fruits, vegetables, and herbs. Food was laid out to dry inside these houses, and fires were built to enhance the process.

Dried foods, especially fish, were important in feeding not just armies, but also the crews of explorers' ships. Explorers of the New World introduced Europeans to other foods that could be dried—most notably, potatoes. And Native Americans in the New World introduced them to *pemmican*, or dried buffalo meat mixed with herbs and fruits.

Dried foods helped the pioneers explore—and settle—America. They dried foods to sustain themselves during long winters, and the dried foods allowed them to travel westward without going hungry.

In the 1800s, food preservation became more complex with the advent of canning, and the Industrial Revolution led to large-scale food production and packaging, which affected dried foods, too. But it wasn't really until the twentieth century that food drying moved out of the home and into factories. Feeding armies in both world wars, but especially World War II, meant a lot of canned and dried foods.

CHEF'S CHOICE

The first large-scale production of dried potatoes happened in 1942. Food processor John Richard "Jack" Simplot won a government contract to supply dried potatoes to the armed forces, and by 1945, he had produced 33 million pounds of dried potatoes. This development led to what we now know as boxed mashed potatoes.

Renewed interest in home dehydration began in the 1970s, with the health food movement. The very first home food dehydrators made their debut in the 1970s, too. Food dehydration enthusiasm has accelerated in recent years, as the local foodies and do-it-yourselfers have discovered the joys of dehydrating food at home. Vegans and raw foodists also have embraced this ancient art.

The Different Methods of Dehydration

There are three basic methods of drying foods—appliance-enhanced drying, sun-drying, and room-drying—and each has advantages and disadvantages.

Appliance Dehydration

You can dehydrate foods using a dehydrator, your oven, your microwave, or even a stovetop dehydrator. An electric dehydrator is the most versatile appliance for drying foods. You can use it year-round in a variety of climates, and it dries food the fastest.

Electric dehydrators are designed to dry food using an electric heat source, usually a coil. Basic dehydrators are simply stackable drying racks with a coil heat source or fan in the bottom or back. Or they may be a rectangular dryer with an external chamber with a heat source and convection fan. Whatever model you choose, a dehydrator can dry foods 24 hours a day, and you don't have to watch it closely as it works. You prep the food, slip it on the drying racks, turn on the dehydrator, and walk away. The dehydrator dries the food with minimal fuss and minimal energy expenditure. (I talk more about choosing a dehydrator that's right for you in Chapter 2.)

An oven, especially one with a convection fan, is the next best choice for dehydrating. The challenge with oven-drying is that it takes two or three times longer than drying in a dehydrator, and you have to watch the food more carefully and rotate it because it doesn't dry as evenly in the oven as it would in a dehydrator. Some fruits, like plums and cherries, can turn out more brittle when oven dried. Sulfured fruits should never be dried in an oven.

DEHYDRATING DON'T

Never dry sulfured fruits in your oven. Sulfur dioxide fumes created by the oven's higher temperatures can be noxious.

Your oven can be a good choice for dehydrating meat jerkies, however, especially if your dehydrator doesn't have a temperature gauge. For safety, it's recommended that all meat jerkies be finished off in an oven. (More on that in Chapter 3.)

You can use your microwave to dehydrate foods, especially herbs and flowers, but the main problem with dehydrating in a microwave is that most fruits, vegetables, and meats cook, at least partially, before they're completely dried. Dehydrating in a microwave can be hit or miss with most other foods, and it's not recommended.

Before electric food dehydrators were invented, people used to dehydrate foods in stovetop dehydrators. They're not manufactured anymore, but you can find some antiques on eBay. These were used in the days when wood-burning stoves were in vogue, and they're really not compatible with today's stoves, especially because the wood frames on some of them could be a fire hazard. I've never tried this method, and I don't endorse it.

Sun-Drying

There are two basic ways to sun-dry foods: dry them right in the sun or use a solar-hybrid dryer to enhance the sun's natural rays.

Sun-drying is a natural, low-cost way to dry foods, and it's been done for centuries. All you need are drying trays, protective netting to prevent bugs from eating your foods as they dry, and the sun. The main drawback, however, is that to really dry your foods safely and effectively, you need to be in an area that has a dry climate, with temperatures regularly in the 90s or 100s. It's also preferred that you don't have a lot of pollution because that could affect the purity of your sun-drying.

Not all types of foods can be safely dried in the sun. Most fruits, especially those with high sugar and acid levels, can be sun-dried. Vegetables can be dried, especially if the temperatures soar above 100°F. Meats and fish cannot be safely dried in the sun, unless they're packed with such high levels of salt and preservatives that they would basically be inedible. With sun-drying, you need to turn the fruits or vegetables three or four times a day, and it takes days, not hours, to dry them.

Solar food dryers are like electric food dehydrators, except they use the sun's rays to dry the foods instead of electricity. Many of them look like wooden cabinets, lined with aluminum foil to reflect the rays onto the foods, and some have a backup electric heat source. They dry foods faster than pure sun-drying alone, but they're not as fast as electric dehydrators. They also take up a lot more space than regular dehydrators, and you typically have to assemble them yourself.

Room-Drying

Room-drying, like solar-drying, has been done for centuries. Fruits and vegetables can be dried using this method, but like microwave drying, it's most effective for herbs and flowers. The room in question must be 80°F or above, very low in humidity, and as dust free as possible.

Like microwave-drying, room-drying can be hit or miss, and like sun-drying, it can take days, not hours. Even if you cover the food with bags or netting, the food will probably still get some dust on it. And the main problem with this method is that there's a much bigger chance for spoilage.

Although I'm not a big fan of room dehydration, it can be a fun method to use for bouquets, herb sachets, and the leftover palms from Palm Sunday.

The Least You Need to Know

- Drying your own foods is easy, and home-dried foods taste better—and contain more nutrients—than commercially prepared dried foods.
- Home-drying your fruits and vegetables can prevent waste and save you money.
- All cultures, since the beginning of civilization, have dried food to preserve it.
- There are three basic methods of dehydration—by appliance, sun-drying, or room-drying.
- Oven-drying and microwave-drying are not as effective nor as easy as using an electric dehydrator.

The Dehydrator's Kitchen

In This Chapter

- Shopping for a dehydrator
- Keeping your dehydrator clean
- Dehydrating equipment you'll want
- The importance of quality storage supplies
- What food should you dry?

It doesn't take a lot of equipment to begin your adventures in home drying. All you need is a dehydrator and some food-storage supplies, and you're good to go. But there are a lot of different dehydrators on the market, and depending on your needs and level of interest, it may be hard to choose one that's right for you.

Never fear. In this chapter, I discuss the basic features offered in different dehydrators so you can choose one that best suits your needs. After you select your dehydrator, you also need to know how to keep it clean, so that's another topic I go over.

I also discuss other dehydrator-specific equipment you might want to make dehydrating easier, and I explain what storage supplies you might need, too. Lastly, I discuss food shopping with home dehydrating in mind.

Choosing the Right Dehydrator for You

Home dehydrators come in two basic styles: round stackable dehydrators and cabinet-style box dehydrators.

Round, Stackable Dehydrators

A basic, stackable, no-frills dehydrator is just that: a plastic dehydrator with an electric coil on the bottom. The heat rises to the top, dehydrating the food in the trays stacked above it, and exits through the holes at the top. This type of dehydrator doesn't have a timer or thermostat. You'll have to use a thermometer to check its temperature, and although it's a little bit more of a hassle for dehydrating produce, it's a definite no-no for making meat jerkies.

This inexpensive dehydrator can dry more or less food, simply by stacking on more plastic trays.
(Photo by Kyle Edwards)

 DEHYDRATING DON'T

Meats must be dehydrated at a temperature of at least 145°F. It's not safe to dry meats at any lower temperatures, so if your dehydrator doesn't get that hot, make your meat jerkies in your oven instead.

A basic, stackable unit starts out at about $30 to $40, whereas a box-style dehydrator typically costs between $100 and $200. More sophisticated dehydrators and commercial styles cost anywhere from $300 to $2,000. The cheaper units don't have any accessories, and their heating wattage is lower than those of more expensive models.

My very first dehydrator was an inexpensive stackable model, and it did the job just fine. But I did two things to make the process smoother.

The first was to test my dehydrator's temperature, without any food in it. I learned its temperature hovered in the 130°F to 135°F range. This was perfect for dehydrating fruits and vegetables, but it was a bit high for herbs, which should be dried at 90°F. To compensate, when I dried herbs, I checked them every 1 or 2 hours to see how they were doing. You can also rotate the trays if you so desire.

Checking the dried foods in this type of dehydrator is also important because some layers will dry more quickly than others. Just set a timer to go off every 2 hours to remind you to check them.

This isn't practical when drying foods overnight, though. To compensate for this, I used a timer—the kind you might use to have your lights turn on when you're on vacation—and set it to turn off at the appropriate time so I could still get my beauty sleep. The thing to note, though, is that as soon as the dehydrator is turned off, moisture can re-enter the dried foods. It's best to be there to turn it off or to take out the food when the dehydrator turns off.

I was quite happy dehydrating fruits and vegetables in this dehydrator. Because of the safety concerns about drying meats at too low a temperature, I didn't use it to dry meats. I used my oven for making jerkies instead.

Cabinet-Style Box Dehydrators

My world changed when I got my Excalibur cabinet-style dehydrator. Not only did it have a temperature-controlled thermostat, but it also had a built-in timer. And because it had a convection fan, my foods dried more evenly, across the board, and more quickly.

It was easier to use, too, so I ventured into other areas of dehydration—like making raw food crackers—and I switched to making jerkies in my dehydrator. Whereas dehydrating times were more hit or miss in my hand-me-down stackable dehydrator, they were more exact in my box dehydrator.

Because its convection fan is in the back of the dehydrator, this allows for a much more effective method of air flow than a dehydrator with a fan in the bottom. The fan is a big component of how fast or evenly food dehydrates.

If you decide to purchase this type of dehydrator, you'll want to evaluate how often you'll use it and what volume of foods you'll dehydrate. I have a five-tray version, which meets all my home-drying needs, but I know other home dehydrating enthusiasts and raw foodists who prefer using a nine-tray dehydrator. I even know of some big enthusiasts who have multiple dehydrators!

This cabinet-style dehydrator has a fan, thermostat, and timer.
(Photo by Kyle Edwards)

I should mention that you can find fancy stackable dehydrators, with a fan, thermostat, and timer. You don't have to go more upscale just with a cabinet style.

If you're just starting out, my advice is to start small and start slow. If you're only going to make a few fruit leathers or dry the dill that's taken over your garden, an inexpensive dehydrator works just fine. But if you think this is something you're going to do frequently, or you think you really would appreciate having a timer, thermostat, and fan, then go with a more expensive unit. For a good dehydrator, you shouldn't have to spend more than $100 to $200, and it should last you a long time.

And if beef jerky is your thing, investing in a dehydrator with temperature controls is a must. You really can't safely dehydrate meats at a lower temperature, and you're going to want to be sure the dehydrator is hot enough to kill the bacteria in the meat as it dries.

CHEF'S CHOICE

The University of Wisconsin Extension Office did a study on dehydrators and temperature controls. The only two brands they recommend for making meat jerky are Excalibur and Gardenmaster.

Cleaning Your Dehydrator

Cleaning your dehydrator is usually very simple. Most dehydrator trays and mesh inserts are dishwasher safe, but it's important to read your specific dehydrator's owner's manual to be sure. Because the trays and inserts are plastic, I would wash them in the upper dishwasher rack only. (Some of my plastic utensils and bowls have melted in the bottom rack.) It's also pretty easy to wash your dehydrator trays and inserts by hand, using hot water and mild soap. If you do make jerky, I would include a wipe-down with bleach water, too.

Sometimes, the interior of your dehydrator gets dirty, especially if it's a stackable unit. Fruit or vegetable drippings can goop it up. Mild detergent, mixed with water, and a damp sponge can usually clean up any mess you might encounter.

Even if your trays look perfectly clean after you've dehydrated something, it's a good idea to rinse them with hot water and a little bit of detergent anyway. You can let them air-dry or wipe them with a clean cloth.

Other Handy Equipment to Have

You don't need much other special equipment beyond your dehydrator, but the following sections give you a few suggestions for helpful tools and equipment you might want.

Tray Liners

If you want to make fruit or vegetable leathers, you'll need something to line the dehydrator trays. Otherwise, the purée would drip through and cake on the trays—what a mess!

Most dehydrator manufacturers also sell silicone liners especially for making leathers that exactly fit your dehydrator's trays. These inserts cost about $5 to $10 each, so they're not a bad investment if you plan to make a lot of leathers. They're also great when you're dehydrating finely diced vegetables or fruit, like shallots and garlic.

If you're not sure how much leather you're going to make or don't want to invest in the liners, you can use silicone baking mats instead, if they fit your dehydrator trays. Or you can line your trays with plastic wrap or parchment paper.

Mandoline

If you're planning on chopping a lot of fruits and vegetables, a *mandoline* is a handy tool to have. Mandolines help you cut very uniform slices, more quickly than using a knife. Mandolines are perfect for creating evenly sliced zucchini, potatoes, carrots, and more.

A basic mandoline typically costs about $20 or more. You can find them at most kitchen supply stores and home stores.

DEFINITION

A **mandoline** is a kitchen tool used for slicing. It has two parallel working surfaces you can adjust for different widths of cuts. As you slice the food along one of the surfaces, it comes in contact with a sharp blade, which cuts the food.

Vacuum Sealer

If you plan on dehydrating a lot of foods, you'll need a reliable method for long-term storage. Air, especially oxygen, can get in (and is already present in) regular zipper-lock plastic bags and even glass jars and cause your dried foods to go stale more quickly. Therefore, a vacuum sealer might be a smart investment.

A good vacuum sealer costs anywhere from $50 to $200 (some go even higher, into the $400s), and I've found it handy not just for dried foods, but also frozen foods because it prevents freezer burn.

Jerky Gun

For making meat jerkies, you might want to invest in a jerky gun. A jerky gun looks like a pastry or dough shooter, but it's made especially for meats.

Some dehydrating supply websites and most sausage-making supply websites sell them, but you can also find them at some outdoor hunting and fishing–type stores. They cost about $15 to $25, and they allow you to make finer, more evenly seasoned pieces of jerky than simply cutting the meat in strips.

Storage Supplies

You don't need any special equipment to store dried foods. As mentioned earlier, a vacuum sealer can be handy, and the bags or jars that come with it offer clean, air-tight containers.

Good-quality plastic bags that zip close are another option, especially for shorter-term storage. They are the simplest and easiest storage system to use, but they, along with the plastic baggies for a vacuum sealer, aren't really eco-friendly.

The other problem with plastic bags is that if you don't eat the foods relatively quickly, air will get to them. For example, if you dry banana slices until they're crisp and then place them in a plastic bag without removing the air from the bag, the bananas will start to absorb moisture from the air, and they'll get so sticky they'll stick together. This can also create bacterial contamination concerns. (More on this in Chapter 3.)

Nothing beats jar storage. Clean, sterilized canning jars work quite well for storing all sorts of dried foods. But you can also use clean storage jars of any type. When I dry herbs, I use sanitized glass spice jars. They fit perfectly into my spice shelf. Many vacuum storage systems work with special jars, sucking out all the air. This is especially nice when you're storing vegetables and fruits, which go bad much more quickly in jars that aren't vacuum sealed.

The main thing to keep in mind when storing dehydrated foods is that air and light can cause them to deteriorate faster. Obviously, you want to do all you can avoid that. You also want to avoid heat, rodents, bugs, and of course, moisture. To avoid heat, store dried foods in a cool place. To keep the pests away, put the sealed bags or jars inside Mylar bags. Mylar bags can't be broken into, and they also keep out all light. To avoid oxygen, vacuum seal your bags or jars.

Picking Perfect Ingredients

One of the reasons the fruits and vegetables I dehydrate myself taste so much better than anything I can buy commercially dried is because I start with high-quality fresh ingredients. My old cooking mentor, Jill Prescott, always stressed the importance of starting with high-quality ingredients. You can always ruin good ingredients by bad cooking, but good cooking can never elevate inferior ingredients.

> **DRYING TIP**
>
> If you start with beautiful fresh foods, you'll end up with beautiful dried foods. The fresher and more delicious something tastes, the better it will taste when it's dehydrated.

Dehydrating concentrates the flavors of the foods you begin with. A sweet carrot, for example, tastes even sweeter when it's dried. A mouth-puckering lime tastes even more puckering when it's dehydrated. When water is removed from foods, their underlying flavors are intensified.

Most of the fruits and vegetables I dry are organic and local ingredients I've purchased directly from a farmer at a local farmers' market or produce a friend or I have grown. The farther a fruit or vegetable has to travel to reach you, the more nutrients—and taste—gets lost along the way.

Although I buy local as much as I can, some foods I love to dry aren't grown in Wisconsin, where I live. I can't dry locally grown mangoes or pineapple or bananas, and my son loves these fruits dried. So for these, I try to go organic, but when I can't get organic, I go with what looks and smells the freshest.

I make it a point to get to know the clerks at all the grocery stores where I shop. Befriending your produce manager and butcher is one of the best decisions you can make as a shopper. If you're friendly and ask questions, they'll remember you, and when they see you, they'll likely tell you what's new or fresh or just came in. The same goes for farmers at your local farmers' market.

Beyond befriending your grocery or farmers' market employees, use your senses when you shop. Look for the best-looking, unbruised fruits. Smell the melons. Pick through the bin of peppers to get the freshest-looking ones you can find. Use your eyes, your fingers, and your nose to lead you to the best ingredients.

With meats, I also try to buy local and organic. There's a great stand-alone butcher in my neighborhood. I like to talk to him and learn which farmers he buys his meats from. Because the meats are local, they're fresher, not frozen or refrozen, and taste better when I make homemade jerkies.

DEHYDRATING DON'T

Just because something is labeled organic or local doesn't mean it's good. If something looks bad, chances are, it will taste bad as well. Use your common sense when shopping for ingredients, and don't buy something just because it's on sale.

I don't spend hours hovering over the banana bin, trying to select the most perfect bananas to dry. I buy quality, but I don't labor over the selection. I also don't overspend. If I can't afford certain vegetables or fruits—especially when they're out of season—I don't buy them. And sometimes, if the organic or local costs way too much for my designated budget, I make do with the conventional.

Food preparation, especially dehydration, should be fun, and selecting the foods you want to dry should be enjoyable, too. Just do your best to select the highest-quality foods you can afford, and don't sweat the rest.

The Least You Need to Know

- Food dehydrators come as either a round, stackable unit or a cabinet-style unit.
- An inexpensive dehydrator works fine for produce and herbs, but only use a dehydrator with a thermostat for drying jerky.
- You don't need a lot of extra equipment to dehydrate food. Silicone mats for making fruit leather and a mandoline are a good investment.
- The easiest way to store dried foods for the short term is to use zipper-lock plastic bags. For longer-term storage, vacuum sealed is the way to go.
- Starting with good-quality fresh food results in good-quality dehydrated food.

Food Safety and Storage

In This Chapter

- Kitchen sanitation and safety
- Good food-handling techniques
- Safe pretreatment practices
- Proper packaging

I can't emphasize enough the importance of kitchen safety and sanitation. Proper sanitation becomes even more of a priority when you're preserving food, and that's especially true when you're drying meats. Incorrect handling of raw meat can promote bacterial growth quickly and all too easily.

Food dehydration involves some kitchen prep work, and much of that involves the use of knives and other sharp utensils, increasing the possibility for making mistakes. Fortunately, basic sanitation and safety practices are easy to learn and follow, and they do prevent most problems.

In this chapter, I show you how to keep everything clean and sanitized and explain how to pretreat your foods to prevent bacterial growth. And so all your dehydrated bounty lasts until you're ready to eat it, we take a look at how you should package and store your dehydrated foods.

The Importance of Sanitation

Kitchen sanitation is nothing to take lightly, and it gets even more important when you're preserving food—and again, especially meats. We've all heard of the food poisoning outbreaks caused when food handlers forget to wash their hands or clean their equipment and the recalls of everything from peanut butter to spinach. But sometimes we forget, in the midst of cooking dinner or prepping ingredients, to follow basic kitchen hygiene.

Fortunately, basic food sanitation and safety isn't difficult. The following guidelines are easy to practice and can help you stay safe.

Wash Your Hands

Food safety starts with clean hands. If you wash your hands, they won't be covered with harmful bacteria, and the foods you touch won't be contaminated either.

How easy is it for one little bit of bacteria to cause infection? A friend of mine suffered food poisoning simply because, while handling raw chicken, she wiped the back of her hand on her face. It's that easy to get sick. But if you remember to wash your hands, it's also that easy to prevent contamination and illness.

Before you even take the food out of your shopping bags to put away or to begin the dehydration process, stop and wash your hands. This very basic hygiene rule will prevent a lot of contamination.

This rule is vitally important to follow when you handle raw meat while making jerky. If you touch raw meat, stop. Before you do anything else, wash your hands. Use hot water and soap, and scrub them for at least 15 seconds or the time it takes you to sing the first stanza of "Happy Birthday." Dry your hands on a clean towel before continuing.

> **CHEF'S CHOICE**
>
> Some people prefer to wear gloves when handling meat. But you're not invincible when wearing them. It's no good to use gloves to handle your meat and then do something else while still wearing them. If you wear gloves when handling raw meat, remove them when you're done, and before you touch or do anything else, throw away the gloves and wash and dry your hands. Be sure the gloves you use are food grade. And latex-free gloves may be a good bet in case you share your sausage with anyone who has a latex allergy.

Keep Your Kitchen Clean

Your kitchen needs to be clean, too. It's a good idea to scrub your countertops before you even take your foods out of their containers. Your counters need to be clear of stains and crumbs, too, which could contaminate your foods.

When making jerkies and other dried meat products, there's a chance you could spill some of the meat somewhere along the way, so always wash down your whole counter with soap and water—before and *after* making the meats. Afterward, rinse or wipe them with a mixture of 1 part bleach to 10 parts water. Do the same for your sink.

> **DRYING TIP**
>
> Keep a small spray bottle of bleach in your kitchen to clean your counters. You can use it to disinfect your cutting boards, knives, and sink, too.

You also need to clean your cutting boards with bleach. Some people like to keep one or two cutting boards reserved just for cutting meat. After you use your cutting board—whether for meat or produce—clean it. If you chopped meat on your board, you also need to clean it (and then the sink) with a bleach mixture. "The sink is the area people need to be most reminded to clean," says Patricia Kendall, professor of nutrition and food science at Colorado State University.

After you clean your kitchen and equipment, clean your towels, apron, and sponges, too. You don't want them to recontaminate an area when you're cleaning it. You can clean your sponges by putting them in your dishwasher or microwaving them on high for 1 minute.

Good Hygiene Tips

Restrain your hair while you're working in the kitchen. Whether you opt to wear a hairnet, don your favorite team's baseball cap, or pull it up in a ponytail, be sure there's no way your hair can fall into your food.

Also remove your rings before you start prepping the foods. That way, they won't be contaminated by food particles, and you also won't have to worry about them getting caught on anything in the kitchen.

If you have long fingernails, keep a nailbrush next to your kitchen sink to scrub out any food or crumbs that could get trapped. And of course, remember to regularly wash that brush with hot water, soap, and bleach.

Lastly, consider the footwear you'll be wearing when you're dehydrating foods. While you're peeling, chopping, and slicing three bushels of apples or tomatoes, you'll want to wear comfortable, closed-toe shoes. The closed-toe rule is important because you don't want any knives that accidentally fall to cut your feet. Comfortable gym shoes are a good choice.

Everything Within Reach

After you've cleaned your kitchen, but before you take out your foods and get started, set up your kitchen so it's easy to work in. Take out all the equipment you need for each step, and set it up before you get started so you won't have to stop and look for that peeler or knife later. The French call this concept *mise-en-place*, which can be loosely translated as "get your stuff together."

DEFINITION

Mise-en-place is a French term that means "everything in its place." Almost every French cooking lesson starts with a mini lecture on the importance of everything—tools, ingredients, recipes—being ready to use before you even start making a dish.

Getting everything organized and close to your workspace can prevent strains and work-related injuries.

Watch the Clock When Handling Meat

With raw meat, most bacteria start out on the surface. When you cook the meat, you kill the bacteria. The same thing happens when you dehydrate meat at the proper temperatures.

Before you cook that steak or slice it into jerky, you must keep it cold until you get it in the oven or dehydrator. Raw meat, poultry, and seafood should only be kept at room temperature for a *total of 4 hours* before cooking. That doesn't leave much time to let the meat sit on the counter.

So if it takes you 30 minutes to finish shopping and get home after you remove your meat from the meat case; you spend 60 minutes deboning (if you have a bone-in roast), slicing, and putting the meat into a marinade; and allow yourself 30 minutes to package the meat after it's dehydrated, your meat has been out of refrigeration for 2 hours. That leaves you with a 2-hour fudge factor. The salt and spice mixes you use to make your marinade extend this 4-hour safety window some, but it's important to minimize any unnecessary time your meat is unrefrigerated.

When you first start your journey in drying meats, these individual steps may take a bit more time than the estimated time per step. That's why it's so important for you to put your meat back in the refrigerator after each and every step in the process.

It's equally important to clean your counters, your equipment, and your hands after each step in the process. After you cut and slice your meat, put it in the refrigerator and clean up. After you mix your marinade and pour it over your meat, put it in the refrigerator and clean up. Prepare and then clean. Cook and then clean.

DEHYDRATING DON'T

Be sure your dirty knives, cutting boards, and other used equipment don't come in contact with a clean counter or clean dishes. Be aware of where your used equipment is and what it's touching—bacteria can spread just as easily from dirty dishes as they can dirty hands.

Check Your Temperature

Meat must be dehydrated at hotter temperatures than other foods—at 145°F to 155°F. If your dehydrator doesn't heat that hot, it's probably still okay to dehydrate the basil you picked from your garden, but it isn't safe enough to make beef jerky.

If you'd like to make jerky, first check the temperature of your dehydrator to be sure it gets hot enough. Check the temperature when you're dehydrating another food and again when it's empty. If your dehydrator doesn't reach 145°F to 155°F, get another dehydrator or use your oven for making jerky.

According to Barbara Ingham, food scientist at the University of Wisconsin-Extension, you should only use dehydrators with temperature controls you can set, not dehydrators with preset temperature controls you can't increase or decrease. Ingham also recommends drying your jerky in a dehydrator for 4 hours and then finishing it in your oven at 275°F for 10 minutes. "If you use a high-quality dehydrator with temperature controls you can set and then put your jerky in the oven for ten minutes, you will meet the safety standards of the meat industry," Ingham says.

Pretreat Your Vegetables and Fruits

Until very recently, people and even food experts, assumed dried foods, especially vegetables and fruits, were at little risk for bacterial contamination because their low water content was believed to inhibit microbes from growing. Many dried food enthusiasts believed this, too.

However, two recent Colorado State University studies discovered that both salmonella and E. coli could survive basic drying methods. "We did these studies after there were a couple of outbreaks associated with E. coli and salmonella in both home prepared and small commercially prepared beef jerkies," says study author Kendall. "In our studies, we found that if you have a vegetable or fruit that is contaminated with a pathogen, then the scenario is the same is it is with the meat."

You can get sick after eating fresh foods that are contaminated, but if the dried foods contain bacteria, the bacteria forms a biofilm so it's still there, months later, when you eat the dehydrated food. "The people who are most susceptible to food poisoning and to its potentially deadly effects are pregnant women, the elderly, and children up to the age of six," Kendall says.

Fortunately, Kendall and other researchers discovered that blanching or soaking produce in a solution of water and either citric or *ascorbic acid* effectively kills or prevents the growth of many bacteria and prevents future bacteria growth.

DEFINITION

Ascorbic acid is another name for vitamin C.

Although I didn't always pretreat my fruits and vegetables when I first began dehydrating foods, I do now. Pretreating isn't difficult and only adds 10 to 20 more minutes to your prep work. (I talk more about pretreating in Chapter 4.)

Vacuum Seal for Safety

Pretreating foods before dehydrating them inhibits much bacterial growth, but vacuum sealing also helps the process.

Removing oxygen—which is what proper vacuum sealing does—inhibits bacterial growth. If you properly dehydrate and then properly vacuum seal foods, they'll get a double dose of protection.

Safety Around Sharp Tools

As you'll learn in Chapter 4, you'll do some slicing, chopping, and other food prep before you dehydrate your fruits, vegetables, and other foods. That means you'll need a good knife.

Before you get out your knife, be sure there's nothing on the floor you could potentially trip over—that includes any throw rugs, step stools, or the family dog or cat. If you trip while you're holding something sharp, you could get hurt.

When setting down a knife, always lay it on its side. Never leave the blade pointed up. That's an accident waiting to happen.

It's important to keep your knife sharp. Dull knives cause more accidents than sharp knives. Ever have a knife slip off a slippery tomato skin while you're trying to cut it? That happens when the knife is dull, not sharp. (More on this in Chapter 4.)

Knives aren't the only pieces of equipment you need to be careful using. Mandolines, blenders, and food processors should also always be used with care.

Besides keeping your mandoline blade sharpened as you would your knives, always pay attention when you use it. If you get distracted while slicing, the mandoline can easily slice your hand instead of the produce.

The main rule of thumb—to keep your thumbs attached!—is to never, ever reach down into a blender or food processor while it's running. Do not do this with a knife, a wooden spoon, or anything else. Always turn off the equipment and unplug it if you need to clean off a blade or scrape down the side of blender or the processor.

DEHYDRATING DON'T

All the safety equipment, all the cleaning supplies in the world, all the best practices in the world—none of it matters if you don't use them correctly.

Safe Storage Suggestions

Usually, when you dehydrate foods, you don't plan on eating them right away. Proper storage, then, is important.

In general, you should store dehydrated foods in clean plastic bags, plastic or glass containers, or glass jars. If you plan on storing your foods in jars, be sure to sanitize and dry the jars first. Any moisture in the glass containers could promote bacterial growth. A quick bath in boiling water after washing them works nicely, but you can also sanitize them in the dishwasher, as long as you ensure no cleaning residue is left behind.

Zipper-lock plastic bags are good for short-term storage.

> **CHEF'S CHOICE**
>
> Even in zipped-up plastic baggies, air can affect your dried foods so a vacuum sealer is a worthwhile investment. Vacuum sealers suck out the excess air and seal the bags or containers shut. Not only does this prevent air—and bacteria— from getting in, but it also ensures freshness of taste. Vacuum sealers help prevent freezer burn and make foods more portable.

Before you place your dehydrated foods in a bag or jar, let them cool to room temperature. Warm foods retain more moisture, and even a miniscule amount of moisture, trapped in a bag or jar, can be fodder for mold.

Different types of food can be stored safely at room temperature for different lengths of time. Herbs, for example, last a long time, while meat jerkies do not. The following table offers basic storage time lengths.

Different types of food can be stored safely at room temperature for different lengths of time. Herbs, for example, last up to 12 months, while meat jerkies keep for 2 weeks at room temperature, 3 to 6 months in the refrigerator, or 12 months in the freezer. Fruits and vegetables keep for 6 to 12 months, fruit leathers keep for 6 to 12 months in the refrigerator or freezer, and died cheeses keep for 6 to 12 months in the refrigerator or freezer.

Be sure to label and date your dehydrated goodies after you've packaged them. After sealing your dehydrated foods, store them away from heat and sunlight. This ensures they'll stay fresher longer.

The Least You Need to Know

- When preparing food to be dehydrated, wash your hands frequently, especially before and after you touch raw meat and equipment used to process the meat.
- Use a mixture of 1 part bleach to 10 parts water to wipe down your counters and clean your other kitchen equipment, especially after handling meat.
- Always dehydrate meat at the proper temperature—145°F to 155°F.
- Pretreating most fruits and vegetables before dehydrating them, using proper sterilization techniques, and correct storage all help prevent bacterial growth.
- Properly package your dehydrated foods to keep them fresh longer.
- Label and date your packaged dehydrated foods.

Special Cooking Techniques

In This Chapter

- Basic prep work
- Knife-handling tips
- Pretreating fruits, veggies, and more
- Some thoughts on sulfur
- The rehydration process
- Putting your home-dried foods to use

The biggest cooking challenge when dehydrating foods is not the actual drying of the foods. It's the cutting, peeling, pitting, and more that comes beforehand. Any way you slice it (pun intended), the preparation for dehydrating foods takes the most work.

In this chapter, we explore the basic prep work necessary before your foods are ready for the dehydrator, including some handy ways to remove pits from fruits. I also share some knife-handling tips and other techniques to help speed along the preparation process.

We also look at pretreating—the most important step in the prep process—in this chapter. The way you pretreat your foods determines how long they'll keep, and how *safely* they'll keep. In addition, I share some thoughts on whether or not to use sulfur for food preservation.

Lastly, I explain how you can properly rehydrate your dried foods before eating or cooking, and I offer some useful suggestions on incorporating your home-dried foods in your meals.

Pitting, Peeling, and Other Prep Work

The first step in preparing your fruits and vegetables for dehydrating is to clean them. Wash them with water to remove dirt, bugs, and anything else that shouldn't be on them. Cut away bruised or soft spots with a sharp paring knife.

Then you're ready for more advanced prep work.

Perfect Pitting and Seeding

If you're working with fruit and it contains pits or stems, those need to be removed. Cherry pitters pop the pits out of cherries, and some fancy ones even remove the pits from a bunch of cherries at a time, but you don't need to purchase such gadgets to pit your cherries. You can use a straw instead.

Just pull out the stem, and press a straw through the point where the stem was attached to the cherry. When the straw catches the pit, you can push it out through the bottom of the cherry. You'll need a thick, sturdy straw for this. Flimsy straws won't be strong enough to push through the cherry. It's much easier to remove the pits with a straw than slicing the cherries and cutting out the pits.

One thing to note about cherry pitting: if you blanch the cherries before you dehydrate them, remove the stems and pits after blanching. If you boil them with holes in them, you'll lose the cherries' sweet juice and their important nutrients.

To remove the pit from peaches, apricots, avocadoes, and plums, slice the fruit in half, cutting all the way through until you reach the pit and cutting all around the circumference of the fruit. Twist both halves of the fruit around, and pull the halves apart. The pit will stay in one of the halves. Gently use the tip of your knife to loosen the ends of the pit from the fruit and use your thumb to pry it away.

 DRYING TIP

If your fruit isn't ripe enough, the pit will tend to stick to the fruit. Be sure your fruit is ripened properly before you prepare it for dehydration.

Mangoes present a bit more of a challenge because they have a large, flat seed right in the middle. Choose a mango that's firm, but not too firm; an overripe mango won't work for this seed-removal technique. Slice the mango lengthwise along the flat side, right next to the seed. Turn over the mango, and repeat with the other side. Some fruit will still be attached to the seed, so cut the remaining fruit from the outer edge of the seed, cutting it into long strips. Score the fruit with the peel attached to it lengthwise, but don't cut all the way through to the skin. Then invert the skin, pushing the fruit outward. Cut the skin away from the fruit, and it will fall off the skin in strips you can dehydrate.

Peeling Pointers

Some fruits and vegetables have peels you'll need to remove before cutting them. If you're planning on dehydrating a lot of fruits or vegetables, it's important to invest in a good peeler that feels comfortable in your hands. You don't have to keep all the peel in one strip or use a special crank or apple peeler. There's no wrong or right way to peel an apple or a cucumber. Just peel the produce as efficiently as you can.

When you're drying fruits with tough skins such as grapes, plums, cherries, nectarines, figs, and firm berries, you need to *crack* the skin to allow the moisture inside to evaporate while the fruit is being dehydrated.

To crack the skins, bring a pot of water to boil over medium-high heat. Drop the fruit in the boiling water for 30 to 60 seconds. Then, drain the fruit and place it in a bowl of ice-cold water for 30 seconds. Drain on absorbent towels and then place in the dehydrator.

DEFINITION

To **crack** the skin of fruit is to soften or tenderize it so moisture can escape more easily when the fruit is dehydrated. The best way to crack the skin is to soften it through boiling and then stopping the cooking process by soaking it in ice-cold water.

Instead of cracking the skin, you can also poke holes in the skin with a pin or a fork.

When prepping tomatoes for the dehydrator, you may want to remove the skin first. Using a paring knife, remove the core at the top of the tomato. Then, score the bottom of the tomato with an X mark. Bring a large pot of water with a little bit of lemon juice to a boil over medium-high heat. Drop in the tomatoes, let them boil for 1 or 2 minutes, and remove with a slotted spoon. Immediately plunge them into a bath of ice-cold water with ice cubes floating in the bowl. After a minute or two, remove the tomatoes from the water, drain, and peel off the skins.

DRYING TIP

Peels often contain a lot of vitamins and fiber, so don't throw them out! Dry the peels and then grind them into a powder. Ground orange peels, for example, are great to add to flavor dishes.

Cutting, Slicing, and Dicing

Cutting up loads of fruits and vegetables before you dehydrate them is a lot of work. But don't just chop things willy-nilly. Be sure you chop or slice your produce in uniform sizes and shapes. This isn't just because they'll look prettier; when cut about the same size and shape, fruit and vegetable pieces dry more consistently. One giant slice of apple and one super-thin slice of apple won't dry well together. If you remove them from the dehydrator at the same time, one will be completely dried or one will be underdried.

A food processor, fitted with a standard slicing blade, can help you chop up a bunch of veggies or fruits, but sometimes, the appliance doesn't chop as uniformly as you'd like it to. If, when you remove your fruits or veggies from the processor, some pieces vary greatly in size or shape, cut them down to size with a knife.

The Importance of a Sharp Knife

If you plan on slicing your produce by hand, be sure you're using a sharp knife. Chef Roberto Martin, Ellen DeGeneres's personal chef, says almost every "bad" home cook he's ever met uses dull knives.

It's a good idea to have your knives professionally sharpened at least once a year. Some specialty kitchen and gourmet food stores like Sur la Table offer this service. You will also want to hone your knives before each use with a *steel* or a metal rod. If you don't have a steel, you can sharpen your knives regularly on a home knife sharpener, but this doesn't hone them quite as well.

DEFINITION

A **steel** is a rod you can use to sharpen your knife. Just rub the edge of the blade along the steel.

Here's how to hone your knife on a steel:

1. Plant the tip of the rod on a cutting board using your nondominant hand to hold the handle. Your thumb should be up, with your palm facing inward.

2. While holding the steel firmly, use your dominant hand to set the knife blade against the steel at a 20-degree angle.

3. Start with the heel of the blade at the top of the steel, and run the blade down and across the steel so the tip of your knife comes off near the bottom. Your stroke should be gentle and smooth.

4. Repeat this process on the other side of the blade.

5. Now, repeat each side 10 times each.

This might take some getting used to, but it's well worth it to learn. If this process still seems a little unclear to you, you can find video tutorials online. If you search "how to steel a knife," you can find several videos that demonstrate different techniques. Use whichever one feels best to you.

The Knives You Need

The two knives you'll use the most when prepping foods for dehydrating are a paring knife and a chef's knife. You'll use the paring knife to core or pare vegetables and fruits, while the chef's knife will be your tool of choice for most chopping, dicing, and cutting.

Besides keeping your knives sharp and honed, it's important that you hold your knife correctly. Always grasp your knife by the handle, or hilt, between your thumb and four fingers. Do not put your index finger on top of the blade to guide it. Instead, your finger should be against the side of the blade. That gives you much more control than just gripping the knife.

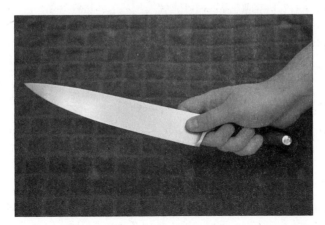

Grasp the knife between your index finger and thumb and wrap your other three fingers around the hilt, or handle.
(Photo by Kyle Edwards)

Dicing Details

When dicing an onion, instead of just randomly chopping it, try this:

1. After removing the skin, slice the onion in half lengthwise, cutting from the top to bottom. Then chop off the top tip—the part that sometimes has some brown skin attached—but leave the root alone.

This is how you begin to slice an onion.
(Photo by Kyle Edwards)

2. Following the natural grooves of the onion, slice into them lengthwise. Again, keep the root intact.

Next, slice lengthwise into the natural grooves on the onion, but don't cut through the root.
(Photo by Kyle Edwards)

3. Finally, cut horizontally, creating perfectly diced onion pieces. Discard the root.

When you slice horizontally into your already-cut lengthwise pieces, you get a perfectly diced onion.
(Photo by Kyle Edwards)

Always remember, whether slicing an onion or anything else, to curl the tips of your fingers back so they don't get accidentally cut when you're slicing.

When you're dicing garlic, use the back of your chef's knife to smash it first. This makes it easier to chop. For most dehydrating, however, you just want to slice the garlic.

This is the correct way to hold a piece of produce while slicing. Notice your fingers should be curled back from the knife.

(Photo by Kyle Edwards)

Slicing Strategies

When julienning potatoes, carrots, and other vegetables that are cylindrical, cut a little bit off one side so it doesn't wobble before you begin slicing the rest of it.

For very thin slices of potatoes, apples, cucumbers, and other fruits and vegetables, a mandoline can be a very useful tool. The main thing you want to remember when using a mandoline, however, is you should cut the last slice with a knife. Pushing that last piece of potato through the mandoline is a sure-fire way to end up cutting yourself yourself.

DEHYDRATING DON'T

Although it's tempting to slice a fruit or a vegetable until there are no more slices to be had, restrain yourself. Discard or cut by hand that last piece of potato instead of pushing it through the mandoline and risking cutting your hand.

Pretreating Fruits

Pretreating fruits before dehydrating them is an important step. Not only does it prevent oxidation or browning, but it also inhibits bacterial growth. Pretreating also helps fruits dehydrate faster, too.

Researchers at the University of Colorado discovered that acidic baths are some of the best ways to prepare fruits for dehydration. For fruits, there are two basic bath options: an ascorbic acid (vitamin C) bath or a citric acid and water bath. Soaking your fruits for 10 minutes in one of these baths usually does the trick.

You can find ascorbic acid or vitamin C in powder form at health food stores and some groceries such as Whole Foods. You can also crush vitamin C tablets to make a powder. The pretreatment recipe, from the University of Colorado, is $2\frac{1}{2}$ tablespoons pure ascorbic acid crystals mixed with 1 quart cold water.

Citric acid is sold at some grocery stores that have canning equipment because it's often added to canned tomatoes. The recipe for a citric acid bath is $\frac{1}{4}$ teaspoon citric acid per 1 quart water.

Instead of straight citric acid, you can also use a mixture of lemon juice and water. Lemon juice contains a lot of citric acid. For a lemon juice pretreatment bath, combine 1 cup lemon juice with 1 cup water.

DRYING TIP

Instead of lemon juice, you can also substitute orange or pineapple juice. Both contain citric acid and prevent oxidation. Use the same ratio as with the lemon juice formula.

With each bath recipe, soak the whole fruit, or peel the fruit and cut directly into the bath, for 10 minutes. Remove with a slotted spoon, drain well, and immediately place in the dehydrator.

Another method some dehydrating enthusiasts like is to spray fruits with lemon juice. Instead of soaking, simply fill a spray bottle with 100 percent lemon juice. If you decide to spray instead of soak, thoroughly spritz each fruit piece with the juice before dehydrating.

Fruits that already contain citric acid, like pineapples and oranges, don't need to be soaked in an acid bath prior to dehydration. Canned fruits also do not need to be pretreated.

Whether you use ascorbic acid, citric acid or lemon juice is a personal preference. Durham Herzog, an avid home dehydrator and instructor in Wisconsin, prefers ascorbic acid. She believes it doesn't leave a flavoring on the fruits. Professor Patricia Kendall, of the University of Colorado, likes straight citric acid for the same reason. I use both, depending on which I have on hand.

Pretreating Vegetables

University researchers developed a slightly different treatment method for preparing vegetables for dehydration. For many vegetables, it's recommended that you *blanch* them in a water and acid mixture.

DEFINITION

Blanching is a cooking technique in which you plunge vegetables into boiling water and then immediately cool or refresh them in a bowl of ice-cold water to stop the cooking process.

Use ¼ teaspoon lemon juice per 1 quart water, ¼ teaspoon citric acid per 1 quart water, or 1 teaspoon ascorbic acid per 1 quart water. Bring the water to a boil over medium-high heat and then blanch your vegetables for about 4 minutes. Delicate greens only need about 1 or 2 minutes. For potatoes, blanch for 7 minutes. Drain the vegetables and cool in a bowl of ice-cold water for at least 4 minutes. Drain on towels and then place the vegetables in the dehydrator.

The exception to the rule is mushrooms. Mushrooms don't need to be blanched, but they should be soaked in a mixture of water and acid, using the same acid-to-water ratios, for 10 minutes. Drain them, and they're ready to be dehydrated.

Some home dehydrators prefer to steam-blanch their vegetables or place the veggies in a steamer basket over boiling water. You can use this method, but it doesn't result in the same even heat penetration as direct water blanching.

DEHYDRATING DON'T

If you're blanching several batches of vegetables, you'll need to add more citric acid to the water after two or three batches. The boiling will destroy its effectiveness by then.

Pretreating Herbs

University researchers have discovered that bacteria can survive on parsley through the dehydrating process.

To pretreat herbs, combine ¼ teaspoon lemon juice, ¼ teaspoon citric acid, or 1 teaspoon ascorbic acid in 1 quart water. Add your herbs, and soak for 2 minutes. Pat dry, and your herbs are ready to dehydrate.

It's important to note that herbs shouldn't be cut or crumbled before dehydration. Cutting releases oils, and the final, dried product won't be as flavor packed.

Pretreating Fruit and Vegetable Leathers

Fruit and vegetable leathers are easy to make and enable you to create many different variations. They do, however, require a few extra steps.

You need to cook the fruits or vegetables you're using in your leathers before you purée them. After pitting, coring, or peeling your fruits or vegetables, cut them into chunks and put them in the top of a double boiler. Fill the bottom of the double boiler with water, and bring it to a boil over medium-high heat. Cover and steam the fruits or vegetables for 15 to 20 minutes or until the fruit or vegetable is soft and a thermometer placed into the mixture reads 160°F.

Place the cooked fruit or vegetables into a blender or food processor fitted with a standard blade. Add ½ teaspoon ascorbic acid crystals, ¼ teaspoon citric acid, or 2 tablespoons lemon juice per 2 cups produce to protect the color and help destroy bacteria during dehydration. Process until smooth.

CHEF'S CHOICE

Canned fruit does not need to be pretreated or cooked because the canning process already destroyed any bacteria.

To Sulfur or Not to Sulfur?

Sulfur is a chemical element that's long been used in drying fruits to ensure their longevity and prevent oxidation or browning. Most commercially dried peaches, golden raisins, apricots, and even some "sun-dried" tomatoes are treated with sulfur to prevent them from browning and spoiling.

Apricots that aren't treated with sulfur, for example, turn quite brown, and their color doesn't resemble fresh apricots at all. They taste the same, but the color is off-putting to some consumers, so manufacturers treat them with sulfur.

Do you really need to sulfur your fruit? Most home dehydration experts definitively say no. It's not necessary. Pretreating with citric acid adequately prevents oxidation and spoilage. And according to one study done by researchers at the University of Colorado, acidic treatments of apple and peach slices better prevented the growth of salmonella bacteria than sodium metabisulfite treatment. Although both sulfur and acidic treatments initially reduced bacteria counts in the fruit slices, after 28 days, only the acidic-treated slices had no detectable levels of bacteria.

DEHYDRATING DON'T

Sulfur compounds can cause severe allergic reactions in some people, and if you have asthma, it's a definite cause for concern. The U.S. Department of Agriculture prohibits the use of sulfur to treat fresh and raw fruits and vegetables, but it permits it for dried produce, saying that consuming small amounts is safe for most individuals. However, some researchers have seen a correlation between sulfur compounds and cancer.

I don't recommend using sulfur to pretreat your fruits. But if you do plan on sulfuring your fruits, whether for aesthetic or spoilage concerns, you need to do it correctly.

When big companies sulfur fruits, often they expose the fruits to sulfur dioxide fumes. That's definitely *not* a recommended treatment for home drying fruits because the fumes are potentially toxic. Instead, according to the University of Colorado, if you choose to sulfur your fruits, use a U.S.P. or food-grade sodium metabisulfite, not Practical Grade, which is not safe for food use. You can purchase sodium metabisulfite at pharmacies and winemaking supply stores.

The recommended sulfur treatment is to dissolve 1 tablespoon sodium metabisulfite in 1 quart cold water. Cut the peeled fruit directly into the sulfur water, soak it for 10 minutes, remove the fruit, and drain it well before dehydrating it.

Rehydrating Dried Foods

The simplest way to rehydrate dried foods is to use cold or hot water. The general rule is to use 1 cup water per 1 cup dried foods. Hot liquids rehydrate foods more quickly than cold liquids, and smaller pieces and powders of dried foods rehydrate more quickly than larger pieces. Diced shallots and powdered celery, for example, rehydrate almost instantly in cold or hot liquid, whereas dried portobello mushroom slices can take up to an hour.

Foods that were blanched prior to drying also rehydrate more quickly than raw foods. The blanching process breaks down the cell structure of the foods, allowing them to rehydrate faster.

When rehydrating, I suggest adding the liquid slowly, ¼ or ⅛ cup at a time. Besides using water, you can also rehydrate foods using fruit juices, wine, milk, or liquor. I'm partial to rehydrating mushrooms with red wine, especially if I'm going to use them to top steak. I also like rehydrating fruits in fruit juices. That gives them an extra jolt of flavor and sweetness. You can also add spices or vanilla extract to the rehydrating liquid.

DEHYDRATING DON'T

You can add any spices, herbs, or flavorings at the beginning of the rehydration process, but do not add sugar or salt at this time. Salt and sweeten the dried fruits only *after* they're rehydrated; otherwise, you could add too much. The salt and sugar also may slow down the rehydrating process.

Besides rehydrating directly with liquid, you can also rehydrate foods with steam. Steam rehydration takes anywhere from 5 to 30 minutes, depending on the size of the food pieces. Simply place the pieces of food in a steamer basket over water or place them in an electric steamer or rice cooker, and steam until rehydrated.

You can also add dried fruits and vegetables directly to soups, stews, or sauces as you're cooking them. But some vegetables such as beans, carrots, and corn can toughen if they're quickly cooked before being fully rehydrated. Instead of just dropping them in your soup and continuing with your recipe, add them to the soup and turn off the heat for 5 to 10 minutes, stirring the dried vegetables occasionally as they begin their rehydration process. The vegetables will fill with water and lighten in color as they rehydrate. If they're still shrunken and dark in color after 5 to 10 minutes, they need a few extra minutes. When the vegetables are rehydrated, turn the heat back on and resume cooking.

Most rehydrated vegetables and fruits resume their predried appearance, but some, like melons and tomatoes, don't look exactly the same. And in my opinion, some vegetables and fruits taste better after they're rehydrated than fresh produce. Carrots taste a little sweeter, for example, and rehydrated apples have more flavor.

You can cook with rehydrated foods pretty much the same way you use fresh, except when you've blanched the produce before drying, it will cook more quickly after it's rehydrated—it's already halfway cooked. It's also best to cook the rehydrated foods with the leftover rehydrated liquid, rather than pour it out and add more milk, wine, etc.

When baking with dried fruits and vegetables, you can add the dried vegetable or fruit pieces directly to the batter, or you can rehydrate them first. Again, when you rehydrate them first, save any extra liquid to add to the batter, to retain the carrot or apple flavor. Reduce the amount of milk or water in the batter accordingly. If you add dehydrated foods directly to your batter, you might want to add a little extra water to your recipe, too.

One important safety note: after you rehydrate your foods, don't let them sit around for long periods of time before you eat them or cook with them. Bacteria that may have been inhibited when the foods were dried could start to grow when water is added.

Using Your Home-Dried Foods

You can use home-dried foods in exactly the same way you'd use commercially dried foods. Throw some dehydrated cranberries into your scones, snack on dried apples, and take that beef jerky along on your camping trip.

You'll soon find that when you dry foods yourself, you discover new and creative uses for your dried bounty. For example, dried celery isn't something you'd usually find on your grocery shelves. However, I dry celery and add it to soups, roasted meat dishes, sauces, and even tuna salads. I also grind it to a powder to flavor soups and stews. It's something that's quickly developed into a pantry necessity.

I also love using my dried mushrooms, not just for soups, sauces, and meat dishes. A few chopped, dried mushrooms adds an *umami* touch to omelets and casseroles. In fact, I consider dried mushrooms and mushroom powder my "secret" ingredient to pump up the taste of various dishes that need a savory flavor note.

DEFINITION

Umami is considered the fifth taste. It's a savory flavor that doesn't neatly fall into the other sweet, salty, sour, and bitter categories.

You can use dried fruits, after they're rehydrated and puréed, to decrease the amount of fat in baked goods. For example, you can replace or reduce the amount of butter or shortening in banana bread by using 1 cup fruit purée. Using fruit purée enables you to reduce the amount of sweetener in a recipe by $\frac{1}{3}$, too. Rehydrated and puréed dried vegetables and fruits also make amazing baby foods. The same is true of rehydrated fruit and vegetable powders.

The more you use your dehydrator, the more you'll start discovering dried foods you love but you never would have tried dried before. I never liked the super-sugary taste of commercially dried pineapple, but I adore homemade dried pineapple slices. They're a decadent treat, and every time I dehydrate pineapple at home, it's gone within a day. My son and I gobble it up, right off the dehydrator trays. I also much prefer my sweet and tender home-dried apple and mango slices to the bland, too-tough, commercially dried versions. Homemade fruit leathers also taste better, as do homemade meat jerkies.

I encourage you to try the dehydrated recipes you think will taste delicious, but I also suggest trying some of the recipes you're not as initially interested in. You might be surprised at what you like, and you'll probably discover some new "family favorite" recipes. Ready to get started and dehydrate some foods?

The Least You Need to Know

- It's important to thoroughly clean your vegetables and fruits before dehydrating them.
- Cut or slice your to-be-dried foods into uniform pieces with a sharp knife so they dehydrate evenly and at the same rate.
- Pretreat your fruits using an acidic bath to prevent oxidation and bacterial growth. Pretreat your vegetables by blanching them in water and lemon juice.
- You need to cook your fruits and vegetables before puréeing them into leathers.
- You don't have to sulfur your fruits if you pretreat them with acid.
- Rehydrate foods with 1 cup water per 1 cup dried foods. Hot liquids rehydrate foods more quickly than cold liquids, and small pieces of dried foods rehydrate faster than big pieces.

Simple and Easy Dehydrated Foods

Part 2 details the basic recipes for dehydrating many kinds of foods. I start with dehydrating fruits and vegetables, from apples to zucchini, and move on to herbs. You learn how to dehydrate cheese, make dehydrator yogurt, and create crème fraîche. I explain how to dry breads and pastas, and I even show you how to make croutons and crackers in your dehydrator. I teach you how to make delicious meat, poultry, and fish jerkies, too.

The chapters in Part 2 offer the easiest recipes and highlight the basic kinds of foods and simple recipes you'll want to use with your dehydrator. These recipes are a great place to start if you've never used a dehydrator before, but they're also perfect to return to any time you dehydrate a vegetable or fruit you haven't dried before.

Sure, you can buy dried onions, raisins, and apples at the grocery store, but when you make them yourself, they taste *so* much better!

Fantastic Dehydrated Fruits

In This Chapter

- Dehydrating fresh fruit
- Sweet and delicious dried fruit
- Cooking with dehydrated fruit
- Grab-and-go sweet snacks

One of the first things you're going to want to dehydrate when you get your dehydrator is fruit. A dehydrator is a great tool to have, especially when you get a bumper crop of cherries or raspberries.

This chapter contains recipes for some of the most common fruits you'll want to dehydrate. All the recipes call for fresh fruit—because fresh fruit tastes fabulous when it's dehydrated—but you can also use frozen and canned fruits. Simply skip the pretreatment steps on the latter two because they're already preserved.

Dried fruits make great snacks, but you can also toss them into cereal, add them to your trail mixes, and even bake with them.

I encourage you to experiment with different fruits to see what you might like best. The easiest fruits to dry, I've found, are apples and bananas—and they taste so sweet when they're done!

One quick note about dehydrating fruits: all the recipes in this chapter recommend drying the fruits between 130°F to 140°F, but some dehydrating enthusiasts prefer to dry their fruits between 120°F and 125°F, with the idea that more nutrients are preserved. If you plan to dry your fruits at a lower temperature, you'll need to tack on at least 2 to 4 more hours drying time.

Apples

Apples are one of the easiest foods to dehydrate. Dried apple slices are so versatile: add them to trail mixes, throw them in scones, bake them in pies, or just snack on them!

Yield:	Prep time:	Dry time:
about 2½ cups	1 hour	7 to 15 hours

4 fresh apples	½ tsp. citric acid or 2½ TB. ascorbic acid
1 qt. water	

1. Peel, core, and slice apples into ¼-inch slices.

2. In a large bowl, combine water and citric acid. Add apple slices, and soak for 10 minutes. Drain.

3. Set the dehydrator to 130°F to 140°F. Evenly arrange apple slices on the dehydrator trays, leaving some space between slices.

4. Dehydrate for 7 to 15 hours. Apples will shrink as they dry, flatten, and have a chewy texture.

5. Store in an airtight container at room temperature for up to 1 year.

> **CHEF'S CHOICE**
>
> For variety, instead of water, use cranberry, orange, pomegranate, or other fruit juices to flavor the apple slices during the citric acid bath. If you don't mind the texture of the peel, you can leave it on.

Apricots

Sweet and chewy dried apricots make great snacks, but they're also great rehydrated as pie and kolache cookie filling.

Yield:	Prep time:	Dry time:
about 1 cup	1 hour	20 to 28 hours

6 fresh apricots	¼ tsp. citric acid or 2½ TB. ascorbic acid
1 qt. water	

1. Slice apricots in half, and remove pits.

2. In a large bowl, combine water and citric acid. Add apricot halves, and soak for 10 minutes. Drain.

3. Set the dehydrator to 130°F to 140°F. Evenly arrange apricots, skin side down, on the dehydrator trays, leaving some space between them.

4. Dehydrate for 20 to 28 hours. After about 10 to 14 hours, flip apricots inside out. Check apricots after about 15 hours, as some might finish earlier than others. Apricots will flatten as they dry, darken to a deep orange, and have a chewy texture.

5. Store in an airtight container at room temperature for up to 1 year.

CHEF'S CHOICE

Apricots, like peaches, darken quite a bit in color when you don't use sulfur as a pretreatment. Just know your homemade dried apricots will look a bit different from the bright orange ones you find at the grocery store. They'll *taste* better though!

Bananas

Dried bananas make a great snack, either by themselves or when tossed with nuts as a trail mix. They also add sweetness to cereals and baked goods.

Yield:	Prep time:	Dry time:
1 cup	30 minutes	8 to 12 hours

6 fresh, but not overripe, bananas, peeled

1 qt. water

¼ tsp. citric acid or 2½ TB. ascorbic acid

1. Slice bananas into ¼-inch slices, and remove any extremely mushy brown spots.

2. In a large bowl, combine water and citric acid. Add banana slices, and soak for 10 minutes. Drain and lightly blot dry with a towel.

3. Set the dehydrator to 130°F to 140°F. Evenly arrange banana slices on the dehydrator trays, leaving some space between them.

4. Dehydrate for 8 to 12 hours. Bananas will shrink to about the size of nickels as they dry and be leathery to the touch.

5. Store in an airtight container at room temperature for up to 1 year.

DRYING TIP

Bananas are a great source of potassium, an electrolyte that helps balance your body's fluids and can help reduce cramps. If you have leg cramps after swimming or hiking, eat a banana.

Blueberries

Dehydrated blueberries taste almost like candy—they're so sweet and easy to pop into your mouth. If you can manage not to eat them all, you can also add them to cereals, baked goods, and trail mixes.

Yield:	Prep time:	Dry time:
1 cup	30 minutes	10 to 18 hours

2 qt. water
¼ tsp. citric acid or 2½ TB. ascorbic acid

1 pt. fresh blueberries

1. In a large bowl, combine 1 quart water and citric acid. Set aside.

2. In a large pot over medium-high heat, bring remaining 1 quart water to a boil. Add blueberries, and boil for 30 seconds. Drain and soak in citric acid bath for 10 minutes. (You may want to add a few ice cubes to help berries cool.) Drain and blot dry with a towel.

3. Set the dehydrator to 130°F to 140°F. Evenly arrange blueberries on the dehydrator trays, leaving some space between them. (Because they're round, blueberries might roll around a bit on the trays.)

4. Dehydrate for 10 to 18 hours. Blueberries will deepen in color as they dry and shrink to the size of pennies or nickels.

5. Store in an airtight container at room temperature for up to 1 year.

DRYING TIP

Besides boiling and cooling your blueberries, you might also want to poke their skin with a toothpick, fork, or tip of a knife. This helps them dry them evenly and completely.

Cherries

Cherries are a terrific fruit to dry. Not only are they less expensive if you dry them yourself, but you also don't have to add the extra sugar, which almost all commercially dried cherries have. Dried cherries are great to add to your breakfast cereal, perfect for baked goods, and wonderful in salads and even baked or roasted meat dishes.

Yield:	Prep time:	Dry time:
about 1 cup	1 hour	20 to 24 hours

2 qt. water	1 lb. fresh cherries
¼ tsp. citric acid or 2½ TB. ascorbic acid	

1. In a large bowl, combine 1 quart water and citric acid. Set aside.

2. In a large pot over medium-high heat, bring remaining 1 quart water to a boil. Add cherries, and boil for 30 to 45 seconds. Drain and soak in citric acid bath for 10 minutes. Drain and blot dry with a towel.

3. Remove stems from cherries, and using a straw or cherry pitter, remove pits. (For more on pitting, see Chapter 4.)

4. Set the dehydrator to 130°F to 140°F. Evenly arrange cherries on the dehydrator trays, leaving some space between them.

5. Dehydrate for 20 to 24 hours, checking cherries after about 10 hours, as some might finish earlier than others. Cherries will darken to almost black in color as they dry and shrink to the size of large raisins.

6. Store in an airtight container at room temperature for up to 1 year.

DRYING TIP

If you choose not to crack the skin of your cherries (step 3), you'll need to add 6 to 8 more hours of drying time.

Citrus Fruits

From oranges to Meyer lemons to limes, dried citrus fruits can add a sweet and sour zing to beverages, savory dishes, and baked goods.

Yield:	Prep time:	Dry time:
about 1½ cups	1 hour	20 hours

1 lb. fresh citrus fruits

1. Scrub outside of fruits to remove wax, and slice in ¼-inch slices. If you're planning to eat finished fruit, like oranges, you can slice the original slices in half and use a paring knife to remove the peel. Set peel aside.

2. Set the dehydrator to 130°F to 140°F. Evenly arrange citrus fruit on the dehydrator trays, leaving some space between them.

3. Dehydrate for 20 hours, checking citrus fruit after about 10 hours, as some might finish earlier than others. Citrus fruit will be almost leathery.

4. Store in an airtight container at room temperature for up to 1 year.

DRYING TIP

Use dried citrus slices to add a lot of aroma to homemade potpourri.

Citrus Peels, Candied

Candied citrus peels are decadently delicious—and they also make a great gift!

Yield:	Prep time:	Dry time:
about 1 cup	1 hour	3 to 8 hours

Leftover peel from 1 lb. citrus fruits   1½ cups sugar or honey
1½ cups water

1. Using a paring knife, remove any fruit and pith still attached to citrus fruit peels. If peels aren't as even as you'd like, slice, in a julienne fashion, to thin them out.

2. In a medium pot over medium-high heat, bring water to a boil.

3. Place sugar in a medium bowl, and stir in 1½ cups boiling water to dissolve. Add citrus fruit peel, and soak for 5 minutes. Remove with a slotted spoon and drain.

4. Set the dehydrator to 130°F to 140°F. Evenly arrange citrus peel slices on the dehydrator trays, leaving some space between them.

5. Dehydrate for 3 to 8 hours, checking slices after 2 hours to see if they're done. Citrus peels will be leathery when done.

6. Store in an airtight container at room temperature for up to 1 year.

DRYING TIP

For extra decadence, melt 1 cup bittersweet or semisweet chocolate in the microwave—about 1½ minutes on high. Dip the candied citrus peels in chocolate, leaving half of each slice bare. For less decadence, just dry the sliced peel without coating it in sugar water. The dried peel can be added to baked goods, teas, and more.

Cranberries

Nothing tastes quite like the bounty of fall than dried cranberries. Eat them as snacks, toss them in salads, or even add them to your Thanksgiving stuffing.

Yield:	Prep time:	Dry time:
½ cup	20 minutes	10 to 18 hours

2 qt. water	1 cup fresh cranberries
Ice cubes	¼ tsp. citric acid or 2½ TB. ascorbic acid

1. In a large bowl, create cold water bath with 1 quart water and some ice cubes.

2. In a large pot over medium-high heat, bring remaining 1 quart water to a boil. Add cranberries and citric acid, and boil for 1½ to 2 minutes, but not more than 2 minutes. Drain and cool in ice water bath until cranberries are room temperature. If their skins haven't cracked or slightly burst, poke them with a toothpick.

2. Set the dehydrator to 130°F to 140°F. Evenly arrange cranberries on the dehydrator trays, leaving some space between them. (Because they're round, cranberries might roll around a bit on the trays.)

3. Dehydrate for 10 to 18 hours, checking every 4 to 6 hours to remove cranberries that are already dried. If some cranberries seem like they're not drying efficiently, poke them again with a toothpick. Cranberries will deepen in color as they dry, shrink like raisins to the size of pennies or dimes, and be a bit crunchy.

4. Store in an airtight container at room temperature for up to 1 year.

> **CHEF'S CHOICE**
>
> If you'd prefer sweetened cranberries, add 2 cups sugar to the water before you boil it. You can use more or less sugar, depending on your taste, and you can substitute honey, agave syrup, or maple syrup for the sugar. After boiling the berries for 1 or 2 minutes in the sugar water, remove the pan from heat, and let the berries steep in the sugar water for about 15 to 20 minutes. Drain and let as much of the sugar syrup drip off before you place the cranberries in the dehydrator. These cranberries will have a more raisinlike texture than their no-sugar counterparts.

Dates

Dates are one of the best fruits to dry. Their sweet, chewy goodness can enliven breads, cereals, and all kinds of baked goodies. You can grind dehydrated dates into date sugar—a healthy substitute for cane sugar.

Yield:	Prep time:	Dry time:
2 cups	10 minutes	8 to 24 hours*

¾ cup "fresh" dates*	¼ tsp. citric acid or 2½ TB. ascorbic acid
1 qt. water	

1. Slice dates in half, and remove pits.

2. In a large bowl, combine water and citric acid. Add dates, and soak for 10 minutes. Drain and lightly blot dry with a towel.

3. Set the dehydrator temperature to 130°F to 140°F. Evenly arrange dates on the dehydrator trays, leaving some space between them.

4. Dehydrate for 8 to 24 hours. Dates will be very chewy when done.

5. Store in an airtight container at room temperature for up to 1 year.

CHEF'S CHOICE

*Most "fresh" dates sold in stores are actually dried or "cured" on the tree. They finish drying in a dehydrator in 5 to 8 hours. Dates that are picked without on-the-tree curing take 18 to 24 hours to dry.

Figs

Figs are a perfect fruit to dry. They not only make great snacks, but they're also fabulous to add to cheese plates.

Yield:	Prep time:	Dry time:
1 cup	30 minutes	24 to 30 hours

1 pt. fresh figs

2 qt. water

¼ tsp. citric acid or 2½ TB. ascorbic acid

1. Slice figs in half or leave whole.

2. In a large bowl, combine 1 quart water and citric acid. Set aside.

3. In a large pot over medium-high heat, bring remaining 1 quart water to a boil. Add figs, and boil for 30 to 45 seconds. Drain and soak in citric acid bath for 10 minutes. Drain and blot dry with a towel.

4. Set the dehydrator to 130°F to 140°F. Evenly arrange figs on the dehydrator trays, leaving some space between them.

5. Dehydrate for 24 to 30 hours. Figs will be dark or almost black in color when dry and shrink to the size of half-dollars.

6. Store in an airtight container at room temperature for up to 1 year.

DRYING TIP

If you choose not to crack the skin of your figs (step 3), add 8 to 10 more hours of drying time.

Grapes

Freshly made raisins taste sweeter than those found boxed in grocery stores. They make great snacks as is, but they're also perfect to toss in trail mixes, in cookies, and on top of oatmeal or cereal.

Yield:	Prep time:	Dry time:
1 cup	30 minutes	24 to 30 hours

2 qt. water

¼ tsp. citric acid or 2½ TB. ascorbic acid

1 lb. fresh, seedless grapes

1. In a large bowl, combine 1 quart water and citric acid. Set aside.

2. In a large pot over medium-high heat, bring remaining 1 quart water to a boil. Add grapes, and boil for 30 to 45 seconds. Drain and soak in citric acid bath for 10 minutes. Drain and blot dry with a towel.

3. Set the dehydrator to 130°F to 140°F. Evenly arrange grapes on the dehydrator trays, leaving some space between them. (Because they're round, grapes might roll around a bit on the trays.)

4. Dehydrate for 24 to 30 hours. Grapes will deepen in color as they dry and shrink to the size of pennies or nickels.

5. Store in an airtight container at room temperature for up to 1 year.

CHEF'S CHOICE

Green grapes become golden raisins when they dry, while red grapes become dark or regular raisins.

Kiwis

Dried kiwis taste a little bit like an exotic SweeTART candy. They make great snacks.

Yield:	Prep time:	Dry time:
1¼ cups	20 minutes	10 to 14 hours

6 fresh kiwis

1 qt. water

¼ tsp. citric acid, 1 tsp. ascorbic acid, or ¼ tsp. lemon juice

1. Peel kiwis using a peeler or a paring knife. Use a paring knife to remove the tough core at the bottom. Slice kiwis in $\frac{1}{2}$-inch-thick rounds.

2. In a large bowl, combine 1 quart water and citric acid. Add kiwis, and soak for 10 minutes.

3. Set the dehydrator to 130°F to 140°F. Evenly arrange kiwis on the dehydrator trays, leaving some space between them.

4. Dehydrate for 10 to 14 hours. Kiwis will shrink to less than half in size as they dry and become sticky. The thinner slices appear a bit translucent, but the middle is slightly chewy. The edible seeds crunch when you bite into a slice.

5. Store in an airtight container at room temperature for up to 1 year.

CHEF'S CHOICE

For an exotic dried fruit salad, mix together equal parts kiwi slices, pineapple slices, and orange slices.

Mangoes

Dried mangoes are one of the sweetest fruit snacks you can make in your dehydrator. They are simply fantastic!

Yield:	Prep time:	Dry time:
1½ cups	20 minutes	18 to 24 hours

2 small fresh mangoes

1 qt. water

¼ tsp. citric acid, 1 tsp. ascorbic acid, or ¼ tsp. lemon juice

1. Slice mangoes lengthwise along the flat side, right next to the seed. Turn over mangoes, and repeat on the other side. Cut away any remaining fruit attached to the seed in long strips. Score fruit with the peel attached to it lengthwise, but don't cut all the way through to the skin. Invert the skin, pushing fruit outward. Then, pare the skin away from fruit, and it will fall off the skin in strips.

2. In a large bowl, combine water and citric acid. Add mangoes, and soak for 10 minutes.

3. Set the dehydrator to 130°F to 140°F. Evenly arrange mangoes on the dehydrator trays, leaving some space between them.

4. Dehydrate for 18 to 24 hours. Mangoes flatten and shrink as they dry and will be a bit leathery.

5. Store in an airtight container at room temperature for up to 1 year.

> **DRYING TIP**
>
> If you're planning to add your dehydrated mango to a trail mix, you can dice the slices smaller before drying them.

Melon

Dried melon slices are sweet treats all by themselves, but they can also be added to gelatin desserts, fruit cups, and other dishes.

Yield:	Prep time:	Dry time:
2 cups	20 minutes	8 to 12 hours

1 medium melon

1. Slice melon in half, and scoop out the seeds. Slice melon into quarters, and using a paring knife, remove the rind. Slice quarters into ¼-inch slices.

2. Set the dehydrator to 130°F to 140°F. Evenly arrange melon on the dehydrator trays, leaving some space between them.

3. Dehydrate for 8 to 12 hours. Melon flattens and shrinks as it dries. Thinner slices will be a bit brittle while thicker slices will remain pliable. Both will be chewy.

4. Store in an airtight container at room temperature for up to 1 year.

> **CHEF'S CHOICE**
>
> You can dehydrate any melon, but watermelon tends to get very, very sticky and overly sweet when dehydrated.

Nectarines

Dried nectarines are a great snack. They're terrific added to pies and breads, too.

Yield:	Prep time:	Dry time:
1 cup	30 minutes	10 to 18 hours

2 qt. water

¼ tsp. citric acid or 2½ TB. ascorbic
    acid

3 or 4 fresh nectarines

1. In a large bowl, combine 1 quart water and citric acid. Set aside.

2. In a large pot over medium-high heat, bring remaining 1 quart water to a boil. Add whole nectarines, and boil for 1 minute. Drain and rinse with cold water for 2 minutes.

3. Slice nectarines in half, remove the pits, and slice nectarines into ¼-inch slices. Soak nectarines in citric acid bath for 10 minutes. Drain and blot dry with a towel.

4. Set the dehydrator to 130°F to 140°F. Evenly arrange nectarines on the dehydrator trays, leaving some space between them.

5. Dehydrate for 10 to 18 hours. About halfway through, invert nectarines to more evenly dry them. Nectarines will turn brown as they dry and almost melt into the dehydrator tray. They should be chewy in texture.

6. Store in an airtight container at room temperature for up to 1 year.

DRYING TIP

Be sure the nectarines you select to dehydrate are ripe, but not overripe. Overripe nectarines can be more challenging to pit.

Papaya

Slightly sweet and aromatic, dried papaya makes a great snack, but it also can be added to trail mixes, baked goods, and even savory curries.

Yield:	Prep time:	Dry time:
1½ cups	20 minutes	18 to 24 hours

1 medium fresh papaya	¼ tsp. citric acid, 1 tsp. ascorbic acid,
1 qt. water	or ¼ tsp. lemon juice

1. Slice papaya in half, and use a spoon to scoop out and discard the seeds. Slice the halves into ¼-inch strips, and cut away the peel.

2. In a large bowl, combine 1 quart water and citric acid. Add papaya, and soak for 10 minutes.

3. Set the dehydrator to 130°F to 140°F. Evenly arrange papaya on the dehydrator trays, leaving some space between them.

4. Dehydrate for 18 to 24 hours. Papaya will flatten and shrink as it dries and have a papery texture.

5. Store in an airtight container at room temperature for up to 1 year.

DRYING TIP

Dried papaya strips can add an exotic note to sangria and fruit punches.

Peaches

Like many other dehydrated fruit, dried peaches make a great snack. They're also amazing in baked goods.

Yield:	Prep time:	Dry time:
1 cup	30 minutes	10 to 18 hours

3 qt. water	Ice cubes
¼ tsp. citric acid or 2½ TB. ascorbic acid	4 fresh peaches

1. In a large bowl, combine 1 quart water and citric acid. Set aside.

2. In a separate bowl, create cold water bath with 1 quart water and some ice cubes.

3. In a large pot over medium-high heat, bring remaining 1 quart water to a boil. Add whole peaches, and boil for 1 minute. Drain and plunge into ice water bath. The peels should slip off.

4. Slice peaches in half, remove the pits, and slice peaches into ¼-inch slices. Soak peaches in citric acid bath for 10 minutes. Drain and blot dry with a towel.

5. Set the dehydrator to 130°F to 140°F. Evenly arrange peaches on the dehydrator trays, leaving some space between them.

6. Dehydrate for 10 to 18 hours. Peaches will brown in color as they dry and almost melt into the dehydrator tray. They should be chewy in texture.

7. Store in an airtight container at room temperature for up to 1 year.

DRYING TIP

Instead of slicing the peaches, you can cut them in half and dry them that way. Add at least 6 to 10 more hours of drying time for halves.

Your peach slices will dry more quickly and evenly if you don't crowd them on the dehydrator tray.
(Photo by Kyle Edwards)

Pears

Dried pears add a depth of sweetness to breads, are a perfect accompaniment to a camping trip, and make great after-school snacks.

Yield:	Prep time:	Dry time:
about 2 cups	1 hour	8 to 16 hours

4 fresh pears	¼ tsp. citric acid or 2½ TB. ascorbic acid
1 qt. water	

1. Peel and core pears, and cut into ¼-inch slices.

2. In a large bowl, combine 1 quart water and citric acid. Add pears, and soak for 10 minutes. Drain.

3. Set the dehydrator to 130°F to 140°F. Evenly arrange pears on the dehydrator trays, leaving some space between them.

4. Dehydrate for 8 to 16 hours, checking pears after 6 hours, as some might finish earlier than others. Pears will shrink as they dry and have a chewy texture when done. The thinner slices will be a bit papery.

5. Store in an airtight container at room temperature for up to 1 year.

> **DRYING TIP**
>
> Instead of using water, you can also use different fruit juices to add a little pizzazz. If you don't mind the peel, you don't have to peel your pears, either.

Pineapple

Pineapple dries extremely well, and home-dehydrated pineapple is more delicious than any store-bought dried pineapple you'll find. Sweet, succulent, and chewy, dried pineapple makes a great snack, and works equally well added to muffins, cakes, and other baked goods.

Yield:	Prep time:	Dry time:
¾ cup	20 minutes	12 to 15 hours

1 fresh pineapple, peeled and cored

1. Remove any tough spots from pineapple, and slice in ½-inch-thick rounds.

2. Set the dehydrator to 130°F to 140°F. Evenly arrange pineapple on the dehydrator trays, leaving some space between them.

3. Dehydrate for 12 to 15 hours. Pineapple will shrink to less than half in size as it dries, becomes sticky, malleable, and chewy.

4. Store in an airtight container at room temperature for up to 1 year.

> **DRYING TIP**
>
> For a pretty fruit treat, place slices of cherries or berries in the middle of the pineapple slices, and dry them together. Maraschino cherries work well for this. If you're using fresh cherries or berries, be sure to pop or crack them so they dry more evenly.

Plums

Dried plums are a perfect grab-and-go treat, and there's a certain satisfaction you get when you make them yourself.

Yield:	Prep time:	Dry time:
1 cup	30 minutes	24 to 30 hours

2 qt. water	8 fresh plums
¼ tsp. citric acid or 2½ TB. ascorbic acid	

1. In a large bowl, combine 1 quart water and citric acid. Set aside.

2. In a large pot over medium-high heat, bring remaining 1 quart water to a boil. Add plums, and boil for 30 to 45 seconds. Drain and soak in citric acid bath for 10 minutes. Drain and blot dry with a towel. Slice plums in half, and remove pits.

3. Set the dehydrator to 130°F to 140°F. Evenly arrange plums on the dehydrator trays, leaving some space between them.

4. Dehydrate for 24 to 30 hours. Plums will darken in color as they dry, shrink to the size of half-dollars, and almost melt into the dehydrator trays.

5. Store in an airtight container at room temperature for up to 1 year.

> **CHEF'S CHOICE**
>
> Regular plums are a different species from prune plums. If you want to make true prunes, buy prune plums. The dehydration directions are the same, but the finished plums will be chewier in texture when they're completely dried.

Raspberries

In my house, dried raspberries usually don't last an hour out of the dehydrator. When I do have extras, they make a great, tart snack and are also great added to cereal. They pair quite well with white chocolate, too, either in trail mixes or baked goods.

Yield:	Prep time:	Dry time:
½ cup	30 minutes	8 to 12 hours

½ pt. fresh raspberries

1 qt. water

¼ tsp. citric acid or 2½ TB. ascorbic acid

1. Wash raspberries in cold water, and set aside.

2. In a large bowl, combine water and citric acid. Add raspberries, and soak for 10 minutes. Drain and blot dry with a towel.

3. Set the dehydrator to 130°F to 140°F. Evenly arrange raspberries on the dehydrator trays, leaving some space between them.

4. Dehydrate for 8 to 12 hours. Raspberries will darken slightly in color as they dry and become leathery in texture, and some of the more fragile ones will almost melt onto the dehydrator trays.

5. Store in an airtight container at room temperature for up to 1 year.

> **DEHYDRATING DON'T**
>
> Raspberries are great to dry, but their cousins, blackberries, are not. Blackberries contain a lot of seeds, and the seeds become more pronounced when they're dried.

Rhubarb

Dried rhubarb is a great addition to scones, breads, and muffins.

Yield:	Prep time:	Dry time:
1 cup	30 minutes	8 to 12 hours

1 lb. fresh rhubarb stalks	¼ tsp. citric acid or 2½ TB. ascorbic acid
1 qt. water	

1. Wash rhubarb with cold water, slice into ¼-inch slices, and set aside.

2. In a large pot over medium-high heat, bring water to a boil. Add rhubarb and citric acid, and blanch rhubarb for about 4 or 5 minutes. Drain, rinse with cold water, and blot dry with a towel.

3. Set the dehydrator to 130°F to 140°F. Evenly arrange rhubarb on the dehydrator trays, leaving some space between them.

4. Dehydrate for 8 to 12 hours. Rhubarb will darken slightly in color as it dries and shrink to the size of dimes.

5. Store in an airtight container at room temperature for up to 1 year.

CHEF'S CHOICE

If straight rhubarb is too tart for your taste buds, add 1½ cups granulated sugar to the water before you bring it to a boil.

Strawberries

Dehydrated strawberries taste of summer. Sweet, tart, and loaded with flavor, they practically melt on your tongue. Besides making a great snack (are you noticing a theme here?), they're also fabulous in cereal and baked goods.

Yield:	Prep time:	Dry time:
1 cup	30 minutes	8 to 12 hours

1 lb. fresh strawberries	¼ tsp. citric acid or 2½ TB. ascorbic acid
1 qt. water	

1. Wash strawberries, and use a paring knife to remove the green leaves. Slice strawberries in ¼-inch slices, or quarter them. (They dry the same, so how you slice them is up to your preference.) Sometimes, really fresh strawberries are smaller, so you can leave them whole or just halve them, depending on their size.

2. In a large bowl, combine 1 quart water and citric acid. Add strawberries, and soak in citric acid bath for 10 minutes. Drain and blot dry with a towel.

3. Set the dehydrator to 130°F to 140°F. Evenly arrange strawberries on the dehydrator trays, leaving some space between them.

4. Dehydrate for 8 to 12 hours. Strawberries will become almost papery thin as they dry and are chewy when done.

5. Store in an airtight container at room temperature for up to 1 year.

Fresh and juicy strawberries can take up a lot of room on a plate, but when dried, they shrink to less than half their original size.
(Photos by Kyle Edwards)

CHEF'S CHOICE

If you don't like strawberry seeds, use a paring knife to gently cut them away along with the outer layer of fruit.

Versatile Dehydrated Vegetables

In This Chapter

- Dehydrating fresh vegetables
- Fun and flavorful veggie chips
- Cooking with dehydrated vegetables
- Simple savory snacks

Looking to make your own vegetable chips? Want to stir up your own dried soup mixes? Long for fresher-tasting onion powder? All these can be yours with dehydrated vegetables.

Dehydrated vegetables add versatility to your cooking repertoire, and the DIY versions taste so much better than their commercial counterparts. I love having dried vegetables on hand when I'm cooking. If I'm making tuna salad sandwiches, for example, and I'm out of fresh celery, I just rehydrate my dried celery. If I'm making soup, stew, or a roast and I'm out of some fresh vegetables, I just throw in some dried vegetables—the dishes taste just as good!

Besides adding dehydrated vegetables to dishes, you can also snack on them, top salads with them, and even throw them into fruit smoothies to kick up the fiber and vitamin content. Dried kale, for example, is a phenomenal addition to smoothies.

Dehydration is also great if you think you won't use up that entire batch of fresh celery, and it's a fabulous tool to have if your green beans have taken over your garden. Even better, drying vegetables is a very easy process.

In this chapter, I share recipes for some of the most common vegetables to dehydrate. I encourage you to start by drying the vegetables you think you'll use the most, but you should definitely experiment with other vegetables, too. My two favorite vegetables to dry are kale and mushrooms, but you might discover you adore dried zucchini or potatoes. Just go with what you like, and have fun!

Dehydrated vegetables—clockwise from top: eggplant, leeks, zucchini, beets, and asparagus—are great to add to soups and casseroles.
(Photo by Kyle Edwards)

In these recipes, I specify fresh vegetables, but you can just as easily dehydrate frozen vegetables. In fact, peas, beans, and corn are easier to dry when you start out with frozen versions instead of fresh because the preparation is easier. Canned veggies, however, contain a lot of salt and are quite mushy, so I don't recommend dehydrating them.

Asparagus

Dehydrated asparagus is a fantastic addition to soups and casseroles, and also works well in salads.

Yield:	Prep time:	Dry time:
½ cup	20 minutes	4 to 6 hours

1 bunch fresh asparagus (about 1 lb.)	Ice cubes
2 qt. water	¼ tsp. citric acid

1. Snap or cut off tough asparagus bottoms, and cut asparagus into 1-inch pieces.

2. In a large bowl, create cold water bath with 1 quart water and some ice cubes.

3. In a large pot over medium-high heat, bring remaining 1 quart water to a boil. Add citric acid and asparagus, and blanch for 4 minutes. Drain and cool asparagus in ice water bath. Drain again, and pat dry with a towel.

4. Set the dehydrator to 125°F. Evenly arrange asparagus on the dehydrator trays, leaving some space between them.

5. Dehydrate for 4 to 6 hours. Asparagus will turn brittle as it dries.

6. Store in an airtight container at room temperature for up to 1 year.

CHEF'S CHOICE

Instead of blanching the asparagus, you also can toss it with sea salt, black pepper, balsamic vinegar, and olive oil and roast it in a pan for 15 minutes at 350°F. Then dehydrate as directed. When rehydrated, this makes a great backpacking dish.

Beans—Green and Other

Dried green beans are great for casseroles and soups, and you can also add them to salads. I think they make a great snack by themselves, too! You can also dry lima beans, purple (green) beans, and wax beans using this recipe.

Yield:	Prep time:	Dry time:
1½ cups	20 minutes	8 to 12 hours

1 lb. fresh green beans	Ice cubes
2 qt. water	¼ tsp. citric acid

1. Remove ends from green beans, and cut to 1-inch pieces.

2. In a large bowl, create cold water bath with 1 quart water and some ice cubes.

3. In a large pot over medium-high heat, bring remaining 1 quart water to a boil. Add citric acid and green beans, and blanch for 4 minutes. Drain and cool in ice water bath. Drain and pat dry with a towel.

4. Set the dehydrator to 125°F. Evenly arrange beans on the dehydrator trays, leaving some space between them.

5. Dehydrate for 8 to 12 hours. Beans will turn brittle as they dry.

6. Store in an airtight container at room temperature for up to 1 year.

CHEF'S CHOICE

For a quick casserole, rehydrate 2 cups dried green beans, 1 cup dried mushrooms, and 4 tablespoons dried onions. Sprinkle with sea salt and freshly ground black pepper, toss with 1 or 2 cups heavy cream, and pour into a casserole dish. Top with breadcrumbs or onion rings, and bake at 350°F for 30 minutes or until bubbly.

Beets

Dried beets are great to use as a cooked vegetable dish, but you can also turn them into borsch. They taste amazing on salads, too.

Yield:	Prep time:	Dry time:
⅔ cup	30 minutes	8 to 12 hours

3 fresh beets

2 qt. water

Ice cubes

¼ tsp. citric acid

1. Cut green tops off beets, peel, and quarter.

2. In a large bowl, create cold water bath with 1 quart water and some ice cubes.

3. In a large pot over medium-high heat, bring remaining 1 quart water to a boil. Add citric acid and beets, and blanch for 4 minutes. Drain and cool in ice water bath. Drain and pat dry with a towel.

4. Slice beets ¼-inch thick.

5. Set the dehydrator to 125°F. Evenly arrange beets on the dehydrator trays, leaving some space between them.

6. Dehydrate for 8 to 12 hours. Beets will deepen to a darker purple in color as they dry and will be leathery.

7. Store in an airtight container at room temperature for up to 1 year.

DRYING TIP

Don't discard those green beet tops! You can dehydrate them, too. Blanch in 1 quart water with ¼ teaspoon citric acid for 2 or 3 minutes. Drain and cool in an ice water bath. Drain, pat dry, and spread leaves evenly on the dehydrator tray. Dehydrate for 3 to 8 hours. They'll be brittle when dried.

Broccoli

Dried broccoli tastes great in soups, adds a little crunch and zip to salads, and is wonderful to add to casseroles. I'm a big broccoli lover so I try to have some dried broccoli on hand at all times.

Yield:	Prep time:	Dry time:
1 cup	20 minutes	10 to 14 hours

1 (1-lb.) head fresh broccoli	Ice cubes
2 qt. water	¼ tsp. citric acid

1. Cut broccoli florets away from stems, and divide florets into smaller, bite-size sections.

2. In a large bowl, create cold water bath with 1 quart water and some ice cubes.

3. In a large pot over medium-high heat, bring remaining 1 quart water to a boil. Add citric acid and broccoli, and blanch for 4 minutes. Drain and cool in ice water bath. Drain and pat dry with a towel.

4. Set the dehydrator to 125°F. Evenly arrange broccoli on the dehydrator trays, leaving some space between them.

5. Dehydrate for 10 to 14 hours. Broccoli will shrink in size as it dries and be brittle.

6. Store in an airtight container at room temperature for up to 1 year.

DRYING TIP

If you're planning to use your dehydrated broccoli in soup, after cutting the florets, throw them into a food processor or blender to chop until you have very small pieces. Blanch as directed, but dry them on a dehydrator tray lined with parchment paper or a specially made liner that fits your dehydrator. The drying time will drop by about 2 to 4 hours.

Cabbage

Dried cabbage is perfect added to soups, cooked with roasted meats, and even rehydrated and used as coleslaw.

Yield:	Prep time:	Dry time:
2½ cups	20 minutes	8 to 12 hours

1 (1½-lb.) head fresh cabbage	Ice cubes
2 qt. water	¼ tsp. citric acid

1. Slice cabbage to ¼-inch thickness—it will start to shred as you slice it, and that's okay. Remove the core.

2. In a large bowl, create cold water bath with 1 quart water and some ice cubes.

3. In a large pot over medium-high heat, bring remaining 1 quart water to a boil. Add citric acid and cabbage, and blanch for 4 minutes. Drain and cool in ice water bath. Drain and pat dry with a towel.

4. Set the dehydrator to 125°F. Evenly arrange cabbage on the dehydrator trays, leaving some space between them.

5. Dehydrate for 8 to 12 hours. Cabbage shreds will shrink as they dry, shrivel, and be brittle.

6. Store in an airtight container at room temperature for up to 1 year.

CHEF'S CHOICE

The dehydrating directions remain the same, whether you use green, red, or Napa cabbage.

Carrots

Dried carrots are so useful. Toss them in salads, sprinkle them in soups, or add them to roasted meats. They're a really great dried veggie to have on hand.

Yield:	Prep time:	Dry time:
¼ cup	20 minutes	6 to 10 hours

½ lb. fresh carrots (about 1½ cups diced)

2 qt. water

Ice cubes

¼ tsp. citric acid

1. Peel and cut carrots into ¼-inch-thick rounds.

2. In a large bowl, create cold water bath with 1 quart water and some ice cubes.

3. In a large pot over medium-high heat, bring remaining 1 quart water to a boil. Add citric acid and diced carrots, and blanch for 4 minutes. Drain and cool in ice water bath. Drain and pat dry with a towel.

4. Set the dehydrator to 125°F. Evenly arrange carrots on the dehydrator trays, leaving some space between them.

5. Dehydrate for 6 to 10 hours. Carrots will shrink to about the size of a marker's top as they dry and be brittle.

6. Store in an airtight container at room temperature for up to 1 year.

 DRYING TIP

Rehydrated and puréed carrot slices make an easy and healthy baby food.

Cauliflower

Dried cauliflower florets are fabulous to add to soups and stews.

Yield:	Prep time:	Dry time:
1 cup	20 minutes	4 to 6 hours

1 (1-lb.) head fresh cauliflower	Ice cubes
2 qt. water	¼ tsp. citric acid

1. Cut cauliflower florets away from core and leaves, and chop into smaller florets.

2. In a large bowl, create cold water bath with 1 quart water and some ice cubes.

3. In a large pot over medium-high heat, bring remaining 1 quart water to a boil. Add citric acid and florets, and blanch for 4 minutes. Drain and cool in ice water bath. Drain and pat dry with a towel.

4. Set the dehydrator to 125°F. Evenly arrange cauliflower on the dehydrator trays, leaving some space between them.

5. Dehydrate for 4 to 6 hours. Cauliflower will shrink as it dries and be brittle.

6. Store in an airtight container at room temperature for up to 1 year.

CHEF'S CHOICE

I love rehydrating cauliflower and broccoli in cream or milk and then tossing in a cheese sauce for an easy casserole.

Celery

Dried celery adds a punch of flavor to sauces and soups. It's good when added as a crunchy topping to salads, too.

Yield:	Prep time:	Dry time:
1 cup	30 minutes	6 to 10 hours

1 bunch celery (about 10 stalks)

2 qt. water

Ice cubes

¼ tsp. citric acid, 1 tsp. ascorbic acid, or ¼ tsp. lemon juice

1. Wash celery, making sure no dirt remains on stalks, and cut into ¼-inch-thick slices. If celery starts to get threads, pull them off.

2. In a large bowl, create cold water bath with 1 quart water and some ice cubes.

3. In a large pot over medium-high heat, bring remaining 1 quart water to a boil. Add citric acid and celery slices, and blanch for 3 or 4 minutes. Drain and cool in ice water bath. Drain and pat dry with a towel.

4. Set the dehydrator to 125°F to 130°F. Evenly arrange celery on the dehydrator trays, leaving some space between them.

5. Dehydrate for 6 to 10 hours. Celery will shrink to about half the size of dimes as it dries and be brittle.

6. Store in an airtight container at room temperature for up to 1 year.

CHEF'S CHOICE

Dried celery is perfect for adding to tuna and pasta salads.

Corn

Dried corn is great to include in taco salads. It also adds sweetness to salsas and flavor to soups. I also think it makes a pretty good snack all by itself!

Yield:	Prep time:	Dry time:
⅓ cup	30 minutes	5 to 8 hours

1 qt. water

¼ tsp. citric acid

1 cup fresh corn kernels (shucked and removed from cobs)

1. In a large pot over medium-high heat, bring water to a boil. Add citric acid and corn kernels, and blanch for 2 or 3 minutes. Drain and rinse with cold water. Drain and pat dry with a towel.

2. Set the dehydrator to 125°F. Evenly arrange corn kernels on the dehydrator trays, leaving some space between them.

3. Dehydrate for 5 to 8 hours. Kernels won't really shrink much as they dry but will be brittle.

4. Store in an airtight container at room temperature for up to 1 year.

DRYING TIP

Shucking and removing fresh kernels from the cob is quite time-consuming, so I recommend using frozen corn in this recipe. You don't even have to blanch it before dehydrating.

Cucumbers

You can add dehydrated cucumbers to sauces and salads, and they make a great chip for dipping. Or use a few slices to transform a plain glass of water into a refreshing drink.

Yield:	Prep time:	Dry time:
¼ cup	20 minutes	8 to 10 hours

2 or 3 large, thin, fresh cucumbers
    (or 5 or 6 small ones)
2 qt. water

Ice cubes
¼ tsp. citric acid, 1 tsp. ascorbic acid,
    or ¼ tsp. lemon juice

1. Peel cucumbers and slice into ¼-inch-thick rounds.

2. In a large bowl, create cold water bath with 1 quart water and some ice cubes.

3. In a large pot over medium-high heat, bring remaining 1 quart water to a boil. Add citric acid and cucumber slices, and blanch for 4 minutes. Drain and cool in ice water bath. Drain and pat dry with a towel.

4. Set the dehydrator to 125°F to 130°F. Evenly arrange cucumbers on the dehydrator trays, leaving some space between them.

5. Dehydrate for 8 to 10 hours. Cucumbers will turn almost translucent as they dry and will be brittle.

6. Store in an airtight container at room temperature for up to 1 year.

CHEF'S CHOICE

Instead of using fresh cucumbers, you can use 2 cups pickle slices. You don't have to blanch pickle slices, just drain them and place them in the dehydrator for the same amount of time as for fresh cucumbers. Dried pickle slices are good camping snacks.

Eggplant

You can add dehydrated eggplant to dips like baba ghanoush or toss it in stews and soups.

Yield:	Prep time:	Dry time:
1½ cups	20 minutes	8 to 10 hours

1 medium eggplant

2 qt. water

Ice cubes

¼ tsp. citric acid, 1 tsp. ascorbic acid, or ¼ tsp. lemon juice

1. Peel eggplant and slice to ¼-inch thickness.

2. In a large bowl, create cold water bath with 1 quart water and some ice cubes.

3. In a large pot over medium-high heat, bring remaining 1 quart water to a boil. Add citric acid and eggplant slices, and blanch for 5 minutes. Drain and cool in ice water bath. Drain and pat dry with a towel.

4. Set the dehydrator to 125°F to 130°F. Evenly arrange eggplant on the dehydrator trays, leaving some space between them.

5. Dehydrate for 8 to 10 hours. Eggplant will turn papery as it dries.

6. Store in an airtight container at room temperature for up to 1 year.

CHEF'S CHOICE

Dried eggplant is perfect added to meatballs, meat loaves, and chilies.

Garlic

Dried garlic is a wonderful addition to your spice rack. Use it on garlic bread, sprinkle it in pasta sauces, rub it on steak—the uses are almost endless!

Yield:	Prep time:	Dry time:
about ⅛ cup	20 minutes	6 to 12 hours

1 head fresh garlic
1 qt. water

¼ tsp. citric acid

1. Slice garlic to ⅛- to ¼-inch thickness.

2. In a large pot over medium-high heat, bring water to a boil. Add citric acid and garlic, and blanch for 2 to 4 minutes. Drain and rinse with cold water. Drain and pat dry with a towel.

3. Set the dehydrator to 125°F to 130°F. Evenly arrange garlic on the dehydrator trays, leaving some space between them.

4. Dehydrate for 6 to 12 hours, checking garlic every 1 or 2 hours to be sure it doesn't turn brown. Garlic will turn almost translucent as it dries, shrink, and be brittle.

5. Store in slices in an airtight glass container at room temperature for up to 1 year, and grind or crumble as needed.

CHEF'S CHOICE

Instead of slicing, you can also mince the garlic. Then, after blanching, spread the minced garlic on a dehydrator sheet or piece of parchment paper before dehydrating.

Ginger

Dried ginger is great to add to baked goods, especially pies and breads.

Yield:	Prep time:	Dry time:
¼ cup	20 minutes	4 to 8 hours

1 (6-in.) piece gingerroot	Ice cubes
2 qt. water	¼ tsp. citric acid

1. Peel and slice gingerroot to ⅛- or ¼-inch thickness.

2. In a large bowl, create cold water bath with 1 quart water and some ice cubes.

3. In a large pot over medium-high heat, bring remaining 1 quart water to a boil. Add citric acid and ginger, and blanch for 2 minutes. Drain and cool in ice water bath. Drain and pat dry with a towel.

4. Set the dehydrator to 125°F. Evenly arrange ginger on the dehydrator trays, leaving some space between them.

5. Dehydrate for 4 to 8 hours. Ginger will shrivel up to little bits as it dries and be hard.

6. Store as dried in an airtight container at room temperature for up to 1 year, and grind as needed.

DRYING TIP

If you have an upset stomach, drink a soothing tea made of dried ginger bits. Bring 1 cup water to a boil, pour over 1 teaspoon ginger bits, let steep for 5 to 10 minutes, and drink.

Kale and Other Leafy Greens

Dried kale chips pack a wallop of iron and vitamins, and even with no fat, they make a fabulous substitute for potato chips. Dried kale leaves are also great added to stews and casseroles for a jolt of nutritious goodness, and they can even be crumbled into smoothies.

Yield:	Prep time:	Dry time:
1 cup	15 minutes	3 to 6 hours

1 bunch fresh kale (about ½ lb.)   Ice cubes

2 qt. water   ¼ tsp. citric acid

1. Cut away kale's tough stems about 3 or 4 inches from the bottom.

2. In a large bowl, create cold water bath with 1 quart water and some ice cubes.

3. In a large pot over medium-high heat, bring remaining 1 quart water to a boil. Add citric acid and kale leaves, and blanch for 30 to 60 seconds. Drain and cool in ice water bath for about 3 minutes. Drain and pat dry with a towel.

4. Set the dehydrator to 95°F to 115°F. Evenly arrange kale on the dehydrator trays, leaving some space between them.

5. Dehydrate for 3 to 6 hours. Kale will turn fragile as it dries and be brittle.

6. Store in an airtight container at room temperature for up to 1 year.

CHEF'S CHOICE

Although I love plain kale leaves for cooking and adding to smoothies, I like my snack kale chips with a bit of spice. After draining and patting dry, I sprinkle with 1 teaspoon salt, 1 teaspoon Cajun seasoning, and 1 teaspoon freshly cracked black pepper. Instead of kale, you can use Swiss chard, collard greens, spinach, or even romaine lettuce with this recipe.

Leeks

Dried leeks are amazing in soups and stocks. They add a depth of flavor you just can't get from other vegetables.

Yield:	Prep time:	Dry time:
2 cups	10 minutes	6 to 10 hours

1 large leek	Ice cubes
2 qt. water	¼ tsp. citric acid

1. Cut off leek's green tops, clean dirt from the top, and slice to ¼-inch thickness.

2. In a large bowl, create cold water bath with 1 quart water and some ice cubes.

3. In a large pot over medium-high heat, bring remaining 1 quart water to a boil. Add citric acid and leek, and blanch for 2 minutes. Drain and cool in ice water bath. Drain and pat dry with a towel. (Leek slices might fall apart during the blanching process, and that's okay.)

4. Set the dehydrator to 125°F. Evenly arrange leeks on the dehydrator trays, leaving some space between them.

5. Dehydrate for 6 to 10 hours. Leeks will fall apart into translucent strings as they dry and become papery and brittle.

6. Store in an airtight container at room temperature for up to 1 year.

CHEF'S CHOICE

Rehydrated leeks are great to sauté in butter and serve alongside chicken or fish dishes.

Mushrooms

Dried mushrooms add a punch of umami flavor to stews, soups, and casseroles.
They're even great in meat loaves, burgers, and pizzas.

Yield:	Prep time:	Dry time:
about 1½ cup	20 minutes	8 to 10 hours

24 oz. fresh white, portobello, or
    your favorite mushrooms

1 qt. cold water

¼ tsp. citric acid, 1 tsp. ascorbic acid,
    or ¼ tsp. lemon juice

1. Slice mushrooms to ½-inch thickness.

2. In a large bowl, combine cold water and citric acid. Add mushrooms, and soak
   for 10 minutes. Drain and pat dry.

3. Set the dehydrator to 125°F to 130°F. Evenly arrange mushrooms on the
   dehydrator trays, leaving some space between them.

4. Dehydrate for 8 to 10 hours. Mushrooms will shrink to about a quarter of their
   original size as they dry and be brittle.

5. Store in an airtight container at room temperature for up to 1 year.

CHEF'S CHOICE

When rehydrated, dried mushrooms make the perfect flavorful addition to
omelets and other egg dishes.

Onions

The uses for dried onions are nearly endless—soups, salads, salad dressings, sauces, etc. They're a fantastic staple to have in your cupboard.

Yield:	Prep time:	Dry time:
1 cup	30 minutes	6 to 10 hours

1 very large or 3 small fresh onions

1 qt. water

¼ tsp. citric acid, 1 tsp. ascorbic acid, or ¼ tsp. lemon juice

1. Remove brown outer layer from onions, wash onions, and slice into ¼-inch-thick slices. You can leave your onions sliced or dice them.

2. In a large pot over medium-high heat, bring water to a boil. Add citric acid and onions, and blanch for 3 or 4 minutes. Drain and pat dry with a towel.

3. Set the dehydrator to 125°F to 130°F. Evenly arrange onions on the dehydrator trays, leaving some space between them. If you diced your onions, you'll need to use a silicone drying sheet or parchment paper in the dehydrator trays so onions don't slip through as they dry.

4. Dehydrate for 6 to 10 hours. Onions will shrink quite a bit as they dry and be leathery.

5. Store in an airtight container at room temperature for up to 1 year.

CHEF'S CHOICE

You can dry shallots the same way you dry onions, but there are a couple considerations: shallots dry more quickly than onions, and if you dice them—and I highly recommend dicing them because dried, diced shallots are great to add to salad dressings and sauces—you need to line your dehydrator trays with either a specially fitted sheet or parchment paper.

Peas

Dried peas are fabulous when added to salads, casseroles, and soups. They also make a great kid-size snack!

Yield:	Prep time:	Dry time:
⅓ cup	30 minutes	4 to 6 hours

2 qt. water

Ice cubes

¼ tsp. citric acid

1 cup shelled fresh peas

1. In a large bowl, create cold water bath with 1 quart water and some ice cubes.

2. In a large pot over medium-high heat, bring remaining 1 quart water to a boil. Add citric acid and peas, and blanch for 2 minutes. Drain and cool in ice water bath. Drain again, and pat dry with a towel.

3. Set the dehydrator to 125°F to 130°F. Evenly arrange peas on the dehydrator trays, leaving some space between them. (Because they're round, peas might roll around a bit on the trays.)

4. Dehydrate for 4 to 6 hours. Peas will shrink to about half their original size as they dry and be hard and brittle.

5. Store in an airtight container at room temperature for up to 1 year.

CHEF'S CHOICE

Instead of shelling fresh peas, it's easier to use frozen peas. You don't have to blanch them, either.

Peppers—Bell and Other

Dried peppers, both bell and hot, are perfect for tossing into chilies, salsas, and even salads. I love adding them to bean dishes, too.

Yield:	Prep time:	Dry time:
1 cup	20 minutes	4 to 8 hours

2 fresh green or red bell peppers	Ice cubes
2 qt. water	¼ tsp. citric acid

1. Remove stems, seeds, and white membranes from bell peppers, and slice peppers into ¼-inch slices or rings.

2. In a large bowl, create cold water bath with 1 quart water and some ice cubes.

3. In a large pot over medium-high heat, bring remaining 1 quart water to a boil. Add citric acid and bell peppers, and blanch for 2 minutes. Drain and cool in ice water bath. Drain and pat dry with a towel.

4. Set the dehydrator to 125°F. Evenly arrange bell peppers on the dehydrator trays, leaving some space between them.

5. Dehydrate for 4 to 8 hours. Peppers will turn almost translucent as they dry, shrink to the slice of a nickel or a quarter, and be brittle.

6. Store in an airtight container at room temperature for up to 1 year.

CHEF'S CHOICE

If you're drying hot peppers, you don't need to remove membranes or seeds. You do need to wear gloves while handling, however. Otherwise, you'll suffer a nasty burning sensation from the heat.

Potatoes

Dried potatoes are easily fried, thrown into casseroles, and tossed into soups.

Yield:	Prep time:	Dry time:
2 cups	20 minutes	8 to 14 hours

2 large fresh potatoes	Ice cubes
2 qt. water	¼ tsp. citric acid

1. Slice potatoes to ¼-inch thickness and then slice into matchsticks.

2. In a large bowl, create cold water bath with 1 quart water and some ice cubes.

3. In a large pot over medium-high heat, bring potatoes and remaining 1 quart water to a boil. When boiling, add citric acid, and blanch for 4 to 6 minutes. Drain and cool in ice water bath. Drain and pat dry with a towel.

4. Set the dehydrator to 125°F to 130°F. Evenly arrange potatoes on the dehydrator trays, leaving some space between them.

5. Dehydrate for 8 to 14 hours. Potatoes will shrink as they dry and be brittle.

6. Store in an airtight container at room temperature for up to 1 year.

CHEF'S CHOICE

Instead of matchsticks, you can just dry the potato slices, but that will add at least 2 to 4 hours to the drying time. You can also dry sweet potatoes with this recipe. Sweet potato slices make great, healthy dog treats. The finished slices will be a combination of leathery and brittle when done.

Pumpkin or Squash

Dried pumpkin, once rehydrated, can be added to pies, breads, and other baked goods.

Yield:	Prep time:	Dry time:
1½ cups	65 to 70 minutes	8 to 12 hours

1 lb. fresh baking pumpkin

1. Preheat the oven to 350°F.

2. Slice pumpkin in half, and remove the seeds. Cover pumpkin completely with aluminum foil, and set on a baking sheet. Bake for 45 to 50 minutes or until tender. Let cool to room temperature.

3. Unwrap pumpkin from aluminum foil, cut away rind, and purée flesh in food processor fitted with a standard blade or in a blender until smooth.

4. Set the dehydrator to 125°F. Line the dehydrator trays with sheets of parchment paper, and spread pumpkin purée over sheets, smoothing to an even layer.

5. Dehydrate for 8 to 12 hours. Pumpkin will be leathery when done.

6. Break pumpkin into pieces or roll up with plastic wrap before storing in an airtight container at room temperature for up to 1 year.

CHEF'S CHOICE

Rehydrated puréed pumpkin or squash makes a great and easy baby food. Just rehydrate with a little hot water or broth, and serve.

Rutabagas and Other Root Vegetables

Dried rutabaga, once rehydrated, tastes great mashed. You also can add it to soups and stews.

Yield:	Prep time:	Dry time:
1¾ cups	20 minutes	7 to 12 hours

1 (1½-lb.) fresh rutabaga
2 qt. water

Ice cubes
¼ tsp. citric acid

1. Peel and slice rutabaga to ¼-inch thickness.

2. In a large bowl, create cold water bath with 1 quart water and some ice cubes.

3. In a large pot over medium-high heat, bring remaining 1 quart water to a boil. Add citric acid and rutabagas, and blanch for 4 to 6 minutes. Drain and cool in ice water bath. Drain and pat dry with a towel.

4. Set the dehydrator to 125°F. Evenly arrange rutabagas on the dehydrator trays, leaving some space between them.

5. Dehydrate for 7 to 12 hours. Rutabaga will shrivel as it dries and shrink to about half its size. The edges will be brittle, but the middle of slices will be a bit leathery.

6. Store in an airtight container at room temperature for up to 1 year.

CHEF'S CHOICE

You can also dry parsnips and turnips using this recipe. Rehydrated slices of rutabaga, parsnips, and turnips can make a tasty casserole: after rehydrating, toss with sea salt and freshly cracked pepper. Preheat the oven to 350°F. Line a casserole dish with rehydrated slices, pour 1 or 2 cups heavy cream over slices, top with 1 cup grated Gruyère cheese, and bake for 30 minutes.

Tomatoes

Home-dehydrated tomatoes taste even better than store-bought sun-dried tomatoes. They're amazing with pasta, add zip to salads, and even make a great tapenade spread when ground up with olive oil and Italian herbs such as basil and oregano.

Yield:	Prep time:	Dry time:
1 cup	20 minutes	5 to 10 hours

4 to 6 tomatoes

1 qt. water

¼ tsp. citric acid

1. Remove tomato cores, and slice tomatoes to ¼-inch thickness.

2. In a large bowl, combine water and citric acid. Add tomatoes, and soak for 5 to 10 minutes. Drain and pat dry with a towel.

3. Set the dehydrator to 125°F. Evenly arrange tomatoes on the dehydrator trays, leaving some space between them.

4. Dehydrate for 5 to 10 hours. Tomatoes will turn almost translucent as they dry, shrink to the slice of a nickel or a quarter, and be brittle.

5. Store in an airtight container at room temperature for up to 1 year.

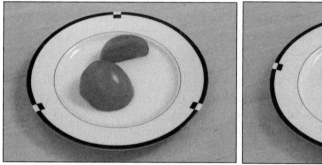

Roma tomatoes, traditionally used to make sun-dried tomatoes, are juicy and firm when fresh. When drying tomatoes, slice them thin or in half. The halves require several hours more drying time.

(Photos by Kyle Edwards)

CHEF'S CHOICE

Roma tomatoes and cherry tomatoes work best when dehydrated tomatoes are your desired outcome. Other varieties have a lot more pulp and water and don't work as well. If you're drying cherry tomatoes, just slice them in half.

Zucchini

Add dried zucchini to stews and casseroles, or use in ratatouille. You can sprinkle slices with spices and make vegetable chips, too.

Yield:	Prep time:	Dry time:
1 cup	20 minutes	8 to 12 hours

2 fresh zucchini	Ice cubes
2 qt. water	¼ tsp. citric acid

1. Slice zucchini to ¼-inch thickness.

2. In a large bowl, create cold water bath with 1 quart water and some ice cubes.

3. In a large pot over medium-high heat, bring remaining 1 quart water to a boil. Add citric acid and zucchini, and blanch for 4 minutes. Drain and cool in ice water bath. Drain and pat dry with a towel.

4. Set the dehydrator to 125°F. Evenly arrange zucchini on the dehydrator trays, leaving some space between them.

5. Dehydrate for 8 to 12 hours. Zucchini will turn almost translucent as it dries, shrink to the slice of a nickel or a quarter, and be brittle.

6. Store in an airtight container at room temperature for up to 1 year.

CHEF'S CHOICE

For a tasty snack, slice zucchini to ⅛-inch thickness or thinner (a mandoline is great for this purpose). After draining, toss with 1 teaspoon garlic powder, Cajun seasoning, or Mexican seasoning; 1 teaspoon salt; and 1 teaspoon freshly ground black pepper. Dehydrate as directed.

Dehydrated Herbs and Blends

In This Chapter

- Herb drying tips
- Drying differences among herbs
- Fun and flavorful uses for dehydrated herbs
- Tasty herb blends

Drying herbs is fun and easy. And when you dry them yourself, your end product packs more flavor than commercially dried and processed versions.

In this chapter, I teach you the basics of drying herbs and explain the similarities and differences among the various herbs you can dry. I also give you some creative ideas for cooking with your dehydrated herbs and some fantastic recipes for herb blends.

What You Need to Know About Drying Herbs

Herbs are probably the easiest things to dehydrate. Fruits and vegetables all have varying drying times and preparation techniques, but you can prep and dry most herbs in a very similar manner. Once you've dried one herb, it's pretty easy to dry another.

The main difference between drying herbs and drying other produce is that you dry herbs at a lower temperature, usually between 90°F and 115°F. In addition, herbs dry faster than produce, with some drying in as little as 3 hours and others drying within 12 hours at most. The stronger and hotter your dehydrator, the quicker the herbs dry. If your dehydrator has a thermostat, your herbs will most likely dry within 2 to 4 hours. A dehydrator without a thermostat will probably dry herbs within 8 to 12 hours.

According to Excalibur Dehydrators, if you're using a dehydrator with a thermostat, and it takes more than 4 hours to dry your herbs, increase the temperature to 125°F. If you live somewhere with high humidity, or if you're drying herbs during a time of year when you experience such a climate, increase the temperature to combat the water in the air.

DRYING TIP

If you have a dehydrator with less *oomph,* check your herbs every 2 hours. Not all the herbs dry evenly, and you should remove the herbs that are already dried so they don't overdry.

Easy Herb Prep

Herbs don't require a lot of advance prep work. They don't need to be blanched, and they don't need to be peeled, cored, or sliced like many fruits and vegetables do.

You can dry fresh herbs you bought at a grocery store or a farmers' market, or you can dry herbs you or a family member or friend have grown in surplus in a garden. You can pick your herbs any time of the day, but many dehydrator experts recommend picking in the morning, just after the dew has evaporated. Other experts also recommend you wear gloves when handling herbs because the natural oils on your skin may adversely affect the taste.

Before you clean your herbs, trim off any brown, dead, or discolored leaves. Clean the herbs of any pieces of dirt and grime, and gently rinse them in a colander to remove any remaining debris. If the herbs' stems are too large to fit in your dehydrator's trays—like some dill plants—cut the stems so they fit.

Then, if you're pretreating your herbs, soak them for 2 minutes in a mixture of ¼ teaspoon lemon juice, ¼ teaspoon citric acid, or 1 teaspoon ascorbic acid and 1 quart water. Drain, pat dry, and place in your dehydrator. It's that simple.

Not Just Leaves

For most of herbs, you'll just dry the leaves. But you can dry the flowers and even the seeds of many herbs, too.

You can dry the flowers of these herbs:

Anise	Mint
Basil	Oregano
Chives	Rosemary
Dill	Sage
Lavender	Savory
Marjoram	Thyme

CHEF'S CHOICE

Flowered herb tops not only taste great in dishes and add color and beauty, but also are fabulous in potpourri, sachets, and dried flower arrangements.

You can dry the seeds of these herbs:

Caraway

Coriander (also known as cilantro)

Cumin

Dill

Instead of drying the leaves, seeds or flowers, for some herbs, you'll want to dry the roots. You can dry the roots of these herbs:

Ginger

Ginseng

Horseradish

You'll need to prepare these latter herbs a little differently. Because they're roots, you should scrub off the dirt, especially if you harvest them yourself or buy them direct from a farmer. You'll also want to use a vegetable peeler or a paring knife to remove the outer, rougher layer and then slice the herbs into $\frac{1}{8}$- or $\frac{1}{4}$-inch slices. If they seem particularly tough, you may also want to blanch them for 1 or 2 minutes in boiling water before soaking in an ice bath with about $\frac{1}{4}$ teaspoon citric acid.

Fresh-to-Dry Measurements

When you're drying herbs, instead of measuring out 1 cup or 1 pound of fresh herbs, it's more likely you'll purchase or harvest a bunch. Estimating how much those fresh herbs will shrink to when dried can seem like guesswork.

As a general rule, 1 tablespoon fresh herbs dehydrates to 1 teaspoon dried herbs. But you don't cut the leaves off the herb stalks before drying, nor do you chop them as you would for cooking, so it's not easy to take a tablespoon measurement. Let's back up and measure by the stalk instead.

I've found that about 1 or 2 stalks yield 1 teaspoon dried herbs. The stalks I used to arrive at this measurement typically measured at least 8 inches long. So if you have bunch of fresh parsley, or about 15 stalks, you'll have about 12 to 15 teaspoons fresh or 3 or 4 tablespoons dried parsley. So if you want a large quantity of dried herbs—enough to fill a 2- or 3-ounce jar—you'll need to start with several bunches of fresh herbs. Filling even a small, 1-ounce jar of herbs likely requires more fresh than you might think.

The nice thing about dried herbs is that a little goes a long way. Dried herbs are anywhere from two to four times stronger or more concentrated in flavor than fresh herbs. Remember, 1 teaspoon dried herbs equals 1 tablespoon fresh herbs.

Cooking with Dried Herbs

Freshly dried herbs add a punch of flavor and zing to any dish. They're perfect crumbled into stews, stuffings, and casseroles; added to sauces and soups; and rubbed on meats or fish before cooking. You can add them to scrambled eggs, quiches, and breakfast casseroles. Thyme, savory, and tarragon all lend themselves nicely to egg dishes. These same herbs taste amazing in salad dressings, too.

Fold herbs into butters, cream cheese, and crème fraîche to add flavor, and stir them into yogurt, homemade fruit smoothies, and fresh lemonade. I like to add mint, thyme, and basil to sweeten dishes. If you make homemade fruit preserves or butters, you can include herbs for a savory dimension.

CHEF'S CHOICE

Try this simple recipe for garlic butter: combine ½ cup unsalted butter, softened, with 1 tablespoon dehydrated garlic, 2 teaspoons dehydrated chives, 1 or 2 teaspoons sea salt, and 1 teaspoon sugar or honey, adding the garlic 1 teaspoon at a time to avoid adding too much garlic.

Dried herbs are fantastic in homemade breads and rolls, and I adore adding them to scones—rosemary-scented scones are perfect for brunch—and chives go great with potato bread recipes. Mix dried herbs with sugar to create herbal flavored sugars. Thyme-scented sugar adds a depth of flavor to coffeecakes and scones.

For flavored vinegars and oils, add rosemary, tarragon, thyme, or savory. I love adding oregano and basil to olive oils and making herbal mustards and mayonnaises. Tarragon adds zip to mustard, while basil makes a great pesto mayo.

Blended dried herbs create lovely teas and tea blends. Chamomile and mint are two obvious choices for making teas, but you can add lavender, ginger, basil, and rosemary to tea blends, too.

 DRYING TIP

Why not add dried herbs to liquor? Mint, for example, transforms vodka into a refreshing mint vodka. Let the herbs soak in the liquor for at least 3 weeks before straining out the herbs.

Cooking and baking with dried herbs doesn't entail any special techniques, and you've probably used commercially dried herbs for years. The thing I've noticed about using homemade dried herbs is that my freshly dried herbs tend to be stronger and more vibrant in color than the herbs I buy at the store. They taste fresher, even when I buy dried herbs from a specialty spice store.

When cooking with herbs, making something like a soup or a sauce, I add them in at the last hour of cooking time. However, the opposite is true for dairy goods. Mix in the herbs to your butter, yogurt, or crème fraîche and chill for at least an hour to let the herbs' flavors infuse the dairy goods. A crème fraîche maker I once interviewed said her secret to great cream soups is to add herbs to her crème fraîche the day before she makes the soups. The flavors are just so fresh and intense after a day's melding. You can do the same with sour cream and yogurt.

Storing Dried Herbs

Dried herbs can last for about a year—sometimes more, sometimes less—in your pantry. I store my dried herbs in glass jars with tight-fitting lids to keep out the air and moisture—both of which will age the herbs. Some experts recommend storing them in dark jars, but I've never found dark-colored glass spice jars. I simply reuse my empty spice jars—after cleaning and sanitizing them completely, of course—and relabeling them.

Although you can use plastic bags, I don't recommend them for herbs. The bags tend to let in air, and herbs go bad faster when more air reaches them.

DRYING TIP

If you have a bumper crop of, say, rosemary, and you know you have more dehydrated rosemary than you'd use within a year, turn the extra rosemary into gifts. Package the dried herb in a pretty bottle with a bow, and you've got a great gift.

I crush and crumble my dehydrated herbs so they fit into the jars, but I don't crumble them completely to the littlest bits possible. Keeping them as whole as possible and then crumbling as you cook with them helps them stay fresher longer.

How can you tell whether your dehydrated herbs should be tossed? Use your nose. If that jar of dried basil smells like basil, it's good to use. If you don't smell basil—or if you only detect a very slight hint of basil—throw it out. The basic rule is, if you can smell it, and I mean really smell it, you can use it. If you can't smell it, toss it.

Never add stale herbs to your dishes. These add nothing, flavor-wise.

Homemade Herbal Blends

One of the nicest things you can do with home-dehydrated herbs is create your own herbal blends. If you have a bunch of basil, oregano, thyme, and rosemary growing in your garden, you can transform them into a dried Italian seasoning.

This is one area where drying your own herbs saves you big money. Commercial dried herbal blends are far more expensive than a single dried herb, so if you can make your own blends, you'll definitely save some cash. You'll also save money because you can mix up only what you need when you need it. When you buy premixed dried herbs, sometimes you'll only use it once or twice, and before you know it, it's gone stale. When you mix it yourself, as you need it, it won't go bad before you can use it.

The other great thing about mixing the herbs yourself is that you can include or omit herbs as you have them on hand or as your taste dictates. Don't like garlic? Don't add it to the Italian seasoning. Don't like lavender? Skip it in the herbes de Provence. Making your own blends allows you the freedom to customize to suit your preferences.

DRYING TIP

If you don't grow one particular herb, such as fennel seeds, and you really want it in your herbes de Provence, you can buy just a little for your own mix.

Basic Dried Herbs

You can use this basic recipe to create just about every dried herb you want in your spice rack.

Yield:	Prep time:	Dry time:
about 3 tablespoons	15 minutes	3 to 12 hours

1 large bunch fresh herbs (about 15 stalks)	1 qt. water ¼ tsp. citric acid

1. Remove any dead or discolored leaves. If herb stalks come in varying lengths, use kitchen shears to trim to even lengths of about 8 inches each. Rinse herbs in cold water, and shake off excess water.

2. In a large bowl, combine water and citric acid. Add herbs, and soak for 1 minute. Drain and lightly pat herbs dry with a towel. If herbs are still wet, stand them in a glass and let them air-dry for 30 minutes. (If they're too wet when you place them in the dehydrator, they'll take twice as long to dehydrate.)

3. Set the dehydrator to 90°F to 115°F. (If your dehydrator's set temperature runs higher than this, leave at least two trays on the bottom, closer to the heat source, empty.) Evenly arrange stalks on the dehydrator trays, leaving some space between them.

4. Dehydrate for 3 to 12 hours. Herbs are done when leaves crumble off stalks as you touch them. Leaves should still be green, not brown in color. After removing and discarding stalks, crumble leaves again with your fingers.

5. Store in a glass jar with a tight-fitting lid for up to 1 year.

CHEF'S CHOICE

Instead of crumbling the leaves off the stems or stalks, you can store the dried herbs whole. Stuff the whole stems of dried thyme, rosemary, and tarragon, for example, directly into a poultry cavity. Add some salt and pepper, pour on a little olive oil or melted butter, and you've got a divine roast bird.

Italian Seasoning

This savory herbal blend richly enhances pasta sauces, pizza, lasagna, and even garlic bread.

Yield:	Prep time:
about ½ cup	5 minutes

2 TB. dehydrated basil	2 tsp. dehydrated savory
2 TB. dehydrated oregano	1 tsp. dehydrated thyme
2 TB. dehydrated minced garlic	1 tsp. dehydrated marjoram
1 TB. dehydrated parsley	1 tsp. dehydrated onion powder

1. In a medium bowl, mix together basil, oregano, garlic, parsley, savory, thyme, marjoram, and onion powder.

2. Store in a glass jar with a tight-fitting lid for up to 1 year.

> **CHEF'S CHOICE**
>
> If you prefer some spice, add 1 teaspoon ground fresh black pepper and ¼ teaspoon cayenne to this blend.

Fines Herbes

This classic French herbal blend steals the show in sauces, egg dishes, and vegetables. It's highly aromatic and almost sweet smelling.

Yield:	Prep time:
about ½ cup	5 minutes

2 TB. dehydrated tarragon	2 TB. dehydrated chervil
2 TB. dehydrated parsley	2 TB. dehydrated marjoram
2 TB. dehydrated chives	

1. In a medium bowl, mix together tarragon, parsley, chives, chervil, and marjoram.

2. Store in a glass jar with a tight-fitting lid for up to 1 year.

> **CHEF'S CHOICE**
>
> You can get creative with this blend, adding savory, dried watercress, and even dried minced garlic, too.

Herbes de Provence

This delicious French blend is great for grilled fish and meats but is also perfect in vegetable stews.

Yield:	Prep time:
about ½ cup	5 minutes

2 TB. dehydrated savory	1 TB. dehydrated marjoram
2 TB. dehydrated thyme	1 tsp. dehydrated fennel seeds
2 TB. dehydrated rosemary	1 tsp. dehydrated lavender flowers

1. In a medium bowl, mix together savory, thyme, rosemary, marjoram, fennel seeds, and lavender flowers.

2. Store in a glass jar with a tight-fitting lid for up to 1 year.

> **CHEF'S CHOICE**
>
> Some versions of herbes de Provence also include 1 or 2 tablespoons dried oregano and dried basil. Feel free to add these if you like.

Bouquet Garni

Traditionally, this blend of herbs is bundled together, tied in a piece of cheesecloth, and added to soups, sauces, or stocks. It's then removed before the dish is served. I especially love using bouquet garni to add zip to my homemade soup stocks.

Yield:	Prep time:
5 bouquets	30 minutes

4 TB. dehydrated parsley

2 TB. dehydrated thyme

2 TB. dehydrated savory

2 TB. whole black peppercorns

10 dehydrated bay leaves

1. In a medium bowl, mix together parsley, thyme, savory, and black peppercorns.

2. Cut 5 (2½- to 3½-inch) squares of cheesecloth. Place 2 bay leaves and 2 tablespoons dried herb mixture in middle of each piece, and tie each with twine.

3. Store in a glass jar with a tight-fitting lid for up to 1 year.

CHEF'S CHOICE

If you'd rather not use cheesecloth, grind the whole black peppercorns and also the bay leaves. Mix everything together, and add about 1 or 2 tablespoons per dish/soup/stock.

Dried Meats and Jerkies

In This Chapter

- Dehydrating meat
- Flavorful beef jerky
- Perfect poultry jerky
- Sensational seafood jerky

In this chapter, we get to the *meat* of using your dehydrator. Homemade meat jerkies taste fresher and are more tender than what you can buy at the grocery store. Plus, you can adapt the flavors and salt content to suit your taste buds.

The delicious recipes in this chapter were developed by my friend and professional chef (and co-author of *The Complete Idiot's Guide to Sausage Making*), Jeff King. Jeff, who makes jerkies and sausages professionally for his Sausage Guys business in Chicago, adapted his recipes for this book.

One of the best uses of your dehydrator is to make different meat jerkies, so after trying out a few of these recipes, be sure to get creative and experiment on your own with different spices, sauces, and marinades.

Classic Beef Jerky

This classic beef jerky has a little bit of a kick from the crushed red pepper flakes.

Yield:	Prep time:	Chill time:	Dry time:	Cook time:
about ¾ pound	60 minutes	25 hours	about 4 hours	10 minutes

2 lb. flank steak

½ cup soy sauce

¼ cup Worcestershire sauce

1 tsp. liquid smoke

2 tsp. freshly ground black pepper

2 tsp. garlic powder

2 tsp. onion powder

1 tsp. chili powder

1 tsp. crushed red pepper flakes

1. Place flank steak in a 1-gallon zipper-lock plastic bag, seal the bag, and place in the freezer for 30 to 60 minutes or until steak is somewhat firm.

2. Meanwhile, in another 1-gallon zipper-lock plastic bag, combine soy sauce, Worcestershire sauce, liquid smoke, black pepper, garlic powder, onion powder, chili powder, and crushed red pepper flakes.

3. Slice chilled flank steak into ¼-inch strips against the grain, at a 45-degree angle, or with the grain, depending on how chewy you want your jerky to be. (Cutting *with* the grain gives you the chewiest option; cutting *against* the grain gives you the most tender jerky.) Add meat to marinade, and refrigerate for 24 hours.

4. Set the dehydrator to 155°F. Evenly arrange strips of meat on the dehydrator trays, leaving some space between them.

5. Dehydrate for about 4 hours, flipping pieces after 2 or 3 hours. Jerky will be dry, tender, and slightly soft but not at all wet or brittle.

6. Check after 4 hours. Remove all finished pieces to a baking sheet lined with aluminum foil. Return all unfinished jerky to the dehydrator for 20 to 30 more minutes before checking for doneness again. Repeat as needed until all pieces are done.

7. When all jerky is dehydrated, finish in a 275°F oven for 10 minutes. Cool to room temperature.

8. Store in an air-sealed or zipper-lock plastic bag or a glass container at room temperature for up to 2 weeks, in the refrigerator for 3 to 6 months, or in the freezer for up to 1 year.

CHEF'S CHOICE

For more or less kick, adjust the amount of crushed red pepper flakes you add.

Teriyaki Beef Jerky

If you like your jerky on the sweet and mild side, this recipe is for you. Sesame seeds give it a decidedly Asian touch.

Yield:	Prep time:	Chill time:	Dry time:	Cook time:
about ¾ pound	60 minutes	25 hours	about 4 hours	10 minutes

2 lb. flank steak

1 cup teriyaki sauce

2 TB. Worcestershire sauce

1 tsp. liquid smoke

3 TB. light brown sugar

2 tsp. freshly ground black pepper

1 tsp. garlic powder

1 tsp. onion powder

½ tsp. toasted sesame oil

2 tsp. sesame seeds

1. Place flank steak in a 1-gallon zipper-lock plastic bag, seal the bag, and place in the freezer for 30 to 60 minutes or until steak is somewhat firm.

2. Meanwhile, in another 1-gallon zipper-lock plastic bag, combine teriyaki sauce, Worcestershire sauce, liquid smoke, light brown sugar, freshly ground black pepper, garlic powder, onion powder, toasted sesame oil, and sesame seeds.

3. Slice chilled flank steak into ¼-inch strips against the grain, at a 45-degree angle, or with the grain, depending on how chewy you want your jerky to be. (Cutting *with* the grain gives you the chewiest option; cutting *against* the grain gives you the most tender jerky.) Add meat to marinade, and refrigerate for 24 hours.

4. Set the dehydrator to 155°F. Evenly arrange strips of meat on the dehydrator trays, leaving some space between them.

5. Dehydrate for about 4 hours, flipping pieces after 2 or 3 hours. Jerky will be dry, tender, and slightly soft but not at all wet or brittle.

6. Check after 4 hours. Remove all finished pieces to a baking sheet lined with aluminum foil. Return all unfinished jerky to the dehydrator for 20 to 30 more minutes before checking for doneness again. Repeat as needed until all pieces are done.

7. When all jerky is dehydrated, finish in a 275°F oven for 10 minutes. Cool to room temperature.

8. Store in an air-sealed or zipper-lock plastic bag or a glass container at room temperature for up to 2 weeks, in the refrigerator for 3 to 6 months, or in the freezer for up to 1 year.

> **CHEF'S CHOICE**
>
> If you'd like to make homemade teriyaki sauce, here's a simple recipe: combine ½ cup soy sauce, ½ cup mirin (a sweet rice wine) or sake, and 2 or 3 tablespoons sugar. You can also add 1 tablespoon fresh, chopped green onions (or 1 teaspoon dried green onions), 1 or 2 teaspoons fresh grated ginger (or ½ to ¾ teaspoon dried ginger powder), 1 or 2 teaspoons dried onion powder, and 1 tablespoon fresh garlic (or 1 teaspoon garlic powder).

Cracked Pepper Beef Jerky

This recipe makes a terrific, peppery jerky. This recipe is similar to the Classic Beef Jerky recipe, but the black pepper flavor really shines through here.

Yield:	Prep time:	Chill time:	Dry time:	Cook time:
about ¾ pound	60 minutes	25 hours	about 4 hours	10 minutes

2 lb. flank steak	2 TB. freshly ground black pepper
½ cup soy sauce	1 tsp. garlic powder
¼ cup Worcestershire sauce	1 tsp. onion powder
1 tsp. liquid smoke	

1. Place flank steak in a 1-gallon zipper-lock plastic bag, seal the bag, and place in the freezer for 30 to 60 minutes or until steak is somewhat firm.

2. Meanwhile, in another 1-gallon zipper-lock plastic bag, combine soy sauce, Worcestershire sauce, liquid smoke, freshly ground black pepper, garlic powder, and onion powder.

3. Slice chilled meat into ¼-inch strips against the grain, at a 45-degree angle, or with the grain, depending on how chewy you want your jerky to be. (Cutting *with* the grain gives you the chewiest option; cutting *against* the grain gives you the most tender jerky. Add meat to marinade, and refrigerate for 24 hours.)

4. Set the dehydrator to 155°F. Evenly arrange strips of meat on the dehydrator trays, leaving some space between them.

5. Dehydrate for about 4 hours, flipping pieces after 2 or 3 hours. Jerky will be dry, tender, and slightly soft but not at all wet or brittle.

6. Check after 4 hours. Remove all finished pieces to a baking sheet lined with aluminum foil. Return all unfinished jerky to dehydrator for 20 to 30 more minutes before checking for doneness again. Repeat as needed until all pieces are done.

7. When all jerky is dehydrated, finish in a 275°F oven for 10 minutes. Cool to room temperature.

8. Store in an air-sealed or zipper-lock plastic bag or a glass container at room temperature for up to 2 weeks, in the refrigerator for 3 to 6 months, or in the freezer for up to 1 year.

CHEF'S CHOICE

For an even stronger black pepper flavor, crack the pepper yourself using a pepper grinder.

Tender (Jerky Gun) Beef or Venison Jerky

This tender, smoky jerky boasts savory onion and garlic flavors. You can change the flavor by swapping out the Worcestershire sauce, liquid smoke, and soy sauce with 3½ tablespoons barbecue sauce, buffalo sauce, or teriyaki sauce.

Yield:	Prep time:	Chill time:	Dry time:	Cook time:
about 2 pounds	60 minutes	30 to 60 minutes	5 to 8 hours	10 minutes

2 TB. kosher salt

1 tsp. *cure powder #1*

2 TB. finely ground black pepper

1 tsp. garlic powder

1 tsp. onion powder

4½ lb. 90 percent lean beef or venison

½ lb. beef or pork fat

1½ TB. Worcestershire sauce

1 TB. soy sauce

1 TB. liquid smoke

1. In a large bowl, combine kosher salt, cure powder #1, black pepper, garlic powder, and onion powder.

2. Cut beef into cubes, add to spices, and toss to evenly coat meat with spice mix. Cover and refrigerate or freeze for 30 to 60 minutes.

3. Set up your meat grinder. Remove beef from the refrigerator or freezer, and grind with fat through a medium plate into a separate large bowl.

4. Add Worcestershire sauce, soy sauce, and liquid smoke to ground meat, and mix for about 5 minutes or until texture is consistent. Cover and refrigerate while setting up jerky gun and dehydrator equipment.

5. Set the dehydrator to 155°F. Load a *jerky gun* with meat, and pipe strips on the dehydrator trays. (If you don't have a jerky gun, line a 9×9-inch baking pan with two layers of plastic wrap 2 feet long. Pack meat mixture into the pan to form a solid loaf with no air pockets. Fold over plastic wrap to seal meat. Freeze loaf pan for about 2 hours or until meat is very firm. Remove meat from the pan, and peel off plastic wrap. Slice meat into ¼-inch-thick pieces, and evenly arrange on the dehydrator trays.)

6. Dehydrate for 5 to 8 hours, flipping pieces after 2 or 3 hours. Jerky will be dry, tender, and slightly soft but not at all wet or brittle. Flip pieces after 2 to 3 hours.

7. Check after 5 hours. Remove all finished pieces to a baking sheet lined with aluminum foil. Return all unfinished jerky to the dehydrator for 30 more minutes before checking for doneness again. Repeat as needed until all pieces are done.

8. When all jerky is dehydrated, finish in a 275°F oven for 10 minutes. Cool to room temperature.

9. Store in an air-sealed or zipper-lock plastic bag or a glass container at room temperature for up to 2 weeks, in the refrigerator for 3 to 6 months, or in the freezer for up to 1 year.

DEFINITION

A **jerky gun** is a piping tool for making beef jerky. It looks similar to a cookie dough shooter or a pastry gun but is used for meat. Curing powders, also sometimes called curing salts, are commercial mixes of table salt, sodium nitrite, and/or sodium nitrate. They prevent botulism when using ground meats and drying them at low temperatures. **Cure powder #1** contains 6.25 percent sodium nitrite, with the remainder table salt, plus a little red food coloring to alert the user it's not table salt.

Easy Chicken Jerky

With only two flavoring ingredients for the marinade, this is the easiest jerky recipe. Choose a good beer and a good teriyaki sauce because those flavors will stand out.

Yield:	Prep time:	Chill time:	Dry time:	Cook time:
about ¾ pound	60 minutes	25 hours	about 4 hours	10 minutes

2 lb. chicken breasts

1½ cups beer

1½ cups teriyaki sauce

1. Place chicken in a 1-gallon zipper-lock plastic bag, seal the bag, and place in the freezer for 30 to 60 minutes or until chicken is somewhat firm.

2. Meanwhile, in another 1-gallon zipper-lock plastic bag, combine beer and teriyaki sauce.

3. Slice chilled chicken into ¼-inch strips against the grain, at a 45-degree angle, or with the grain, depending on how chewy you want your jerky to be. (Cutting *with* the grain gives you the chewiest option; cutting *against* the grain gives you the most tender jerky.) Add chicken to marinade, and refrigerate for 24 hours.

4. Set the dehydrator to 155°F. Evenly arrange chicken on the dehydrator trays, leaving some space between them.

5. Dehydrate for about 4 hours, flipping pieces after 2 or 3 hours. Jerky will be dry, tender, and slightly soft but not at all wet or brittle.

6. Check after 4 hours. Remove all finished pieces to a baking sheet lined with aluminum foil. Return all unfinished jerky to the dehydrator for 20 to 30 more minutes before checking for doneness again. Repeat as needed until all pieces are done.

7. When all jerky is dehydrated, finish in a 275°F oven for 10 minutes. Cool to room temperature.

8. Store in an air-sealed or zipper-lock plastic bag or a glass container at room temperature for up to 2 weeks, in the refrigerator for 3 to 6 months, or in the freezer for up to 1 year.

CHEF'S CHOICE

You can use any beer you like, but lighter beers tend to work better with chicken, so opt for an ale, light lager, or fruit lager. A porter or a stout might overpower the chicken. You also can replace the chicken breasts with turkey breasts.

Teriyaki Barbecue Chicken Jerky

This super simple jerky recipe features a blend of teriyaki, barbecue, and pineapple flavors.

Yield:	Prep time:	Chill time:	Dry time:	Cook time:
about ¾ pound	60 minutes	25 hours	about 4 hours	10 minutes

2 lb. chicken breasts

½ cup teriyaki sauce

½ cup sweet or spicy barbecue sauce

½ cup canned pineapple, finely chopped or blended into a pulp, or canned crushed pineapple

½ tsp. cayenne

1. Place chicken in a 1-gallon zipper-lock plastic bag, seal the bag, and place in the freezer for 30 to 60 minutes or until chicken is somewhat firm.

2. Meanwhile, in a 1-gallon zipper-lock plastic bag, combine teriyaki sauce, barbecue sauce, pineapple, and cayenne.

3. Slice chilled chicken into ¼-inch strips against the grain, at a 45-degree angle, or with the grain, depending on how chewy you want your jerky to be. (Cutting *with* the grain gives you the chewiest option; cutting *against* the grain gives you the most tender jerky.) Add chicken to marinade, and refrigerate for 24 hours.

4. Set the dehydrator to 155°F. Evenly arrange strips of chicken on the dehydrator trays, leaving some space between them.

5. Dehydrate for about 4 hours, flipping pieces after 2 or 3 hours. Jerky will be dry, tender, and slightly soft but not at all wet or brittle.

6. Check after 4 hours. Remove all finished pieces to a baking sheet lined with aluminum foil. Return all unfinished jerky to the dehydrator for 20 to 30 more minutes before checking for doneness again. Repeat as needed until all pieces are done.

7. When all jerky is dehydrated, finish in a 275°F oven for 10 minutes. Cool to room temperature.

8. Store in an air-sealed or zipper-lock plastic bag or a glass container at room temperature for up to 2 weeks, in the refrigerator for 3 to 6 months, or in the freezer for up to 1 year.

CHEF'S CHOICE

Instead of chicken breasts, you can substitute turkey breasts in this recipe.

Lemon Pepper Chicken Jerky

This tasty chicken jerky boasts a bright lemon flavor with a bit of black pepper spice.

Yield:	Prep time:	Chill time:	Dry time:	Cook time:
about ¾ pound	60 minutes	25 hours	about 4 hours	10 minutes

2 lb. chicken breasts

Zest of 2 lemons

Juice of 1 lemon

2 TB. soy sauce

1 TB. Worcestershire sauce

2 tsp. freshly ground black pepper

½ tsp. garlic powder

1 tsp. salt

½ cup water

1. Place chicken in a 1-gallon zipper-lock plastic bag, seal the bag, and place in the freezer for 30 to 60 minutes or until chicken is somewhat firm.

2. Meanwhile, in another 1-gallon zipper-lock plastic bag, combine lemon zest lemon juice, soy sauce, Worcestershire sauce, black pepper, garlic powder, salt, and water.

3. Slice chilled chicken into ¼-inch strips against the grain, at a 45-degree angle, or with the grain, depending on how chewy you want your jerky to be. (Cutting *with* the grain gives you the chewiest option; cutting *against* the grain gives you the most tender jerky.) Add chicken to marinade, and refrigerate for 24 hours.

4. Set the dehydrator to 155°F. Evenly arrange chicken strips on the dehydrator trays, leaving some space between them.

5. Dehydrate for about 4 hours, flipping pieces after 2 or 3 hours. Jerky will be dry, tender, and slightly soft but not at all wet or brittle.

6. Check after 4 hours. Remove all finished pieces to a baking sheet lined with aluminum foil. Return all unfinished jerky to the dehydrator for 20 to 30 more minutes before checking for doneness again. Repeat as needed until all pieces are done.

7. When all jerky is dehydrated, finish in a 275°F oven for 10 minutes. Allow to cool at room temperature.

8. Store in an air-sealed or zipper-lock plastic bag or a glass container at room temperature for up to 2 weeks, in the refrigerator for 3 to 6 months, or in the freezer for up to 1 year.

CHEF'S CHOICE

This is another recipe in which turkey breasts can be used in place of the chicken breasts.

Duck Jerky

If you want all the flavors of a French-style, seared duck breast, try this delicious jerky. Hearty duck sets off the flavors of juniper berries, orange, brandy, and just a touch of thyme.

Yield:	Prep time:	Chill time:	Dry time:	Cook time:
about ¾ pound	60 minutes	25 hours	about 4 hours	10 minutes

2 lb. duck breasts	Juice of ½ orange
¼ cup soy sauce	1 tsp. freshly ground black pepper
¼ cup water	1 tsp. dried thyme
2 TB. brandy	15 juniper berries, crushed
Zest of 1 orange	2 tsp. salt

1. Place duck in a 1-gallon zipper-lock plastic bag, seal the bag, and place in the freezer for 30 to 60 minutes or until duck is somewhat firm.

2. Meanwhile, in another 1-gallon zipper-lock plastic bag, combine soy sauce, water, brandy, orange zest, orange juice, black pepper, thyme, juniper berries, and salt.

3. Slice chilled duck into ¼-inch strips against the grain, at a 45-degree angle, or with the grain, depending on how chewy you want your jerky to be. (Cutting *with* the grain gives you the chewiest option; cutting *against* the grain gives you the most tender jerky.) Add duck to marinade, and refrigerate for 24 hours.

4. Set the dehydrator to 155°F. Evenly arrange strips of duck on the dehydrator trays, leaving some space between them.

5. Dehydrate for about 4 hours, flipping pieces after 2 or 3 hours. Jerky will be dry, tender, and slightly soft but not at all wet or brittle.

6. Check after 4 hours. Remove all finished pieces to a baking sheet lined with aluminum foil. Return all unfinished jerky to the dehydrator for 20 to 30 more minutes before checking for doneness again. Repeat as needed until all pieces are done.

7. When all jerky is dehydrated, finish in a 275°F oven for 10 minutes. Cool to room temperature.

8. Store in an air-sealed or zipper-lock plastic bag or a glass container at room temperature for up to 2 weeks, in the refrigerator for 3 to 6 months, or in the freezer for up to 1 year.

CHEF'S CHOICE

You could also use pheasant in place of the duck.

Fish Jerky

This fish jerky is delicious and features tangy lemon and pepper flavors.

Yield:	Prep time:	Chill time:	Dry time:	Cook time:
about ¾ pound	60 minutes	25 hours	about 4 hours	10 minutes

2 lb. fresh, firm fish fillets, such as trout or bass

Zest of 2 lemons

Juice of 1 lemon

2 TB. soy sauce

1 TB. Worcestershire sauce

2 tsp. freshly ground black pepper

½ tsp. garlic powder

1 tsp. salt

½ cup water

1. Remove skin and bones from fish, and place fish in a 1-gallon zipper-lock plastic bag, seal the bag, and place in the freezer for 30 to 60 minutes or until fish is somewhat firm.

2. Meanwhile, in another 1-gallon zipper-lock plastic bag, combine lemon zest, lemon juice, soy sauce, Worcestershire sauce, black pepper, garlic powder, salt, and water.

3. Slice chilled fish into ¼-inch strips against the grain, at a 45-degree angle, or with the grain, depending on how chewy you want your jerky to be. (Cutting *with* the grain gives you the chewiest option; cutting *against* the grain gives you the most tender jerky.) Add fish to marinade, and refrigerate for 24 hours.

4. Set the dehydrator to 155°F. Evenly arrange strips of fish on the dehydrator trays, leaving some space between them.

5. Dehydrate for about 4 hours, flipping pieces after 2 or 3 hours. Jerky will be dry, tender, and slightly soft but not at all wet or brittle.

6. Check after 4 hours. Remove all finished pieces to a baking sheet lined with aluminum foil. Return all unfinished jerky to the dehydrator for 20 to 30 more minutes before checking for doneness again. Repeat as needed until all pieces are done.

7. When all jerky is dehydrated, finish in a 275°F oven for 10 minutes. Allow to cool at room temperature.

8. Store in an air-sealed or zipper-lock plastic bag or a glass container at room temperature for up to 2 weeks, in the refrigerator for 3 to 6 months, or in the freezer for up to 1 year.

DEHYDRATING DON'T

Do not use frozen fish in this recipe, only fresh, and use the freshest fish possible. If the fish smells fishy in the store, do not buy it. The finished jerky will taste fishy enough by itself. With frozen fish, you never quite know how long it has been frozen, and fish that's been frozen, thawed, and frozen again will have an exceptionally fishy flavor. That flavor will be exponentially stronger in the finished jerky. For a Cajun flair, add 1 tablespoon Cajun seasoning to the marinade.

Crackers, Grains, Granola, and More

In This Chapter

- Crave-worthy crackers and chips
- Crunchy croutons
- Perfect pasta and grains
- Great-tasting granola

If you haven't figured it out by now, your dehydrator is quite a versatile appliance. In this chapter, you discover it's fabulous for making crisp and delicious crackers and ideal for drying bread, fresh pasta, and rice so they'll cook faster for those hurried weeknights when you're trying to get a nutritious dinner on the table or for relaxing camping trips when you don't want to spend all your time cooking. Perfect for recrisping crackers or chips that have lost their crunch, your dehydrator can also help raise bread dough.

I explain how to do all these things in this chapter, and I also share some deliciously simple recipes for homemade crackers, granola, breadcrumbs, and more.

Crisping, Drying, Rising, and More

When crackers, chips, or cereal have started to go stale, don't throw them out. Pop them in your dehydrator to restore their crisp instead! Set the temperature to 145°F, evenly arrange the carbs on the dehydrator trays, and dry them for 1 hour. Your crackers, chips, or cereal will emerge from the dehydrator crisp and crunchy.

You can also dry fresh pasta in your dehydrator. Lay the pasta on the dehydrator trays, set the temperature to 125°F, and within 1 to 4 hours, you'll have dry pasta.

If you're making fresh bread and you have a cabinet-style dehydrator, you can use it to raise the dough. Simply remove the trays, put a pan of water on the bottom, slide in a tray above the pan of water, and place your bowl of dough on top. Set the dehydrator to 110°F to 120°F, and let your dough rise for as long as the recipe requires.

Simple Dehydrator Crackers

These crisp and delicious crackers are great for serving with cheese, sausage, dips, and more.

Yield:	Prep time:	Dry time:
about 40 crackers	20 minutes	6 to 8 hours

1¼ cups white whole-wheat flour	¾ cup warm water
1 tsp. sea or kosher salt	3 TB. extra-virgin olive oil
1 tsp. garlic powder	¾ tsp. sugar
1 tsp. onion powder	

1. In a medium bowl, stir together 1 cup white whole-wheat flour, ½ teaspoon sea salt, garlic powder, and onion powder. Slowly stir in warm water (depending on the humidity, you may need a little more or a little less water), and stir in 1 tablespoon extra-virgin olive oil.

2. Line a dehydrator tray with a liner or parchment paper cut to fit.

3. Roll out dough to ⅛-inch thickness to fit dehydrator trays, using remaining ¼ cup white whole-wheat flour to keep dough from sticking to your fingers and/or rolling pin. Brush rolled-out dough with remaining 2 tablespoons extra-virgin olive oil, and sprinkle with sugar and remaining ½ teaspoon salt.

4. Set the dehydrator to 145°F.

5. Dehydrate for 2 hours. Using a knife or a pizza cutter, score crackers into squares or triangles so they'll break apart more easily when they're dried.

6. Dehydrate for 2 more hours, and flip crackers off the liner or parchment paper and onto the dehydrator tray, so crackers are now upside down. Dry for 2 to 4 more hours. Crackers are done when they're crisp and brittle.

7. Store in an air-sealed or zipper-lock plastic bag at room temperature for up to 1 year.

Kalamata Olive Crackers

These crispy crackers are great to serve with tapenade and other delicious dips.

Yield:	Prep time:	Dry time:
1 (14×14-inch) tray	20 minutes	6 to 8 hours

¼ cup kalamata olives, pitted

1 cup all-purpose flour

¼ cup quick-cooking oats

1 tsp. sea salt

½ cup warm water

1 TB. honey

1 TB. extra-virgin olive oil, plus more as needed

2 tsp. dehydrated chopped shallots (Onions recipe in Chapter 6)

1 tsp. dehydrated minced Garlic (recipe in Chapter 6)

1 tsp. sugar

1. In a food processor fitted with a standard blade, mince kalamata olives. Transfer to a small bowl, and set aside.

2. In a medium bowl, sift together all-purpose flour, quick-cooking oats, and ½ teaspoon sea salt. Add sifted dry ingredients to the food processor, pour in warm water, and pulse and chop until dough starts to form. Add honey, extra-virgin olive oil, shallots, and Garlic, and pulse until well combined. Add kalamata olives, and pulse again until well combined.

3. Line a dehydrator tray with a liner or parchment paper cut to fit.

4. Roll out dough directly onto the lined dehydrator tray. Dough will be very, very sticky. Press dough evenly around the tray and then cover dough with another dehydrator tray liner or a sheet of plastic wrap that's first been rubbed with olive oil. Use a rolling pin to roll dough to $\frac{1}{8}$-inch thickness. Sprinkle with sugar and remaining $\frac{1}{2}$ teaspoon salt.

5. Set the dehydrator to 145°F.

6. Dehydrate for 2 hours. Using a knife or a pizza cutter, score crackers into squares or triangles so they'll break apart more easily when they're dried.

7. Dehydrate for 2 more hours, and flip crackers off the liner or parchment paper and onto the dehydrator tray, so crackers are now upside down. Dry for 2 to 4 more hours. Crackers are done when they're crisp and brittle.

8. Store in an air-sealed or zipper-lock plastic bag at room temperature for up to 1 year.

CHEF'S CHOICE

For extra flavoring, add 1 teaspoon dried or 1 tablespoon fresh chopped rosemary.

Gluten-Free Crackers

These tasty gluten-free crackers are great for serving with cheese, sausage, and dips. They're crisp and delicious.

Yield:	Prep time:	Dry time:
1 (14×14-inch) tray	20 minutes	6 to 8 hours

1 cup cooked quinoa	3 TB. applesauce
$\frac{1}{2}$ cup whole flaxseeds	2 TB. tamari or gluten-free soy sauce
1 small onion	Olive oil

1. In a food processor fitted with a standard blade, pulse and chop cooked quinoa, whole flaxseeds, onion, applesauce, and tamari until well combined and mixture forms dough ball.

2. Line a dehydrator tray with a liner or parchment paper cut to fit.

3. Roll dough out directly onto the lined dehydrator tray. Dough will be very, very sticky. Press dough evenly around the tray and then cover dough with another dehydrator tray liner or a sheet of plastic wrap that's first been rubbed with olive oil. Use a rolling pin to roll dough to $\frac{1}{8}$-inch thickness.

4. Set the dehydrator to 145°F.

5. Dehydrate for 2 hours. Using a knife or a pizza cutter, score crackers into squares or triangles so they'll break apart more easily when they're dried.

6. Dehydrate for 2 more hours, and flip crackers off the liner or parchment paper and onto the dehydrator tray, so crackers are now upside down. Dehydrate for 2 to 4 more hours. Crackers are done when they're crisp and brittle.

7. Store in an air-sealed or zipper-lock plastic bag at room temperature for up to 1 year.

CHEF'S CHOICE

These gluten-free crackers are easy to customize. Add your favorite seasonings to make them your own.

Pita Chips

Forget buying those expensive pita chips at the grocery store. You can make tastier ones in your dehydrator!

Yield:	Prep time:	Dry time:
12 to 14 chips	10 minutes	2 to 5 hours

12 to 14 mini pita rounds $\frac{1}{2}$ tsp. sea salt
2 TB. extra-virgin olive oil

1. Place pita rounds in a large zipper-lock plastic bag. Add extra-virgin olive oil and sea salt, seal the bag, and shake until rounds are well coated with oil and salt.

2. Set the dehydrator to 145°F. Evenly arrange pita rounds on the dehydrator trays, leaving some space between them.

3. Dehydrate for 2 to 5 hours. Pita chips will be crispy.

4. Store in an air-sealed or zipper-lock plastic bag at room temperature for up to 1 year.

CHEF'S CHOICE

Add 1 teaspoon garlic powder and 1 teaspoon onion powder for great garlic-onion pita chips.

Croutons

Once you make your own croutons, you'll never buy them in a box again. These croutons are delicious and perfect for topping salads or making stuffing.

Yield:	Prep time:	Dry time:
5 cups	2 minutes	3 to 5 hours

½ loaf sourdough, country French, or Italian bread, cubed

2 or 3 TB. minced fresh garlic

2 TB. extra-virgin olive oil

½ tsp. sea salt

½ tsp. Cajun seasoning blend

½ tsp. freshly ground black pepper

1. In a 1-gallon zipper-lock plastic bag, combine bread cubes, garlic, extra-virgin olive oil, sea salt, Cajun seasoning blend, and black pepper. Seal the bag, and shake it for 2 minutes to coat all croutons.

2. Set the dehydrator to 145°F. Evenly arrange croutons on the dehydrator trays, leaving some space between them.

3. Dehydrate for 3 to 5 hours.

4. Store in an air-sealed or zipper-lock plastic bag at room temperature for up to 1 year.

CHEF'S CHOICE

Instead of Cajun seasoning, you can use Italian seasoning. Also try onion powder or garlic powder instead of the fresh garlic.

Dried Breadcrumbs

Your dehydrator makes the best, crispiest breadcrumbs you'll ever taste.

Yield:	Prep time:	Dry time:
1 cup	2 minutes	2 to 5 hours

6 slices white, wheat, or rye bread

1. Set the dehydrator to 145°F. Evenly arrange bread slices on the dehydrator trays, leaving some space between them.

2. Dehydrate for 2 to 5 hours.

3. Place dehydrated bread slices in a food processor fitted with a standard blade, and chop until you've got breadcrumbs.

4. Store in an air-sealed or zipper-lock plastic bag at room temperature for up to 1 year.

CHEF'S CHOICE

For seasoned breadcrumbs, combine dried herbs and/or garlic in the food processor when you chop the bread.

Instant Pasta

If you need to have pasta on hand that cooks quickly, this is the recipe for you. By first cooking the pasta and then dehydrating it, you reduce the amount of time necessary to cook it later. You'll still need to boil water for cooking, but not for nearly as long.

Yield:	Prep time:	Cook time:	Dry time:
1 lb. dried	8 minutes	varies	2 to 5 hours

1 lb. pasta

1. Cook pasta according to the package directions, and drain.

2. Set the dehydrator to 145°F. Evenly arrange pasta on the dehydrator trays, leaving some space between them.

3. Dehydrate for 2 to 5 hours.

4. Store in an air-sealed or zipper-lock plastic bag at room temperature for up to 1 year.

> **CHEF'S CHOICE**
>
> Use this recipe to make *Marvelous Mac 'n' Cheese* (see recipe in Chapter 13).

Instant Rice

Dehydrated rice is perfect for camping and backpacking. Just add a little water, set it over the campfire, and you'll have perfectly plump rice in minutes.

Yield:	Prep time:	Dry time:
¾ cup	40 minutes	2 to 5 hours

1 cup cooked rice (your favorite)

1. Line a dehydrator tray with a liner or parchment paper cut to fit.

2. Set the dehydrator to 145°F. Evenly arrange rice grains on the lined dehydrator trays, leaving some space between them.

3. Dehydrate for 2 to 5 hours.

4. Store in an air-sealed or zipper-lock plastic bag at room temperature for up to 1 year.

> **CHEF'S CHOICE**
>
> Dehydrated cooked rice is also great to add when making soup. Add to the soup during the last 30 minutes of cook time.

Instant Quinoa

Quinoa cooks quickly—in about 15 minutes—but when it's dried, it's perfect for adding to quick-cooking soups and other dishes.

Yield:	Prep time:	Dry time:
¾ cup	40 minutes	2 to 5 hours

1 cup cooked quinoa

1. Line a dehydrator tray with a liner or parchment paper cut to fit.

2. Set the dehydrator to 145°F. Evenly arrange quinoa grains on the lined dehydrator trays, leaving some space between them.

3. Dehydrate for 2 to 5 hours.

4. Store in an air-sealed or zipper-lock plastic bag at room temperature for up to 1 year.

DRYING TIP

The grain quinoa (pronounced *KEEN-wah*) contains all eight essential amino acids—the building blocks of protein, which is why it's often included in a vegetarian diet. Rehydrate it with some hot milk to make a healthier version of cream of wheat.

Homemade Granola

Granola you make yourself is so much tastier than anything you can buy at a grocery. It's more fragrant, sweet, delicious, and nutritious.

Yield:	Prep time:	Dry time:
7 cups	5 minutes	8 to 14 hours

3 cups rolled oats

½ cup oat bran

½ cup sunflower seeds

½ cup ground flaxseeds

½ cup blanched, slivered almonds

½ cup dried coconut flakes

½ cup coconut oil

½ cup honey

2 tsp. vanilla extract

½ tsp. sea salt

1. In a large bowl, combine rolled oats, oat bran, sunflower seeds, ground flaxseeds, almonds, coconut flakes, coconut oil, honey, vanilla extract, and sea salt.

2. Set the dehydrator to 145°F. Line the dehydrator trays with liners, and evenly distribute granola mixture on trays.

3. Dehydrate for 8 to 14 hours, stirring at least twice during drying so granola dries evenly.

4. Store in an air-sealed or zipper-lock plastic bag at room temperature for up to 6 months.

DRYING TIP

Pack some of this easy-to-make granola in your backpack before you hit the trail—or your purse or briefcase before you hit the office!

Amaranth Oat Granola

This tasty granola has a crispy bite, thanks to the amaranth and steel-cut oats, and is highlighted with vanilla and cinnamon.

Yield:	Prep time:	Dry time:
8 cups	5 minutes	8 to 14 hours

2 cups instant steel-cut oats	⅓ cup coconut oil
1 cup amaranth	2 tsp. vanilla extract
2 tsp. ground cinnamon	1 cup raisins
¼ tsp. salt	½ cup chopped walnuts
½ cup pure maple syrup	

1. In a large bowl, combine steel-cut oats, amaranth, cinnamon, and salt. Stir in maple syrup, coconut oil, and vanilla extract. Add raisins and walnuts, and stir well to combine.

2. Set the dehydrator to 145°F. Line the dehydrator trays with liners, and evenly distribute granola mixture on trays.

3. Dehydrate for 8 to 14 hours, stirring at least twice during drying so granola dries evenly.

4. Store in an air-sealed or zipper-lock plastic bag at room temperature for up to 6 months.

CHEF'S CHOICE

If you don't like the crunch of steel-cut oats, you can use regular oatmeal. And if you don't care for amaranth, you can substitute ½ cup oat bran and ½ cup ground flaxseeds instead.

Peanut Butter Granola

This granola is so addictive, it'll be hard not to lick the bowl after you mix it together.

Yield:	Prep time:	Dry time:
7 cups	5 minutes	8 to 14 hours

2 cups rolled oats

½ cup oat bran

½ cup dried coconut flakes

½ cup ground flaxseeds

½ cup unsweetened peanut butter

½ cup honey

2 tsp. vanilla extract

1. In a large bowl, combine rolled oats, oat bran, coconut flakes and ground flaxseeds. Stir in peanut butter, honey, and vanilla extract.

2. Set the dehydrator to 145°F. Line the dehydrator trays with liners, and evenly distribute granola mixture on trays.

3. Dehydrate for 8 to 14 hours, stirring at least twice during drying so granola dries evenly.

4. Store in an air-sealed or zipper-lock plastic bag at room temperature for up to 6 months.

CHEF'S CHOICE

To make granola bars, form the granola mixture into 12 (3×1-inch) bars and lightly flatten the bars on the lined trays. You might need to dry the bars 2 or 3 hours longer to ensure they're crispy and completely dried.

Gluten-Free Granola

Chock-full of both quinoa and flax, this granola is not only delicious, it's also nutritious.

Yield:	Prep time:	Dry time:
3 cups	5 minutes	8 to 14 hours

1½ cups cooked quinoa

½ cup sunflower seeds

½ cup ground flaxseeds

½ cup chopped walnuts

½ cup dried coconut flakes

½ cup coconut oil

½ cup honey

2 tsp. vanilla extract

½ tsp. sea salt

1. In a large bowl, combine quinoa, sunflower seeds, ground flaxseeds, walnuts, coconut flakes, coconut oil, honey, vanilla extract, and sea salt.

2. Set the dehydrator to 145°F. Line the dehydrator trays with liners, and evenly distribute granola mixture on trays.

3. Dehydrate for 8 to 14 hours, stirring at least twice during drying so granola dries evenly.

4. Store in an air-sealed or zipper-lock plastic bag at room temperature for up to 6 months.

CHEF'S CHOICE

For extra sweetness, add 1 cup dried raisins or cherries. Or try it with ½ teaspoon cinnamon. Use a high-quality vanilla extract because the vanilla flavor really comes through when you dry granola in a dehydrator.

Dehydrating Dairy

In This Chapter

- Terrific tips for drying dairy
- Tasty dehydrated cheeses
- Yummy yogurts
- Creamy crème fraîche

Dehydrating dairy? you might be thinking. *How can you dehydrate dairy?* You're about to find out!

A dehydrator is ideal for making yogurt, drying yogurt, and even dehydrating cheese. Dehydrated cheese is great to use in place of the dried cheese you find in green plastic bottles on grocery shelves, and it's also perfect for campsite cooking.

In this chapter, I share the basic recipes you'll want to have on hand for drying dairy. I also give you a few hints about what dairy products you shouldn't dehydrate, including milk.

Dairy Do's and Don'ts

Cottage cheese, with its whey drained, and hard cheeses like cheddar or Parmesan are good bets for your dehydrator. Cream cheese is also good to dehydrate—especially as a layer on top of fruit leathers.

Never try drying milk, however. Drying milk isn't an easy—or necessarily safe—process. Most home-dehydrated milk goes bad rather quickly because any fat at all makes the dried milk go bad very quickly. It's easier just to buy dried, nonfat milk powder from the store.

Fresh cheeses and soft cheeses are also hard to dry.

Dehydrated Cheese

Forget processed, commercially dried hard cheeses like Parmesan, Romano, or cheddar. You can make your own dried cheese that tastes so much better!

Yield:	Prep time:	Dry time:
⅛ cup	5 minutes	4 to 8 hours

¼ cup grated Parmesan, Romano,
    cheddar, or another hard cheese

1. Line a dehydrator tray with a liner or parchment paper cut to fit.

2. Set the dehydrator to 145°F. Evenly spread Parmesan cheese on the dehydrator tray.

3. Dehydrate for 4 to 8 hours. Cheese will crumble to even smaller bits between your fingers, but still be slightly oily, when done.

4. Store in an air-sealed or zipper-lock plastic bag at room temperature for up to 1 week or up to 6 months in the refrigerator. Because it still contains fat, it's best to store it in the refrigerator or freezer.

> **DEHYDRATING DON'T**
>
> Do not dehydrate semisoft, fresh, or soft-ripened cheeses, all of which have a higher moisture content. Stick with the harder cheeses. Try an aged gouda!

Dehydrated Cottage Cheese

Dried cottage cheese is delicious and convenient not just for backpacking, but also for flavoring popcorn and chips.

Yield:	Prep time:	Dry time:
1 cup	5 minutes	4 to 8 hours

2 cups low-fat or nonfat cottage
    cheese

1. Line dehydrator trays with liners or parchment paper cut to fit.

2. Drain cottage cheese in a fine-mesh strainer.

3. Set dehydrator to 145°F. Evenly arrange curds on the dehydrator trays.

4. Dehydrate for 4 to 8 hours.

5. Store in an air-sealed or zipper-lock plastic bag at room temperature for up to 1 month.

DRYING TIP

Only use low-fat (1 percent) or nonfat cottage cheese. Cottage cheese with higher fat contents will spoil more easily, and it won't dry as well.

Dehydrated Yogurt

Dried yogurt, or yogurt leather, makes a fantastic grab-and-go snack.

Yield:	Prep time:	Dry time:
1 (14×14-inch) tray	2 minutes	6 to 10 hours

2 cups nonfat yogurt, lightly
   sweetened/flavored or plain

1. Line a dehydrator tray with a liner or parchment paper cut to fit.

2. Set the dehydrator to 140°F to 145°F. Pour yogurt on the dehydrator tray, and smooth with a rubber spatula.

3. Dehydrate for 6 to 10 hours. Yogurt will be leathery and pliable when done.

4. Store in an air-sealed or zipper-lock plastic bag at room temperature for up to 2 weeks at room temperature or up to 1 year in the freezer.

CHEF'S CHOICE

You can rehydrate dried plain yogurt to make a dip or sauce. You also can also make the yogurt into a sauce or dip first and then dry it.

Homemade Dehydrator Yogurt

Your dehydrator can double as a yogurt maker, and once you get the hang of making your own yogurt, you may never buy commercial versions again!

Yield:	Prep time:	Cook time:	Dry time:
1 quart	20 minutes	8 to 10 hours	4 to 6 hours

1 qt. milk (whole to nonfat, your preference)

¼ cup plain yogurt with live, active cultures

½ cup nonfat milk powder (optional)

1. In a medium pot over medium-high heat, heat milk to 200°F, stirring frequently to prevent scorching. As soon as the temperature reaches 200°F on your candy thermometer, immediately remove milk from heat to cool to 115°F. To cool more quickly, put pot in a larger bowl of ice water. (Don't let milk get hotter than 115°F because that could kill the bacteria that makes yogurt, yogurt.)

2. Stir in yogurt and nonfat milk powder (if using), and pour mixture into ramekins or small ceramic bowls.

3. Set the dehydrator to 115°F. Remove some of the dehydrator trays so the ramekins can fit inside your dehydrator.

4. Dehydrate for 4 hours, and check taste. If yogurt's tanginess is to your liking, remove from dehydrator and cool in refrigerator. If not, let it "cook" another 1 or 2 hours. Yogurt will be done when it's tangy and has the consistency of cooked custard.

5. Store in covered containers in the refrigerator for up to 2 weeks.

CHEF'S CHOICE

You can add more or less nonfat milk powder, depending on how thick you like your yogurt. Stir fruit, honey, or fruit jams in the finished yogurt for flavor. Or mix in dehydrated fruits, nuts, and other delicious goodies.

Homemade Dehydrator Crème Fraîche

Crème fraîche, also often known as French sour cream, is silky smooth, tangy, and perfect for adding to soups, desserts, and dips. But it's also expensive—except if you make it yourself, which you can do quite easily in your dehydrator. This homemade version is simply divine!

Yield:	Prep time:	Dry time:	Chill time:
1 pint	20 minutes	12 to 14 hours	4 to 8 hours

1 pt. heavy cream (40% milk fat, free of additives like guar gum)

2 TB. cultured buttermilk

1. In a medium bowl, whisk together heavy cream and cultured buttermilk. Pour into ceramic bowls, ramekins, or glass canning jars.

2. Set the dehydrator to 95°F. Remove some of the dehydrator trays so the ramekins can fit inside your dehydrator.

3. Dehydrate for 12 to 14 hours. Crème fraîche will be tangy like sour cream, but with a more gentle tang than sour cream, when done. (It will thicken like yogurt.)

4. Turn off the dehydrator, and let crème fraîche cool inside for 30 minutes. Remove crème fraîche and refrigerate for 4 to 8 hours so it thickens even more. When it's done, you'll be able to scoop it out with a spoon and it will keep its shape.

5. Store in covered containers in the refrigerator for up to 2 weeks.

CHEF'S CHOICE

If you're planning to make a dip or use the crème fraîche in a soup that has fresh or dried herbs, mix the herbs in the crème fraîche first and then let the flavors combine for an hour in the refrigerator. Also, instead of buttermilk, you can use 2 tablespoons plain, nonfat yogurt with live cultures, although the tang won't be the same. You'll get more of a yogurt with a crème fraîche texture. It's important to use 40% milk-fat heavy cream. Any whipping creams that have guar gum, carrageenan, or other additives don't have that percentage of milk fat.

Dehydrated Tofu

Okay, tofu technically isn't a dairy product, but it is dairy *substitute*, so that's why it's in this chapter. Dried tofu is great for miso soup, but it also can enhance vegetarian casseroles and soups.

Yield:	Prep time:	Dry time:
2 cups	10 minutes	15 to 24 hours

1 lb. firm or extra-firm tofu

1. Let tofu stand in a drainer for 5 minutes. Then, using a towel or paper towel, press out more water.

2. Slice tofu into $\frac{1}{4}$-inch or thinner slices, and cut those into $\frac{1}{2}$-inch-wide strips. Press tofu one more time with a towel or paper towel to remove any excess moisture.

3. Set the dehydrator to 145°F. Evenly arrange tofu strips on dehydrator trays, leaving some space between them.

4. Dehydrate for 15 to 24 hours. Tofu will be brittle when done.

5. Store in an air-sealed or zipper-lock plastic bag at room temperature for up to 1 month, in the refrigerator for 6 months, or in the freezer for up to 1 year.

CHEF'S CHOICE

Tofu is practically tasteless, so you can rub the strips with Cajun seasoning, Italian seasoning, garlic powder, and/or onion powder, depending on how you plan to use the finished product.

Delicious Dried Food Recipes

Part 3 is where you can really get creative. Once you understand the basics of dehydrating foods from Parts 1 and 2, you can expand and try making some very exciting recipes like Peanut Butter Banana Fruit Leather, Vegetable Soup Base, Trail Mix, Onion Soup, and even Backpacker's Burritos.

In Part 3, I show you how to use your dehydrator to create delicious desserts such as meringues and cookies, and I also teach you how to make treats for your dogs and cats. I also explain how to incorporate dried foods into recipes and how to make homemade "instant" foods, soups, and even mac 'n' cheese. This part is definitely recipe-focused, but it also teaches you dehydrating techniques specific to the recipes of each chapter. For example, the fruit leather chapter highlights the cooking technique and practical culinary knowledge you need to make fruit leathers easily and deliciously.

Lastly, Part 3 shows you how to make gifts using your dehydrated foods as well as potpourri and pomander balls. It even includes suggestions on how to best and beautifully package your dehydrated goodness for gift-giving.

Fruit and Vegetable Leathers

In This Chapter

- Tips for making terrific leathers
- Fun and flavorful fruit leathers
- Snack-worthy vegetable leathers
- Sweet yogurt and pudding leathers

Forget the store-bought roll-ups. One bite of your own homemade fruit leathers and any commercial versions you try will pale in comparison.

Homemade fruit leathers not only taste better, they're also much less expensive—and incredibly easy!—to make yourself. In this chapter, I teach you the basics of making fruit and vegetable leathers and give you some easy and delicious recipes to try. Once you know how to make a basic fruit leather, you can make fancy flavored and exotic fruit leathers, as well as nutritious vegetable leather bars. You can even make sweet and delicious pudding leathers!

Making Better Leathers

What exactly is fruit leather? Basically, it's fruit, vegetables, or other ingredients puréed and then dehydrated in thin sheets instead of dehydrated whole or in pieces.

The nice thing about making your own leather is that you control the sweetness, adding as much or as little as you like. What's more, you don't need to include any preservatives or additives in your leathers.

The sky's the limit in terms of colors, flavors, and fruits of homemade fruit leathers.
(Photo by Kyle Edwards)

Lining for Leathers

Nothing about dehydrating foods takes a kitchen full of special equipment, but when making leather, you do need a few other tools on hand.

Besides your dehydrator, you need some sort of liner to keep the fruit purée from congealing and dripping through the dehydrator trays. Most dehydrator manufacturers also make special plastic or silicone liners that exactly fit their dehydrator trays. These liners, sometimes called Teflex liners, are great not only for making leathers, but also for drying any foods that come in small pieces, like chopped garlic or granola.

The liners cost about $10 per sheet, which at first might seem a little expensive for a thin sheet of silicone or plastic, especially if you have a five- or nine-tray dehydrator and you want a liner for each tray. But if you plan on drying leathers or chopped foods with any regular frequency, you'll come to realize they're a good investment, as they're easy to use and practically mess-free.

If you don't have a liner, you can line your dehydrator trays with parchment paper or plastic wrap. Both work, but leathers tend to stick more to plastic wrap than parchment paper. You'll need to use new parchment paper or plastic wrap every time you make leather.

Some experts recommend using zipper-lock plastic bags duct-taped onto your dehydrator trays because they're even easier to use than plastic wrap. Just be sure the printed logo on the bags is on the side facing *away* from the fruit.

If you run out of parchment paper or plastic wrap, do not substitute wax paper. Wax paper bonds with the fruit or vegetable mixtures, and there's no easy way to get it off.

You also can use silicone baking sheets as liners, provided they fit your trays or you can cut them to fit your trays.

To prevent sticking, you can spray a light coat of a neutral oil like grapeseed, unflavored vegetable, or safflower oil on whatever you use to line your dehydrator trays.

DEHYDRATING DON'T

Extra-virgin olive oil has its place in cooking, but never use such a strongly flavored oil with your fruit leathers. Otherwise, your final leather will taste like olive oil.

If the leather still sticks to the liner after it's completely dried, pop it in the freezer for about 10 to 15 minutes. It should then pull away more easily.

A Note About Sugar and Pectin

The sugar and pectin content of the fruits or vegetables you're using will affect the outcome of your leathers. Let's start with the sweet stuff.

The more sugar in the fruit or the more sweetener you add to your fruit purée before you dehydrate it into leather, the longer the necessary drying time. If you add a lot of pure fruit juice concentrates or cups upon cups of sugar to your purée, your leather will be sticky, even after it's fully dried.

Therefore, I recommend using little to no added sugar. When you taste the purée before you dry it into leather, keep in mind that it'll sweeten a great deal as it dries. Add sugars and fruit concentrates judiciously—by the tablespoon, not the cup.

Pectin is what makes your leathers, well, leathery. Apples, pineapples, pears, peaches, apricots, rhubarb, figs, cranberries, and blueberries are all high in pectin. Melons, citrus fruits, strawberries, and cherries don't contain as much pectin, and most vegetables contain very little. My next-door neighbor Terese makes batches and batches of rhubarb leather whenever it comes in season. Unlike applesauce-based leathers, which have an apple flavor, rhubarb leathers don't taste like rhubarb, but instead like whatever other fruit it's paired with.

> **DEFINITION**
>
> **Pectin** is a naturally occurring substance found in plants, especially some fruits—part of their cell walls, actually—that's used to help thicken jams and jellies. It's the reason some fruits are more easily made into leathers than others.

When using a fruit or vegetable without a lot of pectin, you may need to add pectin or another thickener to make your leather more leathery, rather than flaky. You can find pectin in the grocery store with canning ingredients and accessories. When making your leather, add about $1\frac{1}{2}$ tablespoons fruit pectin to 2 cups purée.

Another option is to add more of a pectin-filled fruit such as applesauce. A few teaspoons lemon juice can also help thicken a leather.

Without enough pectin, your leather will flake—which isn't always a bad thing. When making my basic tomato leather, for example, I don't mind it flaking because in the end, I break off chunks of the leather to add to sauces and soups.

Picking Your Produce

You can use fresh, frozen, or canned fruits and vegetables to make leathers.

If you're using fresh fruits, you can use them raw, or you can boil them before puréeing them. Some fruits, like apples or pears, should first be turned into apple or pear sauce. Simply peel, core, chop, and boil them for 10 minutes in 1 quart of water mixed with $\frac{1}{4}$ teaspoon citric acid added. You also can use store-bought applesauce, eliminating the critic acid bath step. Just open a jar and go.

There's a slight difference between using cooked and raw fruit. Some experts prefer boiling the fruit first because it gives the final leathers that clear consistency you'd find in commercially made fruit leathers; raw fruit leathers are more opaque, like the raw fruits themselves.

For safety concerns, if you use fresh fruits or uncooked vegetables, first soak them in 1 quart water mixed with $\frac{1}{4}$ teaspoon citric acid to kill off any germs.

Neat and Smooth Leathers

Because leathers are so thin, you'll want to be sure they're smooth, too. The smoother you can spread the purée, the more evenly the leather will dry, and the more beautiful the finished leather will be.

First, be sure you purée the fruit until it's completely smooth, with no visible chunks or bits of fruit remaining.

You may need to process the fruit at least 2 to 5 minutes to get a perfectly smooth and well-blended purée.
(Photo by Kyle Edwards)

When you pour the leather from the food processor or blender to the lined dehydrator tray, pour it carefully so it doesn't spill over the edges of the tray. Pour directly in the middle of the tray.

Pour the fruit purée directly from the food processor right onto a lined dehydrator tray.
(Photo by Kyle Edwards)

Use a spatula to spread the purée outward from the middle. Be sure the tray is on a level surface like a sturdy table or a counter so the purée doesn't slide around.

Use a rubber spatula to smooth the purée onto the tray.
(Photo by Kyle Edwards)

After your leathers are dried, you can roll them up and store them in air-sealed or zipper-lock plastic bags or even covered containers, or you can cut them into bars. I've found a good pair of kitchen shears is the easiest way to trim leathers into easy-to-eat pieces.

Basic Applesauce Leather

This apple leather is easier to make than apple pie. Simply open a jar of commercial applesauce (or use fresh applesauce you've made yourself), and pour.

Yield:	Prep time:	Dry time:
1 (14×14-inch) tray	2 minutes	8 to 12 hours

2 cups unsweetened applesauce

1. Line a dehydrator tray with a liner or parchment paper cut to fit.

2. Set the dehydrator to 140°F to 145°F. Pour applesauce onto the tray, and using a rubber spatula, smooth to an even layer.

3. Dehydrate for 8 to 12 hours. Leather will be done when it's sticky but doesn't move or jiggle and peels off easily.

4. Store in an air-sealed or zipper-lock plastic bag at room temperature for up to 2 months or in the freezer for up to 1 year.

CHEF'S CHOICE

For cinnamon apple leather, add 1 teaspoon ground cinnamon to the applesauce before pouring on the tray.

Apple Berry Leather

This sweet and delicious fruit leather tastes of fresh, ripe summer berries. It rarely lasts a day in my house!

Yield:	Prep time:	Dry time:
1 (14×14-inch) tray	2 minutes	8 to 12 hours

½ lb. fresh or frozen strawberries or raspberries	1 cup unsweetened applesauce

1. Line a dehydrator tray with a liner or parchment paper cut to fit.

2. In a food processor fitted with a standard blade, purée strawberries until smooth and no lumps remain. Add applesauce, and blend.

3. Set the dehydrator to 140°F to 145°F. Pour purée onto the tray, and using a rubber spatula, smooth to an even layer.

4. Dehydrate for 8 to 12 hours. Leather will be done when it's sticky but doesn't move or jiggle and peels off easily.

5. Store in an air-sealed or zipper-lock plastic bag at room temperature for up to 2 months or in the freezer for up to 1 year.

CHEF'S CHOICE

Add 1 teaspoon vanilla extract for an especially fragrant fruit leather. Tahitian vanilla especially pairs very well with fruits.

Apple Banana Leather

This delicious leather is great to make with bananas that are starting to get overripe. It tastes delicious, and it's a great snack for school-age kids.

Yield:	Prep time:	Dry time:
1 (14×14-inch) tray	2 minutes	8 to 12 hours

3 ripe bananas, peeled   1 cup unsweetened applesauce

1. Line a dehydrator tray with a liner or parchment paper cut to fit.

2. In a food processor fitted with a standard blade, purée bananas until smooth and no lumps remain. Add applesauce, and blend.

3. Set the dehydrator to 140°F to 145°F. Pour purée onto the tray, and using a rubber spatula, smooth to an even layer.

4. Dehydrate for 8 to 12 hours. Leather will be done when it's sticky but doesn't move or jiggle and peels off easily.

5. Store in an air-sealed or zipper-lock plastic bag at room temperature for up to 2 months or in the freezer for up to 1 year.

CHEF'S CHOICE

Cinnamon, even ½ teaspoon, is an easy way to add fragrance and flavor to your fruit leathers. One spice blend I love is Penzeys Cake Seasoning. It's similar to a pumpkin pie spice blend, but it has different proportions of cinnamon, nutmeg, and anise.

Rhubarb Berry Leather

My next-door neighbor Terese Peterson has been making this tasty leather for years. It's a great recipe to have on hand when your rhubarb crop is especially bountiful.

Yield:	Prep time:	Dry time:
2 (14×14-inch) tray	2 minutes	8 to 12 hours

2 cups rhubarb cooked with 1 cup   2 cups fresh or frozen strawberries,
sugar (see following Drying Tip)   raspberries, or blueberries

1. Line a dehydrator tray with a liner or parchment paper cut to fit.

2. In a food processor fitted with a standard blade, purée rhubarb and strawberries until smooth and no lumps remain.

3. Set the dehydrator to 140°F to 145°F. Pour purée onto the tray, and using a rubber spatula, smooth to an even layer.

4. Dehydrate for 8 to 12 hours. Leather will be done when it's sticky but doesn't move or jiggle and peels off easily.

5. Store in an air-sealed or zipper-lock plastic bag at room temperature for up to 2 months or in the freezer for up to 1 year.

> **DRYING TIP**
>
> To cook the rhubarb, clean and chop the fresh rhubarb to yield at least 4 cups. Put in a medium saucepan, and add 1 cup sugar and just enough water to cover the rhubarb. Cook, stirring over medium-high heat for about 10 minutes or until rhubarb falls apart and becomes a fruit purée.

Peanut Butter Banana Leather

This delicious, protein-packed fruit leather is a great snack to take on the go. It's a better-tasting snack than those date-nut snack bars you can buy at organic grocery stores.

Yield:	Prep time:	Dry time:
1 (14×14-inch) tray	2 minutes	8 to 12 hours

3 ripe bananas, peeled

1 cup unsweetened, creamy peanut butter

1 cup unsweetened applesauce

1 TB. honey

1. Line a dehydrator tray with a liner or parchment paper cut to fit.

2. In a food processor fitted with a standard blade, purée bananas until smooth and no lumps remain. Add peanut butter, applesauce, and honey, and blend.

3. Set the dehydrator to 140°F to 145°F. Pour purée onto the tray, and using a rubber spatula, smooth to an even layer.

4. Dehydrate for 8 to 12 hours. Leather will be done when it's sticky but doesn't move or jiggle and peels off easily.

5. Store in an air-sealed or zipper-lock plastic bag at room temperature for up to 2 months or in the freezer for up to 1 year.

CHEF'S CHOICE

Instead of using peanut butter, you can substitute the same amount of almond or cashew butter.

Straight Strawberry Leather

This is my son's favorite fruit leather of all time. He can gobble it up within an hour after it comes out of the dehydrator. It's so sweet and delicious!

Yield:	Prep time:	Dry time:
1 (14×14-inch) tray	2 minutes	8 to 12 hours

1 lb. fresh or frozen strawberries or raspberries

1 TB. plus 1½ tsp. fruit pectin

1. Line a dehydrator tray with a liner or parchment paper cut to fit.

2. In a food processor fitted with a standard blade, purée strawberries with fruit pectin until smooth and no lumps remain.

3. Set the dehydrator to 140°F to 145°F. Pour purée onto the tray, and using a rubber spatula, smooth to an even layer.

4. Dehydrate for 8 to 12 hours. Leather will be done when it's sticky but doesn't move or jiggle and peels off easily.

5. Store in an air-sealed or zipper-lock plastic bag at room temperature for up to 2 months or in the freezer for up to 1 year.

CHEF'S CHOICE

Although strawberries are lower in pectin than some other fruits, if you don't have any pectin on hand, it should still turn out okay. It won't peel as easily off the liner as it would with the pectin, but it tastes just fine.

Strawberry Banana Leather

The twin flavors of strawberry and banana make this leather taste like a fruit smoothie, all rolled up.

Yield:	Prep time:	Dry time:
1 (14×14-inch) tray	2 minutes	8 to 12 hours

2 cups strawberries (½ lb.), green tops removed

2 bananas, peeled

1. Line a dehydrator tray with a liner or parchment paper cut to fit.

2. In food processor fitted with a standard blade, purée strawberries and bananas until smooth and no lumps remain.

3. Set the dehydrator to 140°F to 145°F. Pour purée onto the tray, and using a rubber spatula, smooth to an even layer.

4. Dehydrate for 8 to 12 hours. Leather will be done when it's sticky but doesn't move or jiggle and peels off easily.

5. Store in an air-sealed or zipper-lock plastic bag at room temperature for up to 2 months or in the freezer for up to 1 year.

CHEF'S CHOICE

To make this taste even more like a fruit smoothie, mix in ½ to 1 cup plain nonfat yogurt when you purée the fruit.

Strawberry Kiwi Leather

The sweet and tangy taste of this leather reminds me of Jolly Rancher candies.

Yield:	Prep time:	Dry time:
1 (14×14-inch) tray	2 minutes	8 to 12 hours

1 cup strawberries, green tops removed

3 kiwis, peeled

1 cup applesauce

1. Line a dehydrator tray with a liner or parchment paper cut to fit.

2. In a food processor fitted with a standard blade, purée strawberries, kiwis, and applesauce until smooth and no lumps remain.

3. Set the dehydrator to 140°F to 145°F. Pour purée onto the tray, and using a rubber spatula, smooth to an even layer.

4. Dehydrate for 8 to 12 hours. Leather will be done when it's sticky but doesn't move or jiggle and peels off easily.

5. Store in an air-sealed or zipper-lock plastic bag at room temperature for up to 2 months or in the freezer for up to 1 year.

CHEF'S CHOICE

For strawberry banana kiwi leather, you can replace the applesauce with 3 bananas.

Strawberry Lemonade Leather

This tart and sweet leather tastes of summer. It's very refreshing.

Yield:	Prep time:	Dry time:
1 (14×14-inch) tray	2 minutes	8 to 12 hours

1 cup strawberries, green tops removed

Zest of 1 lemon

Juice of 1 lemon

1¼ cups applesauce

1. Line a dehydrator tray with a liner or parchment paper cut to fit.

2. In a food processor fitted with a standard blade, purée strawberries, lemon zest, lemon juice, and applesauce until smooth and no lumps remain.

3. Set the dehydrator to 140°F to 145°F. Pour purée onto the tray, and using a rubber spatula, smooth to an even layer.

4. Dehydrate for 8 to 12 hours. Leather will be done when it's sticky but doesn't move or jiggle and peels off easily.

5. Store in an air-sealed or zipper-lock plastic bag at room temperature for up to 2 months or in the freezer for up to 1 year.

> **DRYING TIP**
>
> This recipe is a bit on the tart side, so you might want to add 1 or 2 tablespoons sugar to sweeten it a bit. Add the sugar by the teaspoon and then taste the purée so you don't add too much.

Strawberry Merlot Leather

This leather reminds me of a refreshing glass of sangria on a hot summer day.

Yield:	Prep time:	Dry time:
1 (14×14-inch) tray	2 minutes	8 to 12 hours

½ cup strawberries, green tops removed

⅓ cup merlot or other red wine

2 TB. sugar

1 cup applesauce

1. Line a dehydrator tray with a liner or parchment paper cut to fit.

2. In a food processor fitted with a standard blade, purée strawberries, merlot, sugar, and applesauce until smooth and no lumps remain.

3. Set the dehydrator to 140°F to 145°F. Pour purée onto the tray, and using a rubber spatula, smooth to an even layer.

4. Dehydrate for 8 to 12 hours. Leather will be done when it's sticky but doesn't move or jiggle and peels off easily.

5. Store in an air-sealed or zipper-lock plastic bag at room temperature for up to 2 months or in the freezer for up to 1 year.

> **CHEF'S CHOICE**
>
> For strawberry daiquiri leather, replace the merlot with the same amount of rum and add the juice and zest of 1 lime. Keep both of these leathers for adults only.

Pineapple Leather

This delicious leather tastes almost like an exotic cocktail. It's sweet and reminiscent of tropical beaches.

Yield:	Prep time:	Dry time:
1 (14×14-inch) tray	2 minutes	8 to 12 hours

1 (16-oz.) can unsweetened pineapple chunks, drained

1 cup unsweetened applesauce

1. Line a dehydrator tray with a liner or parchment paper cut to fit.

2. In a food processor fitted with a standard blade, purée pineapple chunks until smooth and no lumps remain. Add applesauce, and blend.

3. Set the dehydrator to 140°F to 145°F. Pour purée onto the tray, and using a rubber spatula, smooth to an even layer.

4. Dehydrate for 8 to 12 hours. Leather will be done when it's sticky but doesn't move or jiggle and peels off easily.

5. Store in an air-sealed or zipper-lock plastic bag at room temperature for up to 2 months or in the freezer for up to 1 year.

CHEF'S CHOICE

To make this leather taste even more like an exotic drink, add 1 teaspoon rum extract or sprinkle with ½ cup unsweetened dried coconut.

Mandarin Orange Pineapple Leather

This leather reminds me of my husband's Grandma Marvel's fruit salad. It's sunny and sweet.

Yield:	Prep time:	Dry time:
1 (14×14-inch) tray	2 minutes	8 to 12 hours

1 (20-oz.) can crushed unsweetened pineapple, some juice drained

1 (11-oz.) can mandarin oranges, unsweetened or lightly sweetened, drained

½ cup applesauce

1. Line a dehydrator tray with a liner or parchment paper cut to fit.

2. In a food processor fitted with a standard blade, purée pineapple, mandarin oranges, and applesauce until smooth and no lumps remain.

3. Set the dehydrator to 140°F to 145°F. Pour purée onto the tray, and using a rubber spatula, smooth to an even layer.

4. Dehydrate for 8 to 12 hours. Leather will be done when it's sticky but doesn't move or jiggle and peels off easily.

5. Store in an air-sealed or zipper-lock plastic bag at room temperature for up to 2 months or in the freezer for up to 1 year.

CHEF'S CHOICE

For a more intense orange flavor, add the zest of 1 orange.

Pineapple Kiwi Leather

Tart, sweet, and just a touch exotic, this fruit leather tastes amazing.

Yield:	Prep time:	Dry time:
1½ (14×14-inch) trays	2 minutes	8 to 14 hours

1 (20-oz.) can crushed pineapple	4 kiwis, peeled

1. Line a dehydrator tray with a liner or parchment paper cut to fit.

2. In a food processor fitted with a standard blade, purée pineapple and kiwis until smooth and no lumps remain.

3. Set the dehydrator to 140°F to 145°F. Pour purée onto the tray, and using a rubber spatula, smooth to an even layer.

4. Dehydrate for 8 to 14 hours. Leather will be done when it's sticky but doesn't move or jiggle and peels off easily.

5. Store in an air-sealed or zipper-lock plastic bag at room temperature for up to 2 months or in the freezer for up to 1 year.

 DRYING TIP

This leather is a lovely green, but for a more golden color, use golden kiwis instead.

Piña Colada Leather

If you like piña coladas and getting caught in the rain, you'll love this delicious leather.

Yield:	Prep time:	Dry time:
2 (14×14-inch) trays	2 minutes	8 to 12 hours

1 (20-oz.) can crushed pineapple	½ cup coconut milk
1 banana, peeled	

1. Line a dehydrator tray with a liner or parchment paper cut to fit.

2. In a food processor fitted with a standard blade, purée pineapple, banana, and coconut milk until smooth and no lumps remain.

3. Set the dehydrator to 140°F to 145°F. Pour purée onto the tray, and using a rubber spatula, smooth to an even layer.

4. Dehydrate for 8 to 12 hours. Leather will be done when it's sticky but doesn't move or jiggle and peels off easily.

5. Store in an air-sealed or zipper-lock plastic bag at room temperature for up to 2 months or in the freezer for up to 1 year.

CHEF'S CHOICE

For more of a piña colada taste, add ½ teaspoon rum extract or 1 tablespoon actual rum.

Peach Leather

This light orange leather is sweet and delicious, and it will be hard not to gobble it up all at once.

Yield:	Prep time:	Dry time:
1 (14×14-inch) tray	2 minutes	8 to 12 hours

1½ cups peeled peach slices   1 cup unsweetened applesauce

1. Line a dehydrator tray with a liner or parchment paper cut to fit.

2. In a food processor fitted with a standard blade, purée peach slices and applesauce until smooth and no lumps remain.

3. Set the dehydrator to 140°F to 145°F. Pour purée onto the tray, and using a rubber spatula, smooth to an even layer.

4. Dehydrate for 8 to 12 hours. Leather will be done when it's sticky but doesn't move or jiggle and peels off easily.

5. Store in an air-sealed or zipper-lock plastic bag at room temperature for up to 2 months or in the freezer for up to 1 year.

Raspberry Lime Leather

Sweet, tangy, and delicious, this leather tastes just a bit exotic, while staying familiar at the same time.

Yield:	Prep time:	Dry time:
1 (14×14-inch) tray	2 minutes	8 to 12 hours

½ pt. fresh raspberries	Juice of 1 lime
Zest of 1 lime	1½ cups applesauce

1. Line a dehydrator tray with a liner or parchment paper cut to fit.

2. In a food processor fitted with a standard blade, purée raspberries, lime zest, lime juice, and applesauce until smooth and no lumps remain.

3. Set the dehydrator to 140°F to 145°F. Pour purée onto the tray, and using a rubber spatula, smooth to an even layer.

4. Dehydrate for 8 to 12 hours. Leather will be done when it's sticky but doesn't move or jiggle and peels off easily.

5. Store in an air-sealed or zipper-lock plastic bag at room temperature for up to 2 months or in the freezer for up to 1 year.

Orange Leather

This leather boasts a soft, light-orange color, and a definite sweet citrus taste.

Yield:	Prep time:	Dry time:
1 (14×14-inch) tray	2 minutes	8 to 12 hours

1 orange, peeled	1 cup applesauce

1. Line a dehydrator tray with a liner or parchment paper cut to fit.

2. In a food processor fitted with a standard blade, purée orange and applesauce until smooth and no lumps remain.

3. Set the dehydrator to 140°F to 145°F. Pour purée onto the tray, and using a rubber spatula, smooth to an even layer.

4. Dehydrate for 8 to 12 hours. Leather will be done when it's sticky but doesn't move or jiggle and peels off easily.

5. Store in an air-sealed or zipper-lock plastic bag at room temperature for up to 2 months or in the freezer for up to 1 year.

CHEF'S CHOICE

For a more intense orange flavor, zest the orange before peeling, and add the zest to the purée.

Fruit Cocktail Leather

If you love fruit cocktail, you'll love this fresh, fruity, and delicious leather.

Yield:	Prep time:	Dry time:
1½ (14×14-inch) trays	2 minutes	8 to 14 hours

1 (15-oz.) can no-sugar-added fruit cocktail, with juice	2 bananas, peeled

1. Line a dehydrator tray with a liner or parchment paper cut to fit.

2. In a food processor fitted with a standard blade, purée fruit cocktail, with juice, and bananas until smooth and no lumps remain.

3. Set the dehydrator to 140°F to 145°F. Pour purée onto the tray, and using a rubber spatula, smooth to an even layer.

4. Dehydrate for 8 to 14 hours. Leather will be done when it's sticky but doesn't move or jiggle and peels off easily.

5. Store in an air-sealed or zipper-lock plastic bag at room temperature for up to 2 months or in the freezer for up to 1 year.

> **DRYING TIP**
>
> If you use a fruit cocktail mix with sugar added, your drying time will be anywhere from 2 to 6 hours longer.

Banana Chocolate Coconut Leather

This leather tastes like a chocolate candy bar! It's sweet, fruity, and oh-so-good!

Yield:	Prep time:	Dry time:
1 (14×14-inch) tray	2 minutes	8 to 12 hours

3 bananas, peeled
½ cup coconut milk
¼ cup cocoa powder

2 TB. sugar
¼ tsp. chocolate extract

1. Line a dehydrator tray with a liner or parchment paper cut to fit.

2. In a food processor fitted with a standard blade, purée bananas, coconut milk, cocoa powder, sugar, and chocolate extract until smooth as chocolate sauce and no lumps remain.

3. Set the dehydrator to 140°F to 145°F. Pour purée onto the tray, and using a rubber spatula, smooth to an even layer.

4. Dehydrate for 8 to 12 hours. Leather will be done when it's sticky but doesn't move or jiggle and peels off easily.

5. Store in an air-sealed or zipper-lock plastic bag at room temperature for up to 2 months or in the freezer for up to 1 year.

CHEF'S CHOICE

The chocolate extract intensifies the chocolate flavor, but if you don't have any on hand, you can leave it out, or you can replace it with vanilla extract.

Yogurt and Applesauce Leather

This sweet leather is a healthy substitute for cookies. It's more filling than a plain fruit leather, and it's perfect when you need a quick protein pick-me-up.

Yield:	Prep time:	Dry time:
1 (14×14-inch) tray	2 minutes	8 to 12 hours

2 cups unsweetened applesauce

2 cups lightly sweetened or unsweetened nonfat yogurt

1. Line a dehydrator tray with a liner or parchment paper cut to fit.

2. In a food processor fitted with a standard blade, blend applesauce and yogurt until smooth and no lumps remain.

3. Set the dehydrator to 140°F to 145°F. Pour purée onto the tray, and using a rubber spatula, smooth to an even layer.

4. Dehydrate for 8 to 12 hours. Leather will be done when it's sticky but doesn't move or jiggle and peels off easily.

5. Store in an air-sealed or zipper-lock plastic bag at room temperature for up to 2 months or in the freezer for up to 1 year.

CHEF'S CHOICE

If you use plain or vanilla yogurt, the resulting leather will taste like apples, but you can change the flavor base just by changing the flavor of yogurt you use.

Chocolate Peanut Butter Yogurt Leather

This leather tastes like a chocolate and peanut butter bar. Delicious!

Yield:	Prep time:	Dry time:
1 (14×14-inch) tray	2 minutes	8 to 12 hours

½ cup unsweetened peanut butter

½ cup lightly sweetened or unsweetened nonfat yogurt

¼ cup cocoa powder

2 to 4 TB. sugar

½ tsp. vanilla extract

½ tsp. chocolate extract

1. Line a dehydrator tray with a liner or parchment paper cut to fit.

2. In a food processor fitted with a standard blade, purée peanut butter, yogurt, cocoa powder, sugar, vanilla extract, and chocolate extract until smooth and no lumps remain.

3. Line dehydrator tray with specially fitted sheet or parchment paper cut to fit tray. Pour peanut butter–yogurt mixture on sheet. Smooth down with a rubber spatula. Set the dehydrator to 140°F to 145°F.

4. Dehydrate for 8 to 12 hours. Leather will be done when it's sticky but doesn't move or jiggle and peels off easily.

5. Store in an air-sealed or zipper-lock plastic bag at room temperature for up to 2 months or in the freezer for up to 1 year.

DRYING TIP

You can snip this leather into bars, but I like rolling it up and slicing it into leather-yogurt rolls.

Basic Instant Pudding Leather

Instant pudding leather makes for a fast, sweet, portable snack.

Yield:	Prep time:	Dry time:
1 (14×14-inch) tray	2 minutes	8 to 12 hours

1 (3.56-oz.) pkg. instant pudding
  (any flavor)

½ tsp. vanilla extract

2 cups nonfat milk

1. Line a dehydrator tray with a liner or parchment paper cut to fit.

2. In a medium bowl, whisk together instant pudding, milk, and extract until smooth and no lumps remain.

3. Set the dehydrator to 140°F to 145°F. Pour purée onto the tray, and using a rubber spatula, smooth to an even layer.

4. Dehydrate for 8 to 12 hours. Leather will be done when it's sticky but doesn't move or jiggle and peels off easily.

5. Store in an air-sealed or zipper-lock plastic bag at room temperature for up to 2 months or in the freezer for up to 1 year.

CHEF'S CHOICE

If you use chocolate pudding, you can make a mint chocolate leather by adding mint extract instead of vanilla extract. You can also use chocolate extract to add some *oomph* to the chocolate flavor.

Lactose-Free Fancy Chocolate Pudding Leather

This is my chocoholic-husband's favorite leather, and he once ate the entire batch in one sitting. It tastes sort of like an Almond Joy candy bar.

Yield:	Prep time:	Dry time:
1 (14×14-inch) tray	2 minutes	8 to 12 hours

1 (3.56-oz.) pkg. chocolate instant pudding

2 cups coconut milk

½ tsp. vanilla extract

½ tsp. chocolate extract

6 TB. unsweetened toasted coconut shreds

3 TB. thinly sliced toasted almonds

1. Line a dehydrator tray with a liner or parchment paper cut to fit.

2. In a medium bowl, whisk together instant pudding, coconut milk, vanilla extract, and chocolate extract until smooth and no lumps remain.

3. Set the dehydrator to 140°F to 145°F. Pour purée onto the tray, and using a rubber spatula, smooth to an even layer. Sprinkle coconut shreds and almond slices on top, pressing them into pudding slightly.

4. Dehydrate for 8 to 12 hours. Leather will be done when it's sticky but doesn't move or jiggle and peels off easily.

5. Store in an air-sealed or zipper-lock plastic bag at room temperature for up to 2 months or in the freezer for up to 1 year.

CHEF'S CHOICE

You can use regular, nonfat milk in this recipe, but the coconut milk adds a silky, coconut flavor.

Carrot (Basic Vegetable) Leather

You can easily modify this recipe for carrot leather for other vegetables. Adjusting the applesauce content makes it sweeter or not, depending on your taste.

Yield:	Prep time:	Dry time:
1 (14×14-inch) tray	2 minutes	3 to 6 hours

1 qt. water
½ lb. (about 2 cups) fresh carrots, peeled, cleaned, and chopped

¼ tsp. citric acid
1 TB. plus 1½ tsp. fruit pectin
¼ to ½ cup applesauce

1. Line a dehydrator tray with a liner or parchment paper cut to fit.

2. In a large pot over medium-high heat, bring water to a boil. Add carrots and citric acid, and boil for at least 6 minutes for carrots and most other vegetables but less for greens. Drain and cool to room temperature.

3. In a food processor fitted with a standard blade, purée carrots with fruit pectin until smooth and no lumps remain. Add ¼ cup applesauce, and blend. If purée isn't smooth enough, add another ¼ cup, and blend again.

4. Set the dehydrator to 140°F to 145°F. Pour purée onto the tray, and using a rubber spatula, smooth to an even layer.

5. Dehydrate for 3 to 6 hours, checking every 1 or 2 hours because vegetable leather cooks more quickly than fruit leathers. If you leave it too long, it will chunk off in large flakes. Leather will be done when it's sticky but doesn't move or jiggle and peels off easily.

6. Store in an air-sealed or zipper-lock plastic bag at room temperature for up to 2 months or in the freezer for up to 1 year.

CHEF'S CHOICE

Carrots, squash, and beets make for sweet leathers suitable for snacking while greens and other more bitter vegetables make savory leathers. You can use savory leathers as snacks, but breaking off pieces or slices to add as flavorings to sauces and stews is also a good use.

Tomato Leather

This leather makes a great substitute in recipes for tomato paste. I love using it in recipes where I only need 1 or 2 tablespoons tomato paste. Instead of opening an entire can, I can just break off a few square inches of leather.

Yield:	Prep time:	Dry time:
1 (14×14-inch) tray	2 minutes	8 to 12 hours

1 lb. fresh tomatoes   1 TB. plus 1½ tsp. fruit pectin

1. Line a dehydrator tray with a liner or parchment paper cut to fit.

2. In a food processor fitted with a standard blade, purée tomatoes and pectin until smooth and no lumps remain.

3. Set the dehydrator to 140°F to 145°F. Pour purée onto the tray, and using a rubber spatula, smooth to an even layer.

4. Dehydrate for 8 to 12 hours. Leather will be done when it's sticky but doesn't move or jiggle and peels off easily.

5. Store in an air-sealed or zipper-lock plastic bag at room temperature for up to 2 months or in the freezer for up to 1 year.

CHEF'S CHOICE

Although tomatoes are low in pectin, when I haven't had any on hand, I've just done without. The leather doesn't pull off the sheets smoothly, and it does flake, but because I'm not using it for snacking, I don't mind. Another substitute is to add 1 tablespoon cornstarch dissolved in 1 or 2 tablespoons water. Add the cornstarch mixture to the food processor when you would add the pectin.

Vegetable and Fruit Powders

In This Chapter

- Versatile vegetable powders
- Flavorful fruit powders
- Super soup bases
- Easy and nutritious baby food

One of the best uses of dried vegetables and fruits is to flavor and add a jolt of nutrition to soups, sauces, casseroles, baked goods, and more. But sometimes you want the flavoring without the whole pieces of produce.

That's where vegetable and fruit powders come in handy. Want a little onion flavoring for your steak sauce? Sprinkle on some onion powder. Want a little extra iron in your morning smoothie? Add 1 tablespoon powdered greens. Need some *oomph* in your faux bolognaise spaghetti sauce? Add a little celery powder.

This chapter is all about vegetable and fruit powders. In it, I also share some basic powder recipes you'll enjoy creating, and that are great to have on hand in your pantry.

Making Produce Powders

You can convert all vegetables to powders. Some fruits, too. The best fruits to convert to powder are those that are brittle when they're dehydrated. Berries, rhubarb, and melon are the best fruits to turn into powders. Fruits that still are pliable and sticky won't convert to powders well. If you want a powder substitute for these fruits, chop them finely either before or after you dry them.

To make powder, you'll need to have a food processor, blender, or coffee grinder. All the recipes in this chapter call for a food processor fitted with a standard chopping blade, but you might find one of the other appliances works better for you. You even can use an old-fashioned mortar and pestle to make powders, and for some vegetables, you simply can crumble them with your fingers.

Unless you have a very high-powered food processor or blender, the powders won't be as finely powdered as commercially produced powders, but they'll work just as well—and taste so much better!—than anything made commercially.

Using Produce Powders

Vegetable powders are great to add a jolt of flavor to soups, stocks, casseroles, meat dishes, … the list goes on. Onion, mushroom, and celery powder are the three vegetable powders I use the most, and I like to keep them stocked. I use the onion and celery powders for salad dressings, and the mushroom powder adds flavor to several different stocks and sauces.

Vegetable powders—especially those made from really nutritious vegetables like kale and spinach—also are perfect for sneaking nutrition into foods. Add 1 tablespoon to fruit and yogurt smoothies, toss some into meatball or meatloaf recipes, or even add it to hummus and other dips.

Fruit powders sweeten cooked cereals, and you can also use them to make instant fruit sauces for scones or pancakes.

Both vegetable and fruit powders make an excellent instant baby food, too!

The recipes in this chapter give you a starting point, but I encourage you to experiment with other produce.

Onion Powder

This is one of the most versatile powders ever—toss it in soups, rub it on meats, sprinkle it in salad dressings, and so much more. You'll find you use it all the time.

Yield:	Prep time:
²⁄₃ cup	10 minutes

1 batch dehydrated *Onions* (see recipe in Chapter 6)

1. In a food processor fitted with a standard blade, chop onions until you reach a powdery consistency.

2. Store in an air-sealed or zipper-lock plastic bag or a bottle at room temperature for up to 1 year.

CHEF'S CHOICE

For onion salt, combine the whole batch with ¼ to ½ cup kosher salt.

Garlic Powder

This is another very versatile powder. It's terrific in so many dishes.

Yield:	Prep time:
½ cup	10 minutes

4 bulbs dehydrated *Garlic* (see recipe in Chapter 6)

1. Place garlic in a zipper-lock plastic bag, seal the bag, and break garlic slices into tiny pieces using a mallet.

2. Store in an air-sealed or zipper-lock plastic bag or a bottle at room temperature for up to 1 year.

CHEF'S CHOICE

For garlic salt, combine the whole batch with ¼ to ½ cup kosher salt and 1 or 2 tablespoons dried parsley flakes.

Mushroom Powder

This is my secret ingredient. When I'm cooking a sauce or a casserole and it's missing that savory something (umami), I add 1 tablespoon Mushroom Powder, and it wakes the dish right up.

Yield:	Prep time:
¾ cup	10 minutes

1 batch dehydrated *Mushrooms* (see recipe in Chapter 6)

1. In a food processor fitted with a standard blade, chop mushrooms until you reach a powdery consistency.

2. Store in an air-sealed or zipper-lock plastic bag or a bottle at room temperature for up to 1 year.

CHEF'S CHOICE

Mushroom Powder is great in omelets and other egg dishes. For fantastic scrambled eggs, whisk together 3 eggs, 1 tablespoon Mushroom Powder, and 2 or 3 tablespoons heavy cream. Pour mixture into a medium saucepan or skillet over medium-high heat, add 2 tablespoons butter, and sauté for about 5 to 8 minutes. Drizzle with a little truffle oil to finish.

Celery Powder

This versatile powder is perfect in soups and salad dressings.

Yield:	Prep time:
½ cup	10 minutes

1 batch dehydrated *Celery* (see recipe in Chapter 6)

1. In a food processor fitted with a standard blade, chop celery until you reach a powdery consistency.

2. Store in an air-sealed or zipper-lock plastic bag or a bottle at room temperature for up to 1 year.

CHEF'S CHOICE

Although most celery salts are salt combined with dried celery seeds, you can make a celery salt when you combine 1 batch Celery Powder with about ¼ to ½ cup kosher salt.

Kale Powder

This powder is perfect for sneaking in extra nutrition into smoothies and other dishes.

Yield:	Prep time:
½ cup	5 minutes

2 batches dehydrated *Kale* (see recipe in Chapter 6)

1. Using your fingers, crumble kale into powder.

2. Store in an air-sealed or zipper-lock plastic bag or a bottle at room temperature for up to 1 year.

CHEF'S CHOICE

Add Kale Powder to soups and salad dressings for an extra notch of nutrition.

Tomato Powder

This powder is wonderful in soups, sauces, and more. It's a great powder to have on hand in your pantry, and it's a good substitute for tomato paste.

Yield:	Prep time:
⅓ cup	5 minutes

1 batch *Tomato Leather* (see recipe in Chapter 11),
    without fruit pectin, torn into pieces

1. In a food processor fitted with a standard blade, chop tomato leather until you reach a powdery consistency.

2. Store in an air-sealed or zipper-lock plastic bag or a bottle at room temperature for up to 1 year.

> **DRYING TIP**
>
> You can use 1 batch dehydrated Tomatoes (recipe in Chapter 6), but the *Tomato Leather,* without pectin, reduces to a powder more easily.

Strawberry Powder

Sprinkle this fruit powder on hot and cold cereals, add it to fruit smoothies, and mix it in meat marinades and salad dressings.

Yield:	Prep time:
½ cup	10 minutes

1 batch dehydrated *Strawberries* (see recipe in Chapter 5)

1. In a food processor fitted with a standard blade, chop strawberries until you reach a powdery consistency.

2. Store in an air-sealed or zipper-lock plastic bag or a bottle at room temperature for up to 1 year.

Instead of putting maple syrup on your pancakes or French toast, dissolve 2 tablespoons *Strawberry Powder* in 2 tablespoons boiling water to make a sweet and delicious strawberry syrup.

Vegetable Soup Base

Durham Herzog taught me about the powers of a homemade vegetable soup base. This base adds a lot of flavor and *oomph* to soups, sauces, and entrées. Just 1 or 2 tablespoons can make an entire soup taste so much better.

Yield:	**Prep time:**
3²⁄₃ cups	5 minutes

1 cup *Onion Powder* (see recipe earlier in this chapter)	¹⁄₂ cup dehydrated green beans or greens powder (*Beans—Green and Other,* and *Kale* and *Other Leafy Greens,* see recipes in Chapter 6)
1 cup *Celery Powder* (see recipe earlier in this chapter)	
¹⁄₂ cup *Mushroom Powder* (see recipe earlier in this chapter)	2 or 3 TB. *Garlic Powder* (see recipe earlier in this chapter)
2 batches dehydrated *Carrots* (see recipe in Chapter 6)	1 TB. dried parsley flakes (*Basic Dried Herbs,* see recipe in Chapter 7)

1. In a large bowl, combine onion powder, celery powder, mushroom powder, carrots, green beans, garlic powder, and parsley flakes.

2. Store in an air-sealed or zipper-lock plastic bag or a bottle at room temperature for up to 1 year.

Whenever Durham Herzog has leftover veggies, she tosses them in her dehydrator, turns them into powders, and mixes the powders into a soup base. You can use whatever vegetables or vegetable powders you have on hand, but the base should always contain onion and celery powders.

Basic Baby Food

Vegetable and fruit powders make great instant baby food, and they're easy to travel with. They also don't have all the additives, preservatives, and sugars many commercial baby foods contain.

Yield:	Prep time:
1½ tablespoons	2 minutes

2 tsp. any flavor dried vegetable or fruit powder

2 TB. boiling water

1. In a small bowl, whisk together dried vegetable or fruit powder and boiling water, adding water 1 teaspoon at a time, until desired consistency. (Depending on the thickness of powder, you may use less or more water.)

2. Store in an air-sealed or zipper-lock plastic bag or a bottle at room temperature for up to 1 year.

CHEF'S CHOICE

Carrot, squash, and kale powders all make especially nutritious baby foods. You can also combine powders. Or try sprinkling them onto commercial baby foods or cereals.

Dried Soups, Snacks, and More

In This Chapter

- Sensational soups
- Super snacks
- Delicious dips
- Scrumptious salads

By now, you've probably dried a lot of different kinds of foods, and if you need some dried apricots or ginger, chances are you'll dry it yourself instead of running out to the store to buy some. The more you've dehydrated, the more enthusiastic you've probably become about drying other foods.

The only problem I've found with my own enthusiasm for my dehydrators and the wonderful foods I dry in them—and it really isn't a true *problem*—is that sometimes I dry so many foods, I don't know what to do with all my dehydrated bounty. If you face a similar "problem," you've come to the right place. That's what this chapter is all about—using your dried foods to make different dishes.

In this chapter, I share recipes for using your dried foods and show you some creative ways to use your dehydrator. You can make dried soup mixes, meals to take on camping trips, dried food snacks, and even salads. I encourage you to try the recipes that appeal to you, but use them as a jumping-off point. Experiment with new flavors, and try adapting some of your favorite recipes using dehydrated foods. What new recipes and uses for your dehydrator can you come up with?

Dried Onion Soup Mix

Forget buying packaged mixes to make soups, dips, and meat rubs. This recipe, from Durham Herzog, is quick, easy, and delicious!

Yield:	Prep time:	Cook time:	Serving size:
4½ cups	15 minutes	10 minutes	5 tablespoons

¾ cup diced dehydrated *Onions* (see recipe in Chapter 6)

⅓ cup beef bouillon granules

4 tsp. *Onion Powder* (see recipe in Chapter 12)

¼ tsp. celery salt (see *Celery Powder* recipe in Chapter 12)

¼ tsp. sugar

⅛ tsp. freshly ground white pepper

1. In a large bowl, combine Onions, beef bouillon, Onion Powder, celery salt, sugar, and white pepper.

2. Store in an air-sealed or zipper-lock plastic bag or an airtight container in a cool, dry place for up to 6 months.

3. To make soup, pour 2 cups boiling water over 5 tablespoons soup mix (5 tablespoons soup mix replaces 1 [1.25-ounce] package onion soup mix). For dip, mix 2 cups sour cream with 5 tablespoons soup mix.

CHEF'S CHOICE

You can add in 1 tablespoon dried parsley or other herbs, if you like.

Instant Potato Soup

This recipe makes a hearty and warming soup. Durham Herzog suggests using it as a flavoring for cream soups, too.

Yield:	Prep time:	Cook time:	Serving size:
2½ cups	10 minutes	10 minutes	½ cup

3 cups dehydrated finely diced or grated *Potatoes* (see recipe in Chapter 6)

1 cup nonfat instant dried milk powder

¼ cup chicken bouillon granules

3 TB. dehydrated minced green onions

2 TB. dehydrated minced *Onions* (see recipe in Chapter 6)

1 TB. dehydrated parsley

1 tsp. freshly ground white pepper

½ tsp. dehydrated dill

½ tsp. dehydrated thyme

1. In a large bowl, combine potatoes, milk powder, chicken bouillon, green onions, onions, parsley, white pepper, dill, and thyme.

2. Store in an air-sealed or zipper-lock plastic bag or an airtight container in a cool, dry place for up to 6 months.

3. To make soup, combine 1 cup boiling water with ½ cup soup mix. Let sit for 5 minutes before serving.

CHEF'S CHOICE

Add 2 to 4 tablespoons dried bacon bits or 2 to 4 tablespoons grated fresh cheese such as cheddar, per serving, for a baked potato soup.

Instant Chicken Noodle Soup

Is there anything more comforting than chicken noodle soup? You don't have to be feeling under the weather to enjoy this flavorful soup.

Yield:	Prep time:	Cook time:	Serving size:
about 8 cups	10 minutes	30 minutes	2 cups

4 strips *Easy Chicken Jerky* (see recipe in Chapter 8), diced finely

2 cups dehydrated elbow noodles

¼ cup dehydrated diced *Onions* (see recipe in Chapter 6)

¼ cup dehydrated diced *Celery* (see recipe in Chapter 6)

¼ cup dehydrated diced *Carrots* (see recipe in Chapter 6)

¼ cup dehydrated *Peas* (see recipe in Chapter 6)

¼ cup dehydrated green beans (*Beans—Green* and *Other,* see recipe in Chapter 6)

2 TB. chicken bouillon granules

1 TB. dehydrated parsley

1 TB. dehydrated thyme

1 TB. dehydrated savory

1 dehydrated bay leaf

1 tsp. freshly ground black pepper

1. In a large bowl, combine easy chicken jerky, elbow noodles, onions, celery, carrots, peas, green beans, chicken bouillon, parsley, thyme, savory, bay leaf, and black pepper.

2. Store in a large zipper-lock plastic bag in the refrigerator for up to 1 month.

3. To make soup, bring 8 cups water to a boil in a large pot. Add soup mix, and let boil for 5 minutes. Cover and let stand for 20 minutes before serving. Remove bay leaf, and serve.

DRYING TIP

If you'd rather store this in your cupboard instead of the refrigerator, remove the chicken jerky from the recipe, and add it separately when cooking. Because chicken jerky can still be kind of tough, even when it's chopped and rehydrated, you can sauté 2 medium chicken breasts in 2 tablespoons olive oil or butter over medium-high heat, dice, and add to the boiled soup.

Nearly Instant Vegetable Soup

This quick and easy vegetable soup is deliciously warming and quite satisfying.

Yield:	Prep time:	Cook time:	Serving size:
4 cups	20 minutes	1 hour	1 cup

½ cup dehydrated diced *Onions* (see recipe in Chapter 6)

½ cup dehydrated diced *Potatoes* (see recipe in Chapter 6)

¼ cup dehydrated diced *Celery* (see recipe in Chapter 6)

¼ cup dehydrated *Peas* (see recipe in Chapter 6)

¼ cup dehydrated *Corn* (see recipe in Chapter 6)

¼ cup dehydrated green beans (*Beans—Green* and *Other,* see recipe in Chapter 6)

¼ cup dehydrated diced *Carrots* (see recipe in Chapter 6)

2 cups boiling water

1 qt. tomato juice

½ cup *Vegetable Soup Base* (see recipe in Chapter 12)

2 TB. dehydrated parsley

1 TB. dehydrated thyme

1 dehydrated bay leaf

Sea salt

Freshly ground black pepper

1. In a large bowl, soak onions, potatoes, celery, peas, corn, green beans, and carrots in boiling water for 20 minutes.

2. In a large pot over medium-high heat, warm tomato juice and vegetable soup base. When mixture starts to boil, add rehydrated vegetables and any water still in the bottom of the bowl. Reduce heat to medium, and bring to a simmer. Add parsley, thyme, and bay leaf, season with sea salt and black pepper. Remove bay leaf, and serve.

CHEF'S CHOICE

For extra flavor, you can add canned green beans and canned tomatoes. And to make this a beef vegetable soup, add 2 cups cubed, sautéed stew meat and 2 tablespoons beef bouillon granules.

Nearly Instant Creamy Mushroom Soup

This is better than any canned mushroom soup. Rich and flavorful, it's great to use in casseroles.

Yield:	Prep time:	Cook time:	Serving size:
4 to 6 cups	10 minutes	45 minutes	1 cup

4 TB. unsalted butter

1½ cups dehydrated *Mushrooms* (recipe in Chapter 6)

½ cup dehydrated diced *Onions* (recipe in Chapter 6)

6 TB. white flour

2 cups beef stock

4 cups whole milk

1 TB. dehydrated parsley

1 tsp. dehydrated thyme

Sea salt

Freshly ground black pepper

1. In a large pot over medium-high heat, melt butter. Add mushrooms and onions, and sauté for about 5 minutes.

2. Stir in white flour, and whisk in beef stock and whole milk, pouring in only a little bit at a time and letting the mixture thicken.

3. Bring to a simmer, and reduce heat to medium-low. Stir in parsley and thyme, and season with sea salt and black pepper.

DRYING TIP

If you want to turn this into an instant soup mix to take on camping trips, replace the milk and butter with dried milk powder and dried, powdered butter. You can order both online at honeyvillegrain.com.

Nearly Instant Cabbage Cauliflower Soup

This delicious, stick-to-your ribs soup is chock full of luscious vegetables. To make it vegetarian, omit the sausage and use vegetable stock instead of chicken.

Yield:	Prep time:	Cook time:	Serving size:
4 to 6 cups	15 minutes	45 minutes	1 cup

6 cups chicken stock

2 cups dry red wine (like merlot)

2½ cups dehydrated *Cabbage* (see recipe in Chapter 6)

1 cup dehydrated *Cauliflower* (see recipe in Chapter 6)

½ cup dehydrated *Onions* (see recipe in Chapter 6)

½ cup dehydrated *Instant Rice* (see recipe in Chapter 9)

½ cup *Tomato Powder* (see recipe in Chapter 12) or 1 (12-oz.) can tomato paste

2 TB. *Garlic Powder* (see recipe in Chapter 12)

1 TB. dehydrated parsley flakes

2 tsp. dehydrated savory

2 tsp. dehydrated thyme

Sea salt

Freshly ground black pepper

3 links cooked chicken sausage, sliced into rounds

1. In a large pot over medium-high heat, bring chicken stock and red wine to a boil. Add cabbage, cauliflower, onions, instant rice, and tomato powder. Reduce heat to medium, and simmer, stirring frequently, for 5 to 10 minutes or until all vegetables are rehydrated.

2. Reduce heat to medium-low. Stir in garlic powder, parsley flakes, savory, and thyme, and season with sea salt and black pepper. Add chicken sausage, and serve after warmed up.

DRYING TIP

To make this more of a backpacking recipe, pack all the vegetables and rice in one bag, and pack all the spices in another. In a separate bag, pack enough chicken bouillon to make 8 cups and eliminate the wine and the sausage slices.

Simple Pasta Sauce

This dehydrated pasta sauce is perfect for taking to the campsite—and eliminates the need of carrying a heavy jar!

Yield:	Prep time:	Dry time:	Serving size:
1 (14×14-inch) tray	2 minutes	8 to 12 hours	1 cup (rehydrated)

2 cups pasta sauce

1. Line a dehydrator tray with a liner or parchment paper cut to fit.

2. Set the dehydrator to 140°F to 145°F. Pour pasta sauce onto the tray, and using a rubber spatula, smooth to an even layer.

3. Dehydrate for 8 to 12 hours. Pasta sauce will be done when it's sticky but doesn't move or jiggle and peels off easily. (If it doesn't, stick it in freezer for 5 to 15 minutes. Then it will peel off easily.)

4. Store in an air-sealed or zipper-lock plastic bag at room temperature for up to 2 months or in the freezer for up to 1 year. To rehydrate, add 4 cups boiling water to the whole batch. Let stand for 15 minutes before serving.

CHEF'S CHOICE

Instead of pasta sauce, you can also use this technique for salsa and barbecue sauce. Rehydrate the same way, with boiling water.

Juli's Backcountry Burritos

My friend Juli Hacker and her family are avid campers, and this is one of their favorite recipes. It's absolutely delicious.

Yield:	Prep time:	Cook time:	Serving size:
3 burritos	5 minutes	30 minutes	1 burrito

4 cups dry lentils

¼ cup dehydrated diced *Onions* (see recipe in Chapter 6)

¼ cup dehydrated diced *Tomatoes* (see recipe in Chapter 6)

¼ cup dehydrated diced bell peppers (*Peppers—Bell* and *Other*, see recipe in Chapter 6)

⅛ cup dehydrated diced Carrots (see recipe in Chapter 6)

⅛ cup dehydrated diced *Zucchini* (see recipe in Chapter 6)

3 cloves garlic, minced

½ jalapeño pepper, chopped

1 to 3 shakes Tabasco sauce

1 batch Instant Rice (see recipe in Chapter 9) or 1 cup quick-cooking brown rice

6 (7.5-in.) flour tortillas

1. Before leaving on your camping trip, pack lentils, onions, tomatoes, bell peppers, carrots, and zucchini in one bag. Pack garlic, jalapeño pepper, tabasco sauce, brown rice, and tortillas separately.

2. At camp, place lentils and vegetables in a quart-size wide-mouth plastic bottle, cover with water, and let sit for at least 8 hours. At the end of the day, pour water and lentil-vegetable mixture into a large pot, and bring the mixture to a boil.

3. When soup begins to boil, stir in garlic and jalapeño and season with Tabasco. Cover and simmer for about 10 minutes or until lentils are tender. Set mixture aside.

4. Rehydrate instant rice according to the directions in Chapter 9 or cook quick-cooking brown rice according to the package directions. Invert the lid on vegetable pot, warming tortillas as you cook rice.

5. When rice is done, stir it into vegetable-lentil mixture, and spoon into warm tortillas. Add extra Tabasco, if you like.

CHEF'S CHOICE

This dish is tasty seasoned with dried cilantro and other spices, or you can use any combination of mixed vegetables you'd like, including broccoli or eggplant.

Marvelous Mac 'n' Cheese

This is a much healthier substitute for the boxed neon-orange stuff.

Yield:	Prep time:	Cook time:	Serving size:
6 cups	10 minutes	20 minutes	1 cup

6 cups water

6 cups *Instant Pasta* (see recipe in Chapter 9)

¾ cup nonfat dried milk powder

2 tsp. cornstarch

1 cup dehydrated Cottage Cheese (see recipe in Chapter 10)

2 tsp. *Onion Powder* (see recipe in Chapter 12)

1 tsp. *Garlic Powder* (see recipe in Chapter 12)

1 tsp. dehydrated mustard

½ tsp. freshly ground white or black pepper

6 TB. unsalted butter, cut into chunks, or 6 tsp. butter sprinkles or powdered butter

1. In a medium pot over medium-high heat, bring water to a boil. Add instant pasta, and boil for 6 minutes. Remove from heat, and drain water, reserving 4 cups.

2. Whisk milk powder into reserved pasta water.

3. In a small bowl, dissolve cornstarch in 2 tablespoons milk powder mixture. Whisk cornstarch into remaining milk mixture.

4. Add dehydrated cottage cheese, onion powder, garlic powder, mustard, and white pepper, and let stand for 5 minutes or until mixture begins to thicken.

5. Pour over cooked pasta, top with butter, and let stand for 5 more minutes before serving.

CHEF'S CHOICE

For a quick tuna casserole, add ⅓ cup dehydrated *Peas* (see recipe in Chapter 6) and 1 (5-ounce) can tuna, drained.

Zucchini-Apple Salad

My friend Juli makes this easy and delicious salad before she and her family go camping. You can also have it ready to throw together after a long day of work, too.

Yield:	Prep time:	Dry time:	Cook time:	Serving size:
1⅓ cups	20 minutes	8 hours	30 minutes	⅓ cup

½ cup lemon juice

2 TB. sugar

1 TB. minced fresh ginger

1 large zucchini, shredded

1 large apple, peeled, cored, and shredded

1. In a large bowl, whisk together lemon juice, sugar, and ginger until sugar dissolves.

2. In another large bowl, combine zucchini and apple. Pour in lemon juice mixture, stir, cover, and marinate for at least 24 hours.

3. Line a dehydrator tray with a liner or parchment paper cut to fit.

4. Set the dehydrator to 125°F. Pour salad onto the tray, and using a rubber spatula, smooth to an even layer.

5. Dehydrate for at least 8 hours or until salad ingredients are brittle. Package ⅓ cup in each of 4 plastic bags.

6. To make salad, add ⅓ cup water to each bag of salad, and allow to soak for at least 30 minutes to rehydrate.

CHEF'S CHOICE

This salad also works well with shredded carrots and fresh herbs like thyme or cilantro added.

Salad Crunchies

Instead of croutons or bacon bits, try Durham Herzog's dried veggie mix for a delicious salad topper.

Yield:	Prep time:	Serving size:
4 cups	10 minutes	1 or 2 tablespoons

¾ cup dehydrated diced *Onions* (see recipe in Chapter 6)

½ cup dehydrated diced *Tomatoes* (see recipe in Chapter 6)

½ cup dehydrated grated *Carrots* (see recipe in Chapter 6)

½ cup freshly grated Parmesan cheese

¼ cup dehydrated diced *Broccoli* (see recipe in Chapter 6)

¼ cup dehydrated diced *Celery* (see recipe in Chapter 6)

¼ cup dehydrated diced red bell pepper (*Peppers—Bell* and *Other*, see recipe in Chapter 6)

¼ cup dehydrated diced green bell pepper (*Peppers—Bell* and *Other*, see recipe in Chapter 6)

¼ cup dehydrated parsley

¼ cup unsalted sunflower seeds

1. In a large bowl, combine onions, tomatoes, carrots, parmesan cheese, broccoli, celery, red bell pepper, green bell pepper, parsley, and sunflower seeds.

2. Store in a glass jar with a tightly fitted lid in the refrigerator for up to 2 months.

3. To serve, sprinkle each serving of salad with 1 or 2 tablespoons.

CHEF'S CHOICE

If you'd rather store this at room temperature, or if you're sensitive to dairy, you can omit the Parmesan cheese. You can add other dried vegetables such as peas or corn, too.

Gorp

Gorp—or good ol' raisins and peanuts—is a classic camping treat, but it's also the perfect snack. Plus, it's cheaper than the mixes you can buy at the store.

Yield:	Prep time:	Serving size:
3 cups	5 minutes	½ cup

1 cup dehydrated *Grapes* (see recipe in Chapter 5)

1 cup salted roasted peanuts

1 cup semisweet chocolate chips

1. In a large bowl, combine grapes, peanuts, and chocolate chips.

2. Store in an air-sealed or zipper-lock plastic bag or an airtight container at room temperature for up to 1 year.

CHEF'S CHOICE

Instead of chocolate chips, you can also use coated chocolate candies.

Trail Mix

Sweet and salty, this tasty trail mix is great for camping as well as for parties and after-school snacks.

Yield:	Prep time:	Serving size:
9 cups	5 minutes	½ cup

1 cup dehydrated *Grapes* (see recipe in Chapter 5)

1 cup dehydrated *Cherries* (see recipe in Chapter 5)

1 cup dehydrated *Strawberries* (see recipe in Chapter 5)

1 cup salted, roasted peanuts

1 cup salted, roasted almonds, chopped

1 cup salted, roasted cashews, chopped

1 cup semisweet chocolate chips

1 cup white chocolate chips

1 cup bittersweet or dark chocolate chips

1. In an extra-large bowl, combine grapes, cherries, strawberries, peanuts, almonds, cashews, semisweet chocolate chips, white chocolate chips, and bittersweet chocolate chips.

2. Store in an air-sealed or zipper-lock plastic bag or an airtight container at room temperature for up to 1 year.

CHEF'S CHOICE

To add a little heat, mix in 1 teaspoon Cajun seasoning with the nuts. Mix the nuts and the seasoning first and then add the fruits and chocolate chips.

Dehydrated Raw Foods

In This Chapter

- An introduction to raw foods
- "Dehydrating" raw foods
- Getting to know raw food ingredients
- Tasty raw food recipes

A dehydrator is to raw foodies what an oven is to bakers and what a stove is to chefs. With its low temperatures and even drying capability, a dehydrator dehydrates, instead of cooks, and enables raw food enthusiasts to make crackers, breads, and "cooked" foods—all the while preserving the nutritional integrity of the raw ingredients.

Even if you're a meat-loving, jerky-making carnivorous kind of home cook, you really should try some of the amazing raw food crackers and treats featured in this chapter. If you're at all intimidated by the thought of raw foods, don't be. In this chapter, I show you how fun—and delicious!—raw foods can be! I explain what raw foods are and how a dehydrator fits into that kind of lifestyle. I also detail why you might want to incorporate some elements of the raw food lifestyle into your diet and explain the raw food ingredients—or rather, rules for raw food cooking. Lastly, I share some delicious cracker recipes, "bread" recipes, and snacks that even the most carnivorous of your family and friends might enjoy.

A Raw Foods Primer

You, like my husband, might be wondering: what exactly are *raw foods?* Raw foods are, quite simply, foods that aren't cooked. They remain in their most natural state.

When heated above a certain temperature, food becomes cooked and not raw. This cooking destroys some of the nutritional value of foods such as fruits, vegetables, herbs, seeds, and nuts. Foods in their raw state contain more nutrients such as vitamins and minerals, and the foods' *enzymes* are not destroyed by the cooking process.

But a *raw food diet* requires a little bit more thought than simply not heating your foods and preserving your foods' natural enzymes. In fact, most raw food practitioners also avoid meat, seafood, and dairy, and they don't eat flour, either. Raw food enthusiasts believe that a diet that includes foods in their most natural state is better for health and longevity.

> **DEFINITION**
>
> **Raw foods** are foods that have not been cooked or heated above a certain temperature. A **raw food diet** does not include dairy, meat, seafood, or "cooked" grains. **Enzymes** are the molecules, mostly protein, that perform many of your cells' chemical reactions.

How a Dehydrator Fits into a Raw Food Diet

After reading the definition of raw food, you might be thinking that the only things you can eat on a raw food diet are raw celery and raw apples. That's so not the case.

Although heating foods above 118°F is prohibited, raw foods can be dehydrated, frozen, sprouted, juiced, and fermented. Plenty of fabulous raw food books are available, including *The Complete Idiot's Guide to Eating Raw* by Mark Reinfeld, Bo Rinaldi, and Jennifer Murray, so I'm not going to elaborate on the nondehydrating cooking techniques.

Your dehydrator is essential for making raw crackers, breads, and even "flour." For making crackers and breads, most nuts and seeds are soaked—sometimes sprouted—before being mixed or ground in a food processor with other ingredients. These nuts and seeds are then chopped, combined with vegetables or fruits, and dehydrated. Their texture is very similar to regular crackers, and even my college-age nephew Ryan loves them. I think they make excellent snacks, and they're a great way to sneak in more fruits and vegetables to your diet.

Because some crackers and breads require "flour," you can use your dehydrator to make raw flour. The most common way to make flour is to soak raw grains, dehydrate them, and grind the dried grains in a food processor or blender.

The most common grain "flour" I've seen in raw food recipes is one that starts out as *buckwheat groats*. This is such a useful flour to have in your raw food larder, and I include a nonflour flour recipe later in this chapter.

DEFINITION

Buckwheat groats are a nutty-tasting whole grain. They're not the same as regular wheat. Another name for them is *kasha.*

Raw food chefs also use a dehydrator to dry or partially dry foods instead of cooking them on a stove or in an oven. For example, you can partially dry bell peppers in a way that mimics the texture and taste of cooked bell peppers. You can also dry onions coated with raw flour to simulate the taste of fried onions. The result tastes wonderful—and is so much more nutritious than frying. I include a recipe for this, as well.

Raw Food Ingredients

I've discovered that many raw cracker recipes can be enhanced with a little bit of soy sauce. The depth of flavor and the umami nuances of fermented soy add a wow factor salt simply can't match. If you're strictly following a raw food diet, instead of regular soy sauce, use shoyu, which is a type of soy sauce in which the soy is fermented.

Because butter isn't used in raw food recipes, a good substitute is coconut oil.

Raw honey—not pasteurized honey—is a good sweetener to use instead of sugar, which is prohibited because sugar comes from cooked sugar cane. However, if you're following a more vegan diet, honey is out, too. Try agave syrup instead. Another solution is to dehydrate dates and then grind them into a sugar powder.

If some of these recipes intrigue you, but the lack of these special ingredients is holding you back, I encourage you to substitute with what you have on hand. If you don't have sprouted buckwheat, just use whatever flour you have on hand in your pantry. If you don't have honey or agave syrup, use some maple syrup or a little sugar. The raw food police won't arrest you, and chances are, you might find a new favorite recipe to enjoy!

Many raw food enthusiasts even suggest that if you're interested in a raw food diet, start by simply incorporating a few raw food recipes into your daily life, and little by little, go more raw. The way I see it, most of us could probably stand to eat more vegetables and fruits, and raw food recipes are a delicious way to incorporate more of them into our everyday lives.

Raw Tomato Flaxseed Crackers

This rich and flavorful raw cracker tastes great by itself, but it's also fabulous with all sorts of dips.

Yield:	Prep time:	Dry time:
about 40 crackers or 1 (14×14-inch) tray	30 minutes	6 to 8 hours

½ cup ground flaxseeds

½ cup whole flaxseeds

1 cup warm water

3 medium tomatoes, quartered

½ medium yellow or white onion, cut in ½

6 cloves garlic

1 TB. tamari (wheat-free) soy sauce

1. In a medium bowl, stir together ground flaxseeds, whole flaxseeds, and warm water. Set aside to soak for at least 30 minutes.

2. In a food processor fitted with a standard blade, purée tomatoes, yellow onion, garlic, and tamari soy sauce. Add to flaxseed mixture, and stir to combine.

3. Line a dehydrator tray with a liner or parchment paper cut to fit.

4. Set the dehydrator to 115°F.

5. Pour cracker dough onto the lined dehydrator tray. Use a spatula to smooth and even out dough.

6. Dehydrate for 6 to 8 hours.

7. Store in an air-sealed or zipper-lock plastic bag at room temperature for up to 1 year.

CHEF'S CHOICE

You can add Cajun or Italian seasonings—about 1 or 2 teaspoons—to flavor the cracker dough.

Raw Seeded Crackers

This cracker is a good, basic raw cracker to have in your repertoire. Gluten-free, dairy-free, and vegan, it's quite delicious when served with hummus or guacamole.

Yield:	Prep time:	Dry time:
about 60 crackers or 1½ (14×14-inch) trays	4 hours	8 to 12 hours

1 cup ground flaxseeds	1 large carrot, peeled
½ cup sesame seeds	½ medium yellow or white onion
½ cup pumpkin seeds	2 TB. tamari soy sauce
1½ cups warm water	½ tsp. freshly ground black pepper
1 small or medium red bell pepper, ribs, seeds, and core removed	¼ tsp. sea salt

1. In a medium bowl, stir together ground flaxseeds, sesame seeds, pumpkin seeds, and warm water. Set aside to soak for at least 2 hours.

2. After 2 hours, in a food processor fitted with a standard blade, purée red bell pepper, carrot, and yellow onion. Add tamari soy sauce, black pepper, and sea salt, and mix until well combined. Add to flaxseed mixture, and stir to combine.

3. Line a dehydrator tray with a liner or parchment paper cut to fit.

4. Set the dehydrator to 115°F.

5. Pour cracker dough onto the lined dehydrator tray. Use a spatula to smooth and even out dough.

6. Dehydrate for 3 hours, flip crackers upside down onto the tray, and remove the lining. Dehydrate for 5 to 9 more hours.

7. Store in an air-sealed or zipper-lock plastic bag at room temperature for up to 6 months.

CHEF'S CHOICE

For a little something extra, you can add 2 or 3 cloves garlic, 1 teaspoon Cajun or Italian seasoning, or other spices and flavors to suit your taste.

Raw Cabbage "Lace" Crackers

If you like cabbage, you'll love these crisp and crunchy cabbage crackers.

Yield:	Prep time:	Dry time:
about 40 crackers or 1 (14×14-inch) tray	30 minutes	6 to 8 hours

½ green cabbage head (about 1 lb.)

4 cloves garlic

4 TB. *Raw Buckwheat "Flour"* (see recipe later in this chapter)

1 tsp. sea salt

1. In a food processor fitted with a standard blade, purée cabbage and garlic. Add raw buckwheat "flour" and sea salt, and pulse to combine.

2. Line a dehydrator tray with a liner or parchment paper cut to fit.

3. Set the dehydrator to 115°F.

4. Pour cracker dough onto the lined dehydrator tray. Use a spatula to smooth and even out dough.

5. Dehydrate for 6 to 8 hours.

6. Store in an air-sealed or zipper-lock plastic bag at room temperature for up to 6 months.

CHEF'S CHOICE

For a smoother or more pliable cracker, add 1 or 2 peeled and cored apples to the purée. You can also substitute 3 or 4 medium zucchini for the cabbage.

Raw Red Bell Pepper Cabbage Crackers

This raw cracker is slightly reminiscent of coleslaw but crunchier. It's quite addictive!

Yield:	Prep time:	Dry time:
2 (14×14-inch) trays	45 minutes	8 to 14 hours

1 cup sesame seeds

1/2 cup flaxseeds

1 1/2 cups plus 1/3 cup warm water

1/2 head green cabbage head (about 1 lb.)

1/2 large red bell pepper, ribs and seeds removed

1 large yellow or white onion

1 large apple, peeled and cored

2 TB. shoyu or regular soy sauce

1 TB. honey or agave syrup

1/2 tsp. celery seeds

1. In a medium bowl, stir together sesame seeds, flaxseeds, and 1 1/2 cups warm water. Set aside to soak for at least 30 minutes. Drain water.

2. In a food processor fitted with a standard blade, purée cabbage, red bell pepper, yellow onion, apple, and remaining 1/3 cup warm water. Add shoyu, honey, celery seeds, and sesame-flaxseed mixture, and pulse until well combined and smooth.

3. Set the dehydrator to 115°F.

4. Pour cracker dough onto the lined dehydrator tray. Use a spatula to smooth and even out dough.

5. Dehydrate for 3 hours, flip crackers upside down onto the tray, and remove the lining. Use a knife or pizza cutter to score crackers into "slices." Continue drying for 5 to 9 more hours or until crisp.

6. Store in an air-sealed or zipper-lock plastic bag at room temperature for up to 6 months.

CHEF'S CHOICE

If you like things sweet, add 1 or 2 small peeled carrots.

Raw "Fried" Onions

This crisp "not fried" onion is a low-fat alternative to what you usually think of fried onions. You'll never buy another can of fried onions after you try this recipe—it's that good!

Yield:	Prep time:	Dry time:
1 cup	30 minutes	4 to 6 hours

1 small yellow or white onion

1 tsp. sea salt

1 tsp. Cajun seasoning

2 TB. *Raw Buckwheat "Flour"* (see recipe later in this chapter)

1. Slice onion in paper-thin slices. Separate slices into individual rings, and place rings in a small bowl.

2. Sprinkle rings with sea salt and Cajun seasoning, and toss until well coated. Add raw buckwheat "flour," and toss again until well coated.

3. Set the dehydrator to 115°F. Shake excess flour from rings, and evenly arrange on the dehydrator trays.

4. Dehydrate for 4 to 6 hours.

5. Use immediately or store in an air-sealed or zipper-lock plastic bag in the refrigerator for up to 1 week.

DRYING TIP

These onions make fantastic salad and casserole toppers. They also make a great snack to dunk in fresh dip.

Raw Kale Flax "Bread"

This seeded raw cracker is a good, basic raw cracker to have in your repertoire. It's gluten free, dairy free, and also vegan. Try it with hummus or guacamole.

Yield:	Prep time:	Dry time:
about 60 crackers or 1½ (14×14-inch) trays	30 minutes	8 to 12 hours

½ cup ground flaxseeds

½ cup sesame seeds

1 cup water

1 large bunch fresh kale, thick stems removed

1 large red bell pepper, ribs and seeds removed

½ medium yellow or white onion

4 large strawberries, green tops removed

2 TB. honey or agave syrup

1 TB. shoyu or regular soy sauce

½ tsp. sea salt

1. In a medium bowl, stir together flaxseeds, sesame seeds, and water. Set aside to soak for about 15 minutes. Drain water.

2. In a food processor fitted with a standard blade, purée kale leaves, red bell pepper, yellow onion, and strawberries. Add honey, soy sauce, and sea salt. Add seed mixture, and pulse until well combined.

3. Line a dehydrator tray with a liner or parchment paper cut to fit.

4. Set the dehydrator to 115°F.

5. Pour bread dough onto the lined dehydrator tray. Use a spatula to smooth and even out dough.

6. Dehydrate for 3 hours, flip bread upside down onto the tray, and remove the lining. Use a knife or a pizza cutter to score bread into slices. Dehydrate for at least 5 more hours or until crisp.

7. Store in an air-sealed or zipper-lock plastic bag at room temperature for up to 6 months.

DRYING TIP

Lacinato kale is milder than curly kale, but both types work well for this recipe.

Raw Broccoli Strawberry "Bread"

This raw food "bread" reminds me of a summer salad of broccoli, strawberries, and crunchy seeds. The lemon juice also adds a bright, almost sourdough flavor.

Yield:	Prep time:	Dry time:
about 40 crackers or 1 (14×14-inch) tray	45 minutes	6 to 8 hours

½ cup ground pumpkin seeds

½ cup sunflower seeds

1 cup water

1 small head broccoli florets (about ½ lb.)

1 cup fresh strawberries, green tops removed

Juice of 1 lemon

1 TB. honey or agave syrup

1 tsp. sea salt

1. In a medium bowl, stir together pumpkin seeds, sunflower seeds, and water. Set aside to soak for at least 30 minutes. Drain water.

2. In a food processor fitted with a standard blade, purée pumpkin-sunflower seed mixture. Add broccoli florets, strawberries, lemon juice, honey, and sea salt, and pulse until well combined and smooth.

3. Line a dehydrator tray with a liner or parchment paper cut to fit.

4. Set the dehydrator to 115°F.

5. Pour bread dough onto the lined dehydrator tray. Use a spatula to smooth and even out dough.

6. Dehydrate for 3 hours, flip bread upside down onto the dehydrator tray, and remove the lining. Use a knife or pizza cutter to score bread into slices. Dehydrate for at least 3 more hours or until crisp.

7. Store in an air-sealed or zipper-lock plastic bag at room temperature for up to 6 months.

CHEF'S CHOICE

Instead of strawberries, you can use raspberries or raisins.

Raw Banana Walnut Muffins

If you love banana bread, you'll want to try this raw food version.

Yield:	Prep time:	Dry time:
12 mini muffins	30 minutes	6 to 12 hours

2 very ripe bananas, peeled

1 cup walnuts

½ cup *Raw Buckwheat "Flour"* (see recipe later in this chapter)

4 TB. honey or agave syrup

1 TB. coconut oil

2 tsp. vanilla extract

1 tsp. ground cinnamon

¼ tsp. sea salt

1. In a food processor fitted with a standard blade, purée bananas. Add walnuts and raw buckwheat "flour," and pulse until walnuts are ground, and the walnuts, flour, and bananas are well combined. Add honey, coconut oil, vanilla extract, cinnamon, and sea salt, and pulse until well combined and very smooth.

2. Line 12 mini cupcake tins with paper liners.

3. Set the dehydrator to 115°F.

4. Pour muffin dough into the mini cupcake tins, and set cupcake pan on a dehydrator tray in the dehydrator.

5. Dehydrate for 6 to 12 hours. Muffins will be firm but still moist.

6. Store in an air-sealed or zipper-lock plastic bag at room temperature for up to 1 week.

CHEF'S CHOICE

These muffins aren't very sweet. If you prefer things a little sweeter, you might want to add a little more honey or agave syrup. You can add a few dates to sweeten the batter naturally if you like.

Raw Red Bell Pepper Walnut "Crepes"

This raw "crepe," or wrapper, is delicious served stuffed with guacamole and fresh sliced veggies. Savory and filling, it's wonderful even by itself.

Yield:	Prep time:	Dry time:
2 (14×14-inch) trays	45 minutes	8 to 12 hours

1 cup walnuts

½ cup flaxseeds

1½ cups warm water

½ large red bell pepper, ribs and seeds removed

1 large yellow or white onion

½ lb. fresh white or portobello mushrooms

3 cloves garlic

1 TB. fresh sage

1 TB. fresh thyme

2 TB. shoyu or regular soy sauce

1 TB. honey or agave syrup

1 TB. apple cider vinegar

½ tsp. sea salt

1. In a medium bowl, stir together walnuts, flaxseeds, and warm water. Set aside to soak for at least 30 minutes. Drain water.

2. In a food processor fitted with a standard blade, purée red bell pepper, yellow onion, white mushrooms, garlic, sage, and thyme. Add shoyu, honey, apple cider vinegar, and sea salt, and pulse until well combined and smooth.

3. Line a dehydrator tray with a liner or parchment paper cut to fit.

4. Set the dehydrator to 115°F.

5. Pour crepe dough onto the lined dehydrator tray. Use a spatula to smooth and even out dough.

6. Dehydrate for 3 hours, flip crepes upside down onto the dehydrator tray, and remove the lining. Dehydrate for 5 to 9 more hours. Crepes will be flexible and chewy.

7. Store in an air-sealed or zipper-lock plastic bag at room temperature for up to 1 month.

CHEF'S CHOICE

Instead of walnuts, you can also use pecans.

Raw Buckwheat "Flour"

Use this "flour" in any raw food recipe that mimics baked goods or requires flour of any kind.

Yield:	Prep time:	Dry time:
1¼ cup	24 hours	8 to 10 hours

1 cup raw buckwheat groats	1 or 2 cups water

1. In a small bowl, place buckwheat groats. Cover with water, cover the bowl with parchment paper or plastic wrap, and set aside to soak for 24 hours. Drain water.

2. Line a dehydrator tray with a liner or parchment paper cut to fit.

3. Set the dehydrator to 105°F.

4. Pour groats onto the lined dehydrator tray. Use a spatula to smooth an even layer.

5. Dehydrate for 8 to 10 hours.

6. In a blender or food processor fitted with a standard blade, grind dehydrated groats to a powder.

7. Store in an air-sealed or zipper-lock plastic bag at room temperature for up to 6 months.

CHEF'S CHOICE

You also can use raw oat groats to make raw oat "flour."

Decadent Desserts

In This Chapter

- Why use a dehydrator for desserts?
- What desserts work best in a dehydrator
- Tips for making delicious dehydrator desserts
- Mouthwatering dehydrated desserts

One of the most surprising—and delicious—uses for a dehydrator is making desserts. And I'm not talking about the healthy, fruit leather or granola bar–type sweets. I'm talking about decadent brownies, luscious cookies, and fluffy meringues.

Like many dried food enthusiasts, for years I used my dehydrator to make dozens of savory foods, but excluding a few pudding leathers, I never thought to use it to create desserts. As I began to explore the wider world of dehydrating, I discovered that dehydrators make a delicious difference in dozens of desserts.

In this chapter, I explain the how's and why's of "baking" in your dehydrator. I also help you experiment and explore which types of desserts work best in a dehydrator and which desserts you should steer clear of. You also learn some tips to best use your dehydrator. I even share the expert advice of a pastry chef who regularly uses his dehydrator to create luscious and amazing sweets. Lastly, of course, I give you plenty of yummy treats you'll love to make for your family and friends.

Why Dehydrate Your Desserts?

As a food writer, I regularly interview chefs and cooking experts on a variety of topics. One morning, a press release email came into my inbox about the new desserts Chef Jimmy MacMillan was creating. MacMillan, who is executive pastry chef of the

University Club in Chicago and JMPurePastry, was working with Nielsen-Massey, a vanilla and extract company, and making desserts in a dehydrator. I was immediately intrigued, and I had to talk to him to explore this novel idea—"baking" desserts in a dehydrator.

"I got started making desserts in my dehydrator when we started using the food dehydrator for making garnishes for restaurant-plated desserts," Jimmy told me. Jimmy and his pastry staff combined fruit juice and sugar and then shaped the mixture with a stencil to make crisp "petals." Jimmy then flavored the petals with different kinds of extracts. "We use Nielsen-Massey extracts for just everything," Jimmy gushed. Soon he discovered that the flavors, whether they were vanilla or chocolate or almond or whatever, really shone through when the petals came out of the dehydrator.

That led to experimentation with sheets of meringue, also used for dessert garnishes, and then straight meringue desserts.

"Eventually, we realized what a great kitchen tool the food dehydrator is, and we developed more dessert recipes specifically for the dehydrator," Jimmy says. "I really like using a food dehydrator for making desserts because it doesn't discolor food, and the flavors of the ingredients are more vivid."

After talking with Jimmy, I had to try my hand at making desserts in my own dehydrator. One single batch of meringue kisses had me hooked. The meringues were perfectly fluffed, they were pristinely white, and they dissolved on my tongue in a swirl of vanilla sweetness. Not to mention they also made my entire house smell like a vanilla cupcake!

What I learned from Jimmy and my own experimentation is that dehydrators are a wonderful tool for preserving color and upping the ante on flavor. Because dehydrators operate at lower temperatures than ovens, ingredients like vanilla extract and cinnamon don't get cooked out of a cookie. You really taste the vanilla, and the cinnamon flavor is rich and warm. The flavors truly seem to "pop," and they linger on your tongue.

One thing I really noticed is that when I used different varieties of vanilla extract, I could easily discern the flavor nuances of the various extracts. I also learned that I could use Tahitian vanilla in my dehydrator desserts, which is something I could never use in my regular oven desserts. Tahitian vanilla, which is a really floral vanilla, shouldn't be cooked in the oven because the high heat destroys its delicate aromas.

What's more, meringues don't brown or turn golden in the dehydrator—they stay perfectly white. And they don't wilt or weep. Cookies don't brown, either. Your finished desserts look as good as they taste!

CHEF'S CHOICE

Vanilla comes in a few types. Madagascar, Mexican, and Tahitian are the most common. In your dehydrator, you can really taste the differences. Be sure to try them all!

The Best Desserts to Make in Your Dehydrator

Your dehydrator is perfect for creating delicate desserts like meringues. Because heat can be an enemy of meringues, the lower-temperature dehydrator is superior to ovens, convection and otherwise, for making meringues.

I love making egg- and dairy-free recipes in my dehydrator. I've found that the dairy- and egg-free recipes come out just perfectly. You can use egg and dairy recipes, too.

Chef Jimmy agrees: "Some desserts, like meringues, taste far better when they're made in a dehydrator instead of a conventional oven," he advises. "They just melt in your mouth, and I love making tasty, nondairy desserts in a dehydrator, too."

Gluten-free desserts also work well. Gluten-free flours sometimes act differently in ovens than regular flours, but again, the lower temperatures work in your favor when cooking them in a dehydrator.

Many cookies work well in the dehydrator, and I particularly love that the chocolate-chip cookies I make come out perfectly gooey.

Any dessert that uses extracts—be it vanilla, almond, chocolate, or any other—will come out of the dehydrator with that flavor more prominent than when cooked in a conventional oven. Fruit desserts also seem fruitier when made in a dehydrator.

Raw food desserts are a natural to make in your dehydrator. The lower temperatures are perfect for preserving the integrity of the raw ingredients.

Desserts *Not* to Make in Your Dehydrator

Although I use my dehydrator to make many different desserts, I steer clear of trying to make certain desserts in it. The biggest category of dehydrator no-no's? Anything with leavening. If you want to make cookies or cakes that contain baking soda or baking powder, they'll flop in the dehydrator. The lower temperatures prohibit the chemical interactions that go on inside a higher-temperature oven.

You also shouldn't ever try to make yeast breads, for the same reason. The chemistry of heat and leavening makes a dehydrator a no-go. "You really can't make things like muffins or cakes in a dehydrator because they need high heat," Chef Jimmy says. "The high heat of an oven causes the rise in the dough, and it also gives the baked goods structure."

You want to be careful when using raw, whole eggs, too. Because of salmonella concerns, you really should use pasteurized eggs. If you don't have access to pasteurized eggs, I suggest finding a local egg producer you can talk to directly about safety concerns and whose eggs you can feel confident using.

DRYING TIP

Pasteurized eggs aren't all that hard to find. Davidson's Safest Choice Eggs, for example, are sold at many stores across the country, including Whole Foods and even 7-Eleven.

Regardless of pasteurization concerns, I wouldn't recommend making cream- or egg-heavy desserts like baked custards, flourless chocolate cakes, or crème brûlées in your dehydrator. They just wouldn't work as well as in a conventional oven.

The nice thing about dehydrator desserts is that you can mix the ingredients, place them in the dehydrator, and then let them cook while you go do something else. You don't have to watch the clock or worry about burning anything.

But this advantage can also be a disadvantage. If you want to whip up a batch of cookies, you'll have to wait while they bake. In fact, the quickest dehydrator desserts take a minimum of 4 to 6 hours, and some of them take much longer than that. Even 4 hours is a lot of time for a toddler or a teenager to wait for a cookie, so if a quick, pick-me-up dessert is what you crave, stick to traditional, oven-baked desserts.

Delicious Dehydrator Desserts

Because the flavors are so much more pronounced when cooking in your dehydrator as opposed to baking in your conventional oven, you'll really want to use high-quality ingredients in your dehydrator desserts. Specifically, use good-quality nuts, better-quality flours, and fresher fruits. Any off notes in your foods will be amplified in the dehydrator, so you don't want to use anything that's subpar.

When using nuts, for example, be sure they're fresh. Stale or spoiled nuts will ruin a dehydrated dessert.

Opt for higher-quality extracts and spices, too. Generic vanilla extract will taste like generic vanilla extract.

Although Chef Jimmy endorses Nielsen-Massey, I don't endorse one brand over another. In my own cooking and baking, I use vanilla and other extracts as well as spices from Nielsen-Massey, The Spice House, and Penzeys. You might prefer another brand, and that's fine. The main thing is to go with quality.

DEHYDRATING DON'T

Never use artificial vanilla flavoring in a dehydrator. Although it can taste kind of fake in oven-baked goods, its fakeness really tastes bad in dehydrated desserts.

The dehydrator brings out the subtle nuances of vanilla extracts, so don't be afraid of experimenting with different types of vanilla, such as these:

- *Tahitian vanilla* is very floral and delicate, and it goes exceptionally well with fruity desserts.

- *Madagascar vanilla* is really good for chocolate and creamy desserts.

- *Mexican vanilla* is perfect for spice-studded desserts, enhancing cinnamon and ginger, and pairing with dark chocolate desserts.

Some recipes call for honey. Regular honey works just fine, but some of the more exotic, aromatic honeys work particularly well in the dehydrator—again, because their nuances become even more pronounced in the dehydrator.

You most likely will be using pasteurized eggs in your dehydrator dessert endeavors, so you'll need to whip the egg whites for a longer time than you would if using unpasteurized egg whites—plan on 5 to 10 minutes longer than when using unpasteurized egg whites. You also will need to add cream of tartar to better stabilize them. All the meringue recipes in this chapter call for using cream of tartar. Also, the fresher the eggs are, the better they whip up for meringues.

If you want, you can use dried egg white powder instead.

Madagascar Vanilla Brownies

These brownies are, hands down, one of the most delicious dishes you'll ever make in your dehydrator.

Yield:	Prep time:	Dry time:
1 (11×16-inch) pan brownies	20 minutes	8 to 10 hours

4½ cups almond flour

3 cups cocoa powder

1½ tsp. sea salt

½ tsp. ground Ceylon cinnamon

1 cup maple syrup

½ cup light agave syrup

1½ cups water

1 TB. Nielsen-Massey Madagascar Bourbon Pure Vanilla Extract

1. In a small bowl, and using a rubber spatula, combine almond flour, cocoa powder, sea salt, and Ceylon cinnamon. Add maple syrup, light agave syrup, water, and Nielsen-Massey Madagascar Bourbon Pure Vanilla Extract.

2. Set the dehydrator to 115°F. Pour brownie batter into an 11×16-inch baking pan, and using a rubber spatula, smooth to an even layer.

3. Dehydrate for 8 to 10 hours.

4. Remove brownies from the pan, slice, and serve. Store any leftovers in an airtight container at room temperature for up to 1 week.

CHEF'S CHOICE

Ceylon cinnamon has a delicious, fruity aroma, but you can use another cinnamon if you prefer. Madagascar bourbon vanilla extract also has a unique, fruity aroma, but you can substitute with a different vanilla. You can find almond flour at health food and gourmet groceries—or make your own with blanched almonds!

Chocolate-Chip Cookies

These no-egg, no-butter chocolate-chip cookies are deliciously chocolaty.

Yield:	Prep time:	Dry time:
12 (2×3-inch) cookies	20 minutes	8 to 10 hours

1½ cups all-purpose flour

¼ tsp. sea salt

1 cup brown sugar, firmly packed

½ cup coconut oil

2 TB. rum

2 TB. water

2 tsp. vanilla extract (preferably Madagascar or Mexican)

1 (10-oz.) bag dark chocolate chips

1. Line a dehydrator tray with a liner or parchment paper cut to fit.

2. In a large bowl, combine all-purpose flour and sea salt. Add brown sugar and coconut oil, and mix well. Stir in rum, water, and vanilla extract, and mix well again. Stir in chocolate chips.

3. Set the dehydrator to 145°F.

4. Shape cookie dough into 12 (2×3-inch) cookies, and place on the lined dehydrator tray. If chocolate chips fall out, press them back into cookies. Flatten cookies gently.

5. Dehydrate for 8 to 10 hours.

6. Remove cookies from the tray, and serve. Store any leftovers in an airtight container at room temperature for up to 1 week.

CHEF'S CHOICE

If you'd rather not add the rum, substitute with 2 more tablespoons water. You can also substitute 1 teaspoon rum extract, with the water, to add the rum flavor.

Peanut Butter Cookies

Soft and crumbly, these peanut butter cookies are simply divine.

Yield:	Prep time:	Dry time:
24 (2×3-inch) cookies	20 minutes	8 to 10 hours

1¼ cups all-purpose flour

¼ tsp. sea salt

1 cup plus 2 tsp. sugar

½ cup no-sugar-added smooth peanut butter

½ cup coconut oil

2 TB. water

2 tsp. vanilla extract (preferably Madagascar or Mexican)

1. Line a dehydrator tray with a liner or parchment paper cut to fit.

2. In a large bowl, combine all-purpose flour and sea salt. Add 1 cup sugar, peanut butter, and coconut oil, and mix well. Stir in water and vanilla extract, and mix well again.

3. Set the dehydrator to 145°F.

4. Shape cookie dough into 24 (2×3-inch) cookies, and place on the lined dehydrator tray. Flatten cookies gently, and sprinkle with remaining 2 teaspoons sugar.

5. Dehydrate for 4 or 5 hours, flip over cookies, remove the liner, and dehydrate for 4 or 5 more hours.

6. Remove cookies from the tray, and serve. Store any leftovers in an airtight container at room temperature for up to 1 week.

CHEF'S CHOICE

For peanut butter–chocolate-chip cookies, add 1 (10-ounce) bag chocolate chips to the batter.

Oatmeal Cookies

These crispy, brown sugar–laced oatmeal cookies aren't exactly the kind your grandma made because they lack eggs and butter, but they are still amazing.

Yield:	Prep time:	Dry time:
30 (2×3-inch) cookies	20 minutes	8 to 10 hours

1½ cups quick-cooking oats

½ cup white whole-wheat flour

¼ tsp. sea salt

1 cup brown sugar, firmly packed

½ cup coconut oil

2 TB. water

2 tsp. vanilla extract (preferably Madagascar or Mexican)

2 tsp. ground cinnamon

1. Line a dehydrator tray with a liner or parchment paper cut to fit.

2. In a large bowl, combine oats, white whole-wheat flour, and sea salt. Add brown sugar and coconut oil, and mix well. Stir in water, vanilla extract, and cinnamon, and mix well.

3. Set the dehydrator to 145°F.

4. Shape cookie dough into 30 (2×3-inch) cookies, and place on the lined dehydrator tray. Flatten cookies gently.

5. Dehydrate for 4 or 5 hours, flip over cookies and remove liner or parchment paper, and dehydrate for 4 or 5 more hours.

6. Remove cookies from the tray, and serve. Store any leftovers in an airtight container at room temperature for up to 1 week.

CHEF'S CHOICE

For oatmeal raisin cookies, add 1 cup raisins. Or you could add 1 cup white chocolate chips.

Lime Coconut Cookies

Nutty, coconutty, and tartly sweet, these cookies remind me of Florida and Key lime pie.

Yield:	Prep time:	Dry time:
24 (1-teaspoon) cookies	20 minutes	8 to 10 hours

½ cup cooked quinoa

½ cup all-purpose flour

½ cup almonds

½ cup honey

½ cup coconut oil

¼ cup plus 2 TB. finely chopped coconut

1 tsp. vanilla extract (Tahitian works great with lime)

Zest of 1 lime

Juice of 1 lime

1 tsp. sugar

1. Line a dehydrator tray with a liner or parchment paper cut to fit.

2. In a food processor fitted with a standard blade, pulse together quinoa, all-purpose flour, and almonds a few times. Add honey, coconut oil, and ¼ cup coconut, and pulse a few more times. Add vanilla extract, lime zest, and lime juice, and chop or pulse until dough ball forms. Remove dough from the food processor.

3. Set the dehydrator to 145°F.

4. In a small bowl, combine sugar and remaining 2 tablespoons coconut.

5. Shape cookie dough into 24 teaspoon-size balls. Roll in coconut-sugar mixture, and place on the lined dehydrator tray. Flatten cookies gently.

6. Dehydrate for 4 or 5 hours, flip over cookies, and dehydrate for 4 or 5 more hours.

7. Remove cookies from the tray, and serve. Store any leftovers in an airtight container at room temperature for up to 1 week.

CHEF'S CHOICE

Substitute a gluten-free flour like soy or almond flour for the all-purpose flour, and you have a delicious, gluten-free cookie.

Coconut Jam Thumbprint Cookies

These pretty and tasty bites are perfect to add to a holiday cookie tray.

Yield:	Prep time:	Dry time:
24 (1-teaspoon) cookies	20 minutes	8 to 10 hours

1/3 cup your choice jam (raspberry works well)

1 or 2 tsp. hot water

1 tsp. vanilla extract (Tahitian works great)

1 batch uncooked *Lime Coconut Cookie* dough (see recipe earlier in this chapter), lime zest and juice omitted

1. Line a dehydrator tray with a liner or parchment paper cut to fit.

2. In a medium bowl, whisk together jam, hot water, and vanilla extract. Jam mixture should be thick.

3. Set the dehydrator to 145°F.

4. Shape lime coconut cookie dough into teaspoon-size balls. Roll in coconut-sugar mixture, as directed, and placed on the lined dehydrator tray. Flatten cookies gently and then press your thumb in the middle of each cookie. Scoop about 1/2 teaspoon jam mixture into center of each cookie.

5. Dehydrate for 4 or 5 hours, flip over cookies, and dehydrate for 4 or 5 more hours.

6. Remove cookies from the tray, and serve. Store any leftovers in an airtight container at room temperature for up to 1 week.

DRYING TIP

For a colorful holiday cookie tray, make three batches of this dough, but fill each one with a different jam. Try strawberry, apricot, and blackberry, for example.

Pecan Sandies

You'll love these buttery, crumbly, and nutty shortbread cookies. It's hard to eat only one!

Yield:	Prep time:	Dry time:
30 (1-tablespoon) cookies	20 minutes	8 to 10 hours

1 cup all-purpose flour

½ tsp. sea salt

½ cup plus 2 tsp. sugar

½ cup unsalted butter

2 tsp. vanilla extract (Madagascar works best)

¾ cup chopped pecans

1. Line a dehydrator tray with a liner or parchment paper cut to fit.

2. In a large bowl, combine all-purpose flour and sea salt. Set aside.

3. In a separate large bowl, cream together ½ cup sugar and unsalted butter. Add flour-salt mixture, a little bit at a time, and mix well. Stir in vanilla extract, and mix in pecans.

4. Set the dehydrator to 145°F.

5. Shape cookie dough into 30 (1-tablespoon) cookies, and place on the lined dehydrator tray. Flatten cookies gently. If pecans fall out, press them back into cookies. Sprinkle cookies with remaining 2 teaspoons sugar.

6. Dehydrate for 4 or 5 hours, flip over cookies, and dehydrate for 4 or 5 more hours.

7. Remove cookies from the tray, and serve. Store any leftovers in an airtight container at room temperature for up to 1 week.

CHEF'S CHOICE

Add 1 (10-ounce) bag chocolate chips to make these chocolate-chip sandies.

Vanilla Almond Macaroons

These cookies, by Chef Jimmy MacMillan, are chewy, sweet, and utterly addictive.

Yield:	Prep time:	Dry time:
54 (1-tablespoon) cookies	30 minutes	24 hours

1¾ cups dried coconut shreds

¾ cup ground almonds

¾ cup plus 2 TB. almond or cashew flour

Sprinkle of *Apricot flake salt* (optional)

Pinch sea salt

¾ cup maple syrup

⅓ cup coconut oil

1¼ tsp. Nielsen-Massey Madagascar Bourbon Pure Vanilla Extract

½ tsp. Nielsen-Massey Pure Almond Extract

1. Line a dehydrator tray with a liner or parchment paper cut to fit.

2. In a large bowl, whisk together coconut, almonds, almond flour, apricot flake salt (if using), and sea salt. Stir in maple syrup, coconut oil, Nielsen-Massey Madagascar Bourbon Pure Vanilla Extract, and Nielsen-Massey Pure Almond Extract.

3. Set the dehydrator to 125°F to 150°F.

4. Scoop cookie dough by the tablespoon, and place on the lined dehydrator trays. Sprinkle with a little apricot flake salt (if using), and press down slightly.

5. Dehydrate for 24 hours. Macaroons will be crunchy on the outside but soft inside.

6. Remove cookies from the tray and serve. Store any leftovers in an airtight container at room temperature for up to 1 week.

DEFINITION

Apricot flake salt is an apricot-colored sea salt pastry chefs use to finish and enhance a dessert's flavor. You can purchase it at gourmet stores.

Chocolate Ginger Macaroons

This is another of Chef Jimmy's decadent desserts. Chocolaty, nutty, and fruity, this macaroon makes a great holiday treat.

Yield:	Prep time:	Dry time:
54 (1-tablespoon) cookies	30 minutes	24 hours

1¾ cups dried coconut shreds

¾ cup chopped macadamia nuts

¾ cup plus 2 TB. cocoa powder

1½ tsp. ground ginger

Pinch sea salt

¾ cup maple syrup

¼ cup plus 2 TB. coconut oil

1¼ tsp. Nielsen-Massey Tahitian Pure Vanilla Extract

½ tsp. Nielsen-Massey Pure *Chocolate Extract*

1. Line a dehydrator tray with a liner or parchment paper cut to fit.

2. In a large bowl, whisk together coconut, macadamia nuts, cocoa powder, ginger, and sea salt. Stir in maple syrup, coconut oil, Nielsen-Massey Tahitian Pure Vanilla Extract, and Nielsen-Massey Pure Chocolate Extract.

3. Set the dehydrator to 125°F to 150°F.

4. Scoop cookie dough by the tablespoon, and place on the lined dehydrator trays. Press down slightly.

5. Dry for 24 hours, checking every 6 to 8 hours, until macaroons are crunchy on the outside but soft inside.

6. Remove cookies from the tray and serve. Store any leftovers in an airtight container at room temperature for up to 1 week.

DEFINITION

Chocolate extract is made much the same way vanilla extract is—cocoa beans are soaked in an alcohol solution. It has a really chocolaty aroma, and it's a fantastic way to boost the chocolate flavor of a recipe without adding calories.

Vanilla Meringue Kisses

Meringues and meringue cookies taste so much better when they're made in a dehydrator. These vanilla-rich cookies are melt-in-your-mouth delicious!

Yield:	Prep time:	Dry time:
115 to 120 (1-tablespoon) cookies	20 minutes	5 hours

2 large or 3 medium egg whites

½ tsp. white vinegar

¼ tsp. cream of tartar

¼ cup plus 2 TB. sugar

1 tsp. vanilla extract (I love Tahitian)

1. Line a dehydrator tray with a liner or parchment paper cut to fit.

2. In a large glass or metal bowl, and using an electric mixer fitted with a balloon whisk attachment on high speed, mix egg whites, white vinegar, and cream of tartar. When soft peaks form (like soft foam), slowly pour in ¼ cup sugar and vanilla extract. Whip until shiny, hard peaks form. (Hard peaks hold their shape when you turn the mixer attachment upside down.)

3. Set the dehydrator to 135°F.

4. Scoop egg white mixture by the tablespoon on the lined dehydrator trays. Sprinkle cookies with remaining 2 tablespoons sugar.

5. Dehydrate for 4 hours. Meringues will be hard. Let cool inside the dehydrator for 1 hour.

6. Remove cookies from the tray and serve. Store any leftovers in an airtight container at room temperature for up to 1 week.

DRYING TIP

Instead of scooping the egg white mixture onto the dehydrator trays, you can pipe them. Fit a pastry bag with a large star-shape attachment. Scoop egg white mixture into the bag, and gently squeeze out spiral tablespoon-size cookies. If you don't have a pastry bag, you can use a plastic bag, with one corner cut off to squeeze out the egg white mixture.

The egg white fluff should hold its shape when it's turned on its side or upside down.
(Photo by Kyle Edwards)

Hold your pastry bag steady, and squeeze for the count of 3 seconds, swirling slightly as you push out the meringue.
(Photo by Kyle Edwards)

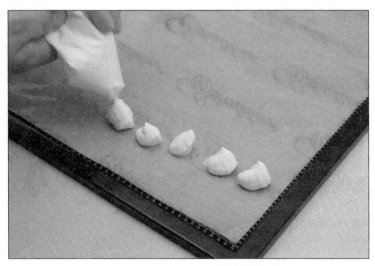

Gently squeeze the meringue out of one corner of a closed plastic bag that you've snipped the corner off of. Hold your hand steady and squeeze for only 1 or 2 seconds, just enough so you squeeze out a small dollop of meringue.
(Photo by Kyle Edwards)

Chocolate Meringue Kisses

These light and fluffy chocolate delights won't last long out of the dehydrator!

Yield:	Prep time:	Dry time:
115 to 120 (1-tablespoon) cookies	20 minutes	5 hours

2 large or 3 medium egg whites

½ tsp. white vinegar

¼ tsp. cream of tartar

2 TB. cocoa powder

¼ cup sugar, optional

½ tsp. chocolate extract

¼ cup mini chocolate chips

1. Line a dehydrator tray with a liner or parchment paper cut to fit.

2. In a large glass or metal bowl, and using an electric mixer fitted with a balloon whisk attachment on high speed, mix egg whites, white vinegar, cream of tartar, and cocoa powder. When soft peaks form (like soft foam), slowly pour in sugar (if using) and chocolate extract. Whip until shiny, hard peaks form. (Hard peaks hold their shape when you turn the mixer attachment upside down.)

3. Set the dehydrator to 135°F.

4. Scoop egg white mixture by the tablespoon on the lined dehydrator trays. Gently press 1 or 2 mini chocolate chips into each cookie.

5. Dehydrate for 4 hours. Meringues will be hard. Let cool inside the dehydrator for 1 hour.

6. Remove cookies from the tray and serve. Store any leftovers in an airtight container at room temperature for up to 1 week.

DRYING TIP

Use a high-quality cocoa powder for these cookies because the chocolate flavor will really shine through. Instead of chocolate chips, you can use mini chocolate-coated candies.

Christmas Meringue Kisses

These peppermint-white chocolate kisses are just divine.

Yield:	Prep time:	Dry time:
115 to 120 (1-tablespoon) cookies	20 minutes	5 hours

2 large or 3 medium egg whites	1 tsp. peppermint extract
½ tsp. white vinegar	¼ cup white chocolate chips
¼ tsp. cream of tartar	2 TB. red sugar
¼ cup sugar	2 TB. green sugar

1. Line a dehydrator tray with a liner or parchment paper cut to fit.

2. In a large bowl, and using an electric mixer fitted with a balloon whisk attachment on high speed, mix egg whites, white vinegar, and cream of tartar. When soft peaks form (like soft foam), slowly pour in sugar and add peppermint extract. Whip until shiny, hard peaks form. (Hard peaks hold their shape when you turn the mixer attachment upside down.)

3. Set the dehydrator to 135°F.

4. Scoop egg white mixture by the tablespoon on the lined dehydrator trays. Gently press 1 or 2 chocolate chips into each cookie, and sprinkle with red and green sugar.

5. Dehydrate for 4 hours. Meringues will be hard. Let cool inside the dehydrator for 1 hour.

6. Remove cookies from the tray and serve. Store any leftovers in an airtight container at room temperature for up to 1 week.

CHEF'S CHOICE

For an extra chocolaty flavor, add ½ teaspoon chocolate extract to cookies. And instead of colored sugars, you can also sprinkle the cookies with crushed peppermint candies.

Cinnamon Kisses

Cinnamon kisses are beautifully fragrant and utterly delicious. Your whole house will smell like cinnamon while they're in the dehydrator.

Yield:	Prep time:	Dry time:
115 to 120 (1-tablespoon) cookies	20 minutes	5 hours

2 large or 3 medium egg whites	1 tsp. vanilla extract (I love Mexican)
½ tsp. cream of tartar	3 tsp. ground cinnamon
¼ cup plus 2 TB. sugar	

1. Line a dehydrator tray with a liner or parchment paper cut to fit.

2. In a large bowl, and using an electric mixer fitted with a balloon whisk attachment on high speed, mix egg whites and cream of tartar. When soft peaks form (like soft foam), slowly pour in ¼ cup sugar, vanilla extract, and 2 teaspoons cinnamon. Whip until shiny, hard peaks form. (Hard peaks hold their shape when you turn the mixer attachment upside down.)

3. Set the dehydrator to 135°F.

4. Scoop egg white mixture by the tablespoon on the lined dehydrator trays. Sprinkle cookies with remaining 2 tablespoons sugar and remaining 1 teaspoon cinnamon.

5. Dehydrate for 4 hours. Meringues will be hard. Let cool inside the dehydrator for 1 hour.

6. Remove cookies from the tray and serve. Store any leftovers in an airtight container at room temperature for up to 1 week.

CHEF'S CHOICE

For fun, press cinnamon red hot candy pieces or cinnamon chips into the cookies before dehydrating them. You'll need about ¼ cup for the whole batch.

Lemon Meringue Puffs

These cookies taste like a bite of lemon meringue pie, but instead of custard, they're a little cloud of sweet, tart, and delicious meringue.

Yield:	Prep time:	Dry time:
115 to 120 (1-tablespoon) cookies	20 minutes	5 hours

2 large or 3 medium egg whites	1 tsp. vanilla extract (I love Tahitian)
½ tsp. cream of tartar	Zest of 1 lemon
¼ cup plus 2 TB. sugar	Juice of 1 lemon

1. Line a dehydrator tray with a liner or parchment paper cut to fit.

2. In a large bowl, and using an electric mixer fitted with a balloon whisk attachment on high, mix egg whites and cream of tartar. When soft peaks form (like soft foam), slowly pour in ¼ cup sugar, vanilla extract, lemon zest, and lemon juice. Whip until shiny, hard peaks form. (Hard peaks hold their shape when you turn the mixer attachment upside down.)

3. Set the dehydrator to 135°F.

4. Scoop egg white mixture by the tablespoon on the lined dehydrator trays. Sprinkle cookies with remaining 2 tablespoons sugar.

5. Dehydrate for 4 hours. Meringues will be hard, but not as hard as some other meringues in this chapter. Let cool inside the dehydrator for 1 hour.

6. Remove cookies from the tray and serve. Store any leftovers in an airtight container at room temperature for up to 1 week.

CHEF'S CHOICE

Instead of lemon zest and juice, you can substitute lime zest and juice in this recipe.

Clouds of Coffee

If you like coffee, you'll love these meringues.

Yield:	Prep time:	Dry time:
115 to 120 (1-tablespoon) cookies	20 minutes	5 hours

2 large or 3 medium egg whites

½ tsp. cream of tartar

¼ cup plus 2 TB. sugar

1 tsp. vanilla extract (I love Mexican)

1 TB. plus 2 tsp. espresso powder

1. Line a dehydrator tray with a liner or parchment paper cut to fit.

2. In a large bowl, and using an electric mixer fitted with a balloon whisk attachment on high, mix egg whites and cream of tartar. When soft peaks form (like soft foam), slowly pour in ¼ cup sugar, vanilla extract, and 1 tablespoon espresso powder. Whip until shiny, hard peaks form. (Hard peaks hold their shape when you turn the mixer attachment upside down.)

3. Set the dehydrator to 135°F.

4. Scoop egg white mixture by the tablespoon on the lined dehydrator trays. Sprinkle cookies with remaining 2 tablespoons sugar and remaining 2 teaspoons espresso powder.

5. Dehydrate for 4 hours. Meringues will be hard. Let cool inside the dehydrator for 1 hour.

6. Remove cookies from the tray and serve. Store any leftovers in an airtight container at room temperature for up to 1 week.

CHEF'S CHOICE

You can add 1 teaspoon ground cinnamon to this recipe, too. And instead of using espresso powder, you can substitute with 1 teaspoon coffee extract.

Schaum Torts

This old-fashioned dessert should be served topped with ice cream, fresh berries, and whipped cream.

Yield:	Prep time:	Dry time:
30 torts	20 minutes	5 hours

2 large or 3 medium egg whites

½ tsp. white vinegar

¼ tsp. cream of tartar

¼ cup plus 2 TB. (optional) sugar

1 tsp. vanilla extract (I love Tahitian)

1. Line a dehydrator tray with a liner or parchment paper cut to fit.

2. In a large bowl, and using an electric mixer fitted with a balloon whisk attachment on high, mix egg whites, white vinegar, and cream of tartar. When soft peaks form (like soft foam), slowly pour in ¼ cup sugar and vanilla extract. Whip until shiny, hard peaks form. (Hard peaks hold their shape when you turn the mixer attachment upside down.)

3. Set the dehydrator to 135°F.

4. Using a pastry bag fitted with a large star-shape attachment or a plastic bag with the corner cut off, squeeze out 3-inch-diameter circles of egg white mixture. Then add 2 more circles on top of the outermost edge of the first circle to create a border. Sprinkle with remaining 2 tablespoons sugar (if using).

5. Dehydrate for 4 hours. Meringues will be hard. Let cool inside the dehydrator for 1 hour before removing and serving.

CHEF'S CHOICE

Strawberry Powder (see recipe in Chapter 12) creates the perfect strawberry sauce for topping Schaum Torts. In a small bowl, combine 2 tablespoons *Strawberry Powder* with 2 tablespoons hot water. Let the powder dissolve and then pour over torts, with fresh or dried berries, ice cream, and whipped cream.

Date Bars

This traditional bar cookie tastes sublime when cooked in a dehydrator.

Yield:	Prep time:	Dry time:
1 (8×8-inch) tray	1½ to 2 hours	4 hours

2 cups dehydrated chopped *Dates*
   (see recipe in Chapter 5)

2 cups water

1 cup almonds

1 cup rolled oats

⅛ cup coconut oil

3 TB. honey or sugar

3 tsp. vanilla extract (Tahitian works
   great with fruit)

1. In a medium bowl, place dates. Cover with water, and set aside to soak for at least 1 or 2 hours.

2. In a food processor fitted with a standard blade, pulse almonds and rolled oats until crumbly. Add coconut oil, honey, and 1 teaspoon vanilla extract. Transfer to a medium bowl, and set aside.

3. Drain water from dates, and reserve date water.

4. In the food processor, purée dates and 1 tablespoon date water. Add remaining 2 teaspoons vanilla extract. (You may need to add a little bit more water to get it to the consistency of peanut butter.)

5. Set the dehydrator to 145°F.

6. Press about ½ of crumble mixture in the bottom of an 8×8-inch pan. Spread date purée on top of crumble mixture, and top with remaining crumble mixture. Set the pan on a dehydrator tray in the dehydrator.

7. Dehydrate for 4 hours.

8. Remove cookies from the tray, slice, and serve. Store any leftovers in an airtight container at room temperature for up to 1 week.

CHEF'S CHOICE

If the date purée isn't sweet enough for you, you can add more honey or sugar, 1 tablespoon at a time.

Quinoa Maple Syrup "Crackers"

These almost-raw crackers are sweet and crunchy, and they make a perfect, light dessert. They're also a fantastic cracker to add to a cheese tray.

Yield:	Prep time:	Dry time:
1 (14×14-inch) tray	20 minutes	8 to 14 hours

½ cup no-sugar-added smooth peanut butter

½ cup maple syrup

2 tsp. vanilla extract (preferably Madagascar or Mexican)

¼ tsp. sea salt

2½ cups cooked quinoa

1. Line a dehydrator tray with a liner or parchment paper cut to fit.

2. In a food processor fitted with a standard blade, purée peanut butter, maple syrup, vanilla extract, and sea salt until smooth. Add cooked quinoa, and pulse to combine.

3. Set the dehydrator to 145°F.

4. Pour cracker dough onto the lined dehydrator tray. Use a spatula to smooth and even out dough.

5. Dehydrate for 8 to 10 hours. About 2 to 4 hours through drying process, use a knife or a pizza cutter to score crackers where you'd like them to slice. About 4 to 6 hours after that, flip over crackers and remove the liner or parchment paper. When crackers are dry, break apart and serve.

6. Store any leftovers in an airtight container at room temperature for up to 1 week.

CHEF'S CHOICE

You can add 2 teaspoons ground cinnamon to make these cinnamon-laced crackers.

Perfect Pet Treats

In This Chapter

- Pet treats from your dehydrator
- Basic guidelines for making pet treats
- Ingredients to avoid
- Dog treat recipes
- Cat treat recipes

For years, I made dog treats in my oven. When I got my dehydrator, I tried making dog treats in that. Now, I won't consider using the oven to make dog treats.

In this chapter, I explain the benefits of making dog treats in your dehydrator. I walk you through the process of making dog and cat treats and give you the basic guidelines so you can create treats based on your pets' preferences. I also tell you what ingredients you should avoid because not all human foods are compatible with pets' tummies. Lastly, I share some pet-tested recipes that will make your cats purr and your dogs drool.

Why DIY Pet Treats?

When I was 7 years old, I used to make "Doggie Delights" for our family dog, Sandy. The "Delights" consisted of cooking canned Cycle dog food on the stovetop and adding eggs and seasonings. Sandy was the best customer to cook for because she never complained, and even if I burned dinner, she'd still gobble it up. I told my mom that when I grew up I was going to write a doggie cookbook. My cooking interests and endeavors have evolved far beyond heating up commercial dog food, but I still cook for my dog.

My dog Olivia loves my homemade dog treats, and I've found that the dehydrator is the best appliance in which to cook them. You can make dog treats in your oven easily, but they don't get as crisp or crunchy as they do when I make them in the dehydrator. Because the dehydrator doesn't cook the aromas out of the treats like an oven does, the treats end up being more aromatic than those you bake, which your pup will appreciate.

CHEF'S CHOICE

Your dog's sense of smell is so acute that smelling is almost like experiencing an emotion.

Another advantage of making treats in your dehydrator is that you can mix the ingredients, fill the dehydrator, and forget about them until the dehydrator dings that it's done. No worries about burning the treats.

The Basics of Dehydrating Pet Treats

You can adapt most dog and cat food treat recipes to work in your dehydrator. But before you throw anything and everything on a dehydrator tray, there are a few ingredients you shouldn't use.

Don't use raw eggs. Egg whites can turn into lovely, cooked meringues in your dehydrator, but when eggs are mixed into a recipe, they never quite get cooked in a dehydrator. In place of raw eggs, you could use dried eggs or egg substitute, but I think it's easier to just add 1 or 2 tablespoons oil or water instead. You also could use ground flaxseeds. When you combine 1 tablespoon ground flaxseeds in 2 tablespoons water, it turns into a goopy, egglike consistency.

You also shouldn't include any leavening agents. As you learned in the desserts chapter, your dehydrator doesn't get hot enough to make cookies or treats rise, so baking soda or baking powder won't work. Just roll your treats out a little thicker instead.

Because I cook using mostly organic and locally sourced ingredients for my family, I do the same when cooking for the animals in my life. I tend to use whole-wheat flour, oats, amaranth, and flaxseeds simply because that's what I have in my pantry most of the time. I also use the same meats, vegetables, and fruits my family eats. My son has snacked on the homemade dog treats, and I don't worry about it because I know they're made with human-grade ingredients.

If your dog or cat has special needs—he's overweight, for example—you might want to use the lower-fat, vegetarian recipes. You can also add ingredients your veterinarian says are especially beneficial to your pet. For example, brewer's yeast can be a natural flea repellent, so add 1 or 2 tablespoons to a recipe if fleas are a problem for your pooch. Cherry juice has been used in some commercial dog treats because of its anti-inflammatory properties. In recipes, you can replace the water or chicken stock called for with cherry juice if you like.

I often use ingredients left over from when I've cooked for my family to make treats for Olivia and the other canines in our lives. Where else can a cup of cooked chicken be just the right amount? It's barely enough for a chicken salad sandwich, but it's perfect for a batch of Chicken Bits. A few slices of liver sausage make for a perfect batch of Liver Sausage Snaps.

There are, however, some leftovers I would never use. And neither should you.

Ingredients to Avoid

Plenty of human foods are also nutritious for your dogs and cats, but some are toxic and could make your pets sick or deathly ill. You've probably heard you shouldn't give your pets chocolate, but there are others.

Here are several human foods you should *never* add to your pet treats:

Alcohol   It can cause vomiting, diarrhea, and death in both dogs and cats. Avoid it.

Artificial sweeteners   These aren't really good for us humans, and they can be toxic to your pets. Xylitol is a known toxin to both dogs and cats.

Avocados   Avocados contain persin, an oil-soluble chemical compound. It's harmless to humans—in fact, it's recently shown some potential breast cancer-fighting effects—but it can cause vomiting, diarrhea, and even death in both dogs and cats.

Chocolate   Chocolate can cause vomiting, diarrhea, and abnormal heart rhythms, along with tremors, seizures, and even death. Avoid it completely. Coffee and caffeinated beverages are bad for dogs for the same reason.

Citrus fruits   The oils in citrus fruits can make your cats throw up. Don't add oranges or lemons to your kitty treats.

Dairy products   Some dogs and most cats are lactose intolerant or sensitive. Many recipes, especially for dog treats, contain milk, yogurt, or cheese, but your pet may be sensitive, so it's best to avoid them.

Macadamia nuts and walnuts   These nuts are toxic to dogs and cats. They contain unknown toxins that can result in muscle weakness and paralysis.

Onions, garlic, and chives   These foods can cause gastrointestinal problems or irritation, and large amounts can damage red blood cells. Cats are more at risk than dogs, but dogs should still avoid them.

Raisins, grapes, and currants   These fruits contain a toxin that can poison both dogs' and cats' kidneys. They are a big no-no.

Salt and sugar   We use salt and sugar to awaken our taste buds. Dogs have less taste buds and a better sense of smell—they "taste" their foods through their noses. They don't need the salt or sugar to make their treats taste better. Neither do cats. Your pets will never miss these ingredients.

Yeast dough   Uncooked yeast dough is toxic and can cause many stomach problems in both dogs and cats.

DEHYDRATING DON'T

Some dog or cat treat recipes call for using prepared, commercial baby food as an ingredient. This isn't always a good idea because some baby foods contain onions or onion powder, as well as excess salt and sugar—all of which are not good for dogs and cats.

Working with Dog and Cat Treat Dough

The best thing about cooking for my dog Olivia is that I don't have to worry about presentation. She doesn't care what her treats look like as long as they smell good and taste good. She'll even eat cat treats!

Dog and cat treat doughs tend to be sticky. I try not to add too much flour or grains because some animal nutritionists say animals shouldn't consume them. But you do need a binder for the meats and vegetables so I use these ingredients sparingly. To deal with the stickiness, you can either dip your fingers in a bowl of water as you form the balls, or you can dust your hands or the countertop with flour.

The easiest method for forming the treats is to roll the dough into balls using your hands and then flatten them, either with your hands or the bottom of a cup. It's that simple.

You can line the dehydrator trays with parchment paper or dehydrator tray liners, but it's best to dry the treats directly on the dehydrator trays because they dry more quickly.

If you want to make cute little bones or hearts or gingerbread men, you can. You can roll out any of the doughs in this chapter's recipes. Then, simply cut them with cookie cutters. Because treat doughs are stickier than cookie doughs, I recommend flattening a ball of dough with your hands and then placing it between two sheets of parchment paper before rolling. Then roll the dough between the paper, going both horizontally and vertically, until the dough is flattened to the thickness you want. When it's flat enough, place the dough—still between the sheets of parchment paper—in the freezer for 5 to 10 minutes. Freezing the dough makes it easier to cut.

Remove the dough from the freezer, peel off the paper, and press the cookie cutters straight down into the dough—no wiggling. After you've finished cutting the treats, lift up the remnant dough and squish it into another dough ball. Repeat the process until you don't have enough dough left over to make it worth your work.

To make pretty cut cat treats, you'll need to add more flour or oatmeal to the dough. Cat treat doughs are just stickier than dog treat dough. Add the flour by the tablespoon until you get the consistency you desire. Then roll out the dough as instructed for the dog treats.

Olivia's Tuna Bites

Named for my own dog, these treats are easy to make, and your dog will absolutely love you for making them.

Yield:	Prep time:	Dry time:
30 treats	15 minutes	8 to 12 hours

1 (5-oz.) can low- or no-salt tuna, with liquid	½ cup quick-cooking oats
½ cup whole-wheat flour	2 TB. extra-virgin olive oil
	3 TB. water

1. In a large bowl, combine tuna, whole-wheat flour, oats, and extra-virgin olive oil. Stir in water a little at a time. You may need to add a little more or less water. Dough should be pliable but not too sticky.

2. Using your hands, form dough into teaspoon-size balls. You might have to wet your hands to keep dough from sticking to your fingers.

3. Set the dehydrator to 145°F. Evenly arrange treats on the dehydrator trays, leaving some space between them.

4. Dehydrate for 8 to 12 hours. Treats will be hard when done.

5. Store in an air-sealed or zipper-lock plastic bag at room temperature for up to 2 weeks or for up to 6 months in the refrigerator.

CHEF'S CHOICE

Cats like this treat, too. You can replace the canned tuna with canned salmon for the felines.

Sweet Potato Sweeties

We aren't the only mammals who think sweet potatoes are delicious. These dog treats are great to make with Thanksgiving leftovers.

Yield:	Prep time:	Dry time:
30 treats	15 minutes	8 to 12 hours

1 cup whole-wheat flour	1 TB. extra-virgin olive oil
½ cup mashed sweet potatoes	¼ cup water

1. In a large bowl, combine whole-wheat flour, sweet potatoes, and extra-virgin olive oil. Stir in water a little at a time. You may need to add a little more or less water. Dough should be pliable but not too sticky.

2. Using your hands, form dough into teaspoon-size balls. You might have to wet your hands to keep dough from sticking to your fingers.

3. Set the dehydrator to 145°F. Evenly arrange treats on the dehydrator trays, leaving some space between them.

4. Dehydrate for 8 to 12 hours. Treats will be hard when done.

5. Store in an air-sealed or zipper-lock plastic bag at room temperature for up to 2 weeks or for up to 6 months in the refrigerator.

DRYING TIP

If you're using leftover sweet potatoes that already have been mashed with butter, do not add the olive oil.

Bring-Home-the-Bacon Bits

What dog doesn't like bacon? What dog wouldn't like these treats?

Yield:	Prep time:	Dry time:
24 to 26 treats	15 minutes	12 to 20 hours

1 cup whole-wheat flour

2 slices bacon, cooked crisp and crumbled fine

2 TB. bacon grease

¼ cup water

1. In a large bowl, combine whole-wheat flour, bacon, and bacon grease. Stir in water a little at a time. You may need to add a little more or less water. Dough should be pliable but not too sticky.

2. Using your hands, form dough into teaspoon-size balls. You might have to wet your hands to keep dough from sticking to your fingers.

3. Set the dehydrator to 145°F. Evenly arrange treats on the dehydrator trays, leaving some space between them. Flatten treats to ¼-inch thickness.

4. Dehydrate for 12 to 20 hours. Treats will be hard. These treats, unless dried for a much longer time than other treats, have a tendency to be softer than most other treats, thanks to the bacon grease. If you take them out of the dehydrator before they're finished, they'll crumble when you break them in half.

5. Store in an air-sealed or zipper-lock plastic bag at room temperature for up to 2 weeks or for up to 6 months in the refrigerator. Because these treats tend to be softer than most other treats, I usually store them in the refrigerator.

CHEF'S CHOICE

You can make these treats without the bacon. Just add 2 more tablespoons bacon grease if so. Your dog will still love them.

Liver Sausage Snaps

Many dogs love liver, and liver sausage mashes easily into dog treat dough. It's a winning combination.

Yield:	Prep time:	Dry time:
30 treats	15 minutes	12 to 20 hours

1 cup whole-wheat flour

4 oz. liver sausage

$\frac{1}{8}$ to $\frac{1}{4}$ cup water

1. In a large bowl, combine whole-wheat flour and liver sausage. Stir in water a little at a time. You may need to add a little more or less water. Dough should be pliable but not too sticky.

2. Using your hands, form dough into teaspoon-size balls. You might have to wet your hands to keep dough from sticking to your fingers.

3. Set the dehydrator to 145°F. Evenly arrange treats on the dehydrator trays, leaving some space between them. Flatten treats to $\frac{1}{4}$-inch thickness.

4. Dehydrate for 12 to 20 hours. Treats will be hard.

5. Store in an air-sealed or zipper-lock plastic bag at room temperature for up to 2 weeks or for up to 6 months in the refrigerator.

CHEF'S CHOICE

Instead of liver sausage, you could use cooked liver. If you use cooked liver, chop it up finely before using. First, chop the liver in a blender or food processor and then add half the water. Add the whole-wheat flour, and add more water after you blend in the flour. You may need to add a little more water to get a dough ball to form in the processor.

Carrot Apple Treats

These sweet treats are low in fat, perfect for the calorie-counting pooch.

Yield:	Prep time:	Dry time:
30 treats	15 minutes	12 to 20 hours

¾ cup grated carrot	1 cup whole-wheat flour
½ cup applesauce	

1. In a food processor fitted with a standard blade, pulse carrots for 1 minute. Add applesauce, and pulse until combined. Add whole-wheat flour, and chop until dough ball forms. Remove dough from the food processor, and transfer to a lightly floured surface. Dough should be pliable but not too sticky.

2. Using your hands, form dough into teaspoon-size balls. You might have to wet your hands to keep dough from sticking to your fingers.

3. Set the dehydrator to 145°F. Evenly arrange treats on the dehydrator trays, leaving some space between them. Flatten treats to ¼-inch thickness.

4. Dehydrate for 12 to 20 hours. Treats will be hard.

5. Store in an air-sealed or zipper-lock plastic bag at room temperature for up to 2 weeks or for up to 6 months in the refrigerator.

 DRYING TIP

Carrots are good for dogs' dental health.

"Here's the Beef" Biscuits

Beef. It's what's for your dog's snack.

Yield:	Prep time:	Dry time:
22 to 24 treats	15 minutes	12 to 20 hours

¾ cup shredded or cubed cooked beef	¼ cup water
	½ cup whole-wheat flour

1. In a food processor fitted with a standard blade, pulse beef for 1 minute. Add water, and chop to a slurry. Add whole-wheat flour, and chop until dough ball forms. Remove dough from the food processor, and transfer to a lightly floured surface. Dough should be pliable but not too sticky.

2. Using your hands, form dough into teaspoon-size balls. You might have to wet your hands to keep dough from sticking to your fingers.

3. Set the dehydrator to 145°F. Evenly arrange treats on the dehydrator trays, leaving some space between them. Flatten treats to ¼-inch thickness.

4. Dehydrate for 12 to 20 hours. Treats will be hard.

5. Store in an air-sealed or zipper-lock plastic bag at room temperature for up to 2 weeks or for up to 6 months in the refrigerator.

CHEF'S CHOICE

Leftover beef works well in this recipe, but you also can use cooked ground beef.

Chicken Bits

This is one of the easiest treats to make, and my dog Olivia loves 'em.

Yield:	Prep time:	Dry time:
26 to 28 treats	15 minutes	12 to 20 hours

½ cup cooked chicken
1 cup whole-wheat flour

½ cup water or chicken stock

1. In a food processor fitted with a standard blade, pulse chicken for 1 minute. Add whole-wheat flour and water, and pulse until combined. Chop until dough ball forms. Remove dough from the food processor, transfer to a lightly floured surface. Dough should be pliable but not too sticky.

2. Using your hands, form dough into teaspoon-size balls. You might have to wet your hands to keep dough from sticking to your fingers.

3. Set the dehydrator to 145°F. Evenly arrange treats on the dehydrator trays, leaving some space between them. Flatten treats to ¼-inch thickness.

4. Dehydrate for 12 to 20 hours. Treats will be hard.

5. Store in an air-sealed or zipper-lock plastic bag at room temperature for up to 2 weeks or for up to 6 months in the refrigerator.

CHEF'S CHOICE

Leftover chicken works well in this recipe. If you have canned chicken, you can use it instead.

Chick'N Bran Biscuits

Which came first, the chicken or the biscuit? In this treat, they both do.

Yield:	Prep time:	Dry time:
24 to 26 treats	15 minutes	12 to 20 hours

½ cup cooked chicken

⅓ cup oatmeal

⅓ cup oat bran

2 TB. chicken stock or water

⅓ cup whole-wheat flour

1. In a food processor fitted with a standard blade, pulse chicken for 1 minute. Add oatmeal, oat bran, and chicken stock, and pulse until combined. Add whole-wheat flour, and chop until dough ball forms. Remove dough from the food processor, and transfer to a lightly floured surface. Dough should be pliable but not too sticky.

2. Using your hands, form dough into teaspoon-size balls. You might have to wet your hands to keep dough from sticking to your fingers.

3. Set the dehydrator to 145°F. Evenly arrange treats on the dehydrator trays, leaving some space between them. Flatten treats to ¼-inch thickness.

4. Dehydrate for 12 to 20 hours. Treats will be hard.

5. Store in an air-sealed or zipper-lock plastic bag at room temperature for up to 2 weeks or for up to 6 months in the refrigerator.

CHEF'S CHOICE

If you have leftover turkey, use it in place of the chicken.

Peanut Butter Bites

My cousins' dog Lassie got her snout stuck in a peanut butter jar once. If your dog likes peanut butter like Lassie did, this is the perfect treat.

Yield:	Prep time:	Dry time:
30 treats	15 minutes	12 to 20 hours

1 cup whole-wheat flour	2 TB. amaranth or wheat germ
$^1/_3$ cup no-sugar-added natural peanut butter	$^1/_2$ cup water

1. In a food processor fitted with a standard blade, pulse whole-wheat flour, peanut butter, and amaranth. Add water, and pulse until dough ball forms. Remove dough from the food processor, and transfer to a lightly floured surface. Dough should be pliable but not too sticky.

2. Using your hands, form dough into teaspoon-size balls. You might have to wet your hands to keep dough from sticking to your fingers.

3. Set the dehydrator to 145°F. Evenly arrange treats on the dehydrator trays, leaving some space between them. Flatten treats to $^1/_4$-inch thickness.

4. Dehydrate for 12 to 20 hours. Treats will be hard.

5. Store in an air-sealed or zipper-lock plastic bag at room temperature for up to 2 weeks or for up to 6 months in the refrigerator.

CHEF'S CHOICE

Almond butter works equally well in this recipe instead of peanut butter.

Pumpkin Bites

Pumpkin is a great food for dogs, especially if their tummy has been upset.

Yield:	Prep time:	Dry time:
30 treats	15 minutes	12 to 20 hours

$^1/_4$ cup cooked pumpkin or squash	$^2/_3$ cup plus 4 TB. whole-wheat flour
$^1/_4$ cup water	

1. In a food processor fitted with a standard blade, pulse pumpkin and water until a slurry forms. Add ²/₃ cup whole-wheat flour, and pulse until dough ball forms. Remove dough from the food processor, and transfer to a lightly floured surface. Dough should be pliable but quite sticky.

2. Using your hands, form dough into teaspoon-size balls, working in remaining 4 tablespoons whole-wheat flour as you form treats. You might have to wet your hands to keep dough from sticking to your fingers.

3. Set the dehydrator to 145°F. Evenly arrange treats on the dehydrator trays, leaving some space between them. Flatten treats to ¼-inch thickness.

4. Dehydrate for 12 to 20 hours. Treats will be hard.

5. Store in an air-sealed or zipper-lock plastic bag at room temperature for up to 2 weeks or for up to 6 months in the refrigerator.

> **CHEF'S CHOICE**
>
> You add more flavor to these treats by using chicken or beef stock instead of the water.

Allegro's "Chocolate" Chippers

When Allegro was a puppy, she managed to eat six squares of unsweetened chocolate. She loved chocolate, but we didn't feed her chocolate—we fed her these treats, flavored with carob (which is okay for pets), instead.

Yield:	Prep time:	Dry time:
24 to 26 treats	15 minutes	12 to 20 hours

½ cup whole-wheat flour	1 or 2 TB. amaranth
¼ cup unsweetened carob chips	½ cup water

1. In a large bowl, combine whole-wheat flour, carob chips, and amaranth. Add water a little at a time until a smooth dough ball forms. Dough should be pliable but not too sticky.

2. Using your hands, form dough into teaspoon-size balls. You might have to wet your hands to keep dough from sticking to it.

3. Set the dehydrator to 145°F. Evenly arrange treats on the dehydrator trays, leaving some space between them. Flatten treats to ¼-inch thickness.

4. Dehydrate for 12 to 20 hours. Treats will be hard.

5. Store in an air-sealed or zipper-lock plastic bag at room temperature for up to 2 weeks or for up to 6 months in the refrigerator.

CHEF'S CHOICE

If you don't have any amaranth on hand, wheat bran or ground flaxseed can add a nice crunch and texture to these treats.

Jordan's Fat Dog Slimmers

My parents' dog, Jordan, is a bit on the hefty size, but he loves broccoli, so these treats are fabulous for his figure.

Yield:	Prep time:	Dry time:
24 treats	15 minutes	12 to 20 hours

1 cup cooked broccoli

¼ cup water

⅔ cup whole-wheat flour

1. In a food processor fitted with a standard blade, pulse broccoli. Add water, and pulse until puréed. Add whole-wheat flour, and pulse until dough ball forms. Remove dough from the food processor, and transfer to a lightly floured surface. Dough should be pliable but not too sticky.

2. Using your hands, form dough into teaspoon-size balls. You might have to wet your hands to keep dough from sticking to it.

3. Set the dehydrator to 145°F. Evenly arrange treats on the dehydrator trays, leaving some space between them. Flatten treats to ¼-inch thickness.

4. Dehydrate for 12 to 20 hours. Treats will be hard.

5. Store in an air-sealed or zipper-lock plastic bag at room temperature for up to 2 weeks or for up to 6 months in the refrigerator.

CHEF'S CHOICE

You can substitute spinach for the broccoli or up the flavor ante by using chicken stock instead of water.

Mint Breathalyzer Bites

Plenty of dogs have, well, dog breath. This treat can help.

Yield:	Prep time:	Dry time:
24 treats	15 minutes	12 to 20 hours

½ cup fresh mint leaves

¼ cup applesauce

3 or 4 TB. whole-wheat flour

1. In a food processor fitted with a standard blade, chop mint leaves until fine. Add applesauce, and pulse for 1 minute until well blended. Add whole-wheat flour, 1 tablespoon at a time, and pulse until well combined. Remove dough from the food processor, and transfer to a lightly floured surface. Dough will be quite sticky.

2. Using your hands, form dough into teaspoon-size balls. You might have to wet your hands to keep dough from sticking to your fingers.

3. Set the dehydrator to 145°F. Evenly arrange treats on the dehydrator trays, leaving some space between them. Flatten treats to ¼-inch thickness, and cut each treat in half.

4. Dehydrate for 12 to 20 hours. Treats will be hard.

5. Store in an air-sealed or zipper-lock plastic bag at room temperature for up to 2 weeks or for up to 6 months in the refrigerator.

DRYING TIP

If your dog managed to eat all the Sardine Stinkers (recipe later in this chapter) you'd planned to give to your cat, you might want to make this treat as an antidote!

Sardine Stinkers

What kitty doesn't like sardines? What kitty wouldn't love these stinky treats?

Yield:	Prep time:	Dry time:
24 treats	15 minutes	12 to 20 hours

1 (3.75-oz.) can sardines packed in water, with water	½ cup oats

1. In a food processor fitted with a standard blade, chop sardines and water from the can until mushy. Add oats, and chop until oats are mixed with sardines. Dough will be quite sticky.

2. Using your hands, form dough into teaspoon-size balls. You might have to wet your hands to keep dough from sticking to your fingers.

3. Set the dehydrator to 145°F. Evenly arrange treats on the dehydrator trays, leaving some space between them. Flatten treats to ¼-inch thickness, and cut each treat in half.

4. Dehydrate for 12 to 20 hours. Treats will be hard.

5. Store in an air-sealed or zipper-lock plastic bag at room temperature for up to 2 weeks or for up to 6 months in the refrigerator.

> **DRYING TIP**
>
> These are perhaps the most aromatic of all the dog and cat treats. I suggest drying them when you're out of the house or putting your dehydrator in the basement when you make them. The aroma is *that* strong.

Shrimp Chips

These little pink kitty treats will have your kitten yowling for more. Some dogs like them, too!

Yield:	Prep time:	Dry time:
30 treats	15 minutes	12 to 20 hours

1 (4-oz.) can tiny shrimp packed in water, with water	¼ cup quick-cooking oats 3 TB. whole-wheat flour

1. In a food processor fitted with a standard blade, chop shrimp and water from the can until mushy. Add oats, and chop until oats are mixed with shrimp. Add whole-wheat flour, 1 tablespoon at a time, and pulse until dough ball forms. Dough will be rather sticky.

2. Using your hands, form dough into teaspoon-size balls. You might have to wet your hands to keep dough from sticking to your fingers.

3. Set the dehydrator to 145°F. Evenly arrange treats on the dehydrator trays, leaving some space between them. Flatten treats to ¼-inch thickness, and cut each treat in half.

4. Dehydrate for 12 to 20 hours. Treats will be hard.

5. Store in an air-sealed or zipper-lock plastic bag at room temperature for up to 2 weeks or for up to 6 months in the refrigerator.

CHEF'S CHOICE

To make these treats more visually attractive, shape the half treats into crescent moons, similar to the shape of shrimp.

Kitty Catnip "Brownies"

If you already feed your cat's addiction with straight catnip, why not cook Kitty a batch of these "brownies"? Your cat will love you for it.

Yield:	Prep time:	Dry time:
50 treats	15 minutes	4 to 10 hours

½ cup fresh catnip leaves

⅛ cup water

3 TB. plus ⅛ to ¼ cup whole-wheat flour

1. In a food processor fitted with a standard blade, chop catnip leaves until fine. Add water, and pulse for 1 minute until well blended. Add 3 tablespoons whole-wheat flour, 1 tablespoon at a time, and pulse until well combined. Remove dough from the food processor, and transfer to a lightly floured surface. Dough will be extremely wet.

2. Using your hands, form dough into teaspoon-size balls, working in remaining ⅛ to ¼ cup whole-wheat flour a little at a time as you form treats.

3. Set the dehydrator to 145°F. Evenly arrange treats on the dehydrator trays, leaving some space between them. Flatten to ¼-inch thickness, and cut each treat in half.

4. Dehydrate for 4 to 10 hours. Treats will be hard.

5. Store in an air-sealed or zipper-lock plastic bag at room temperature for up to 2 weeks or for up to 6 months in the refrigerator.

CHEF'S CHOICE

You can use dried catnip in this recipe, too. If you opt for dried, use about 2 tablespoons instead of ½ cup fresh. You may have to use more or less flour, and instead of chopping in a food processor, just combine in a bowl with a spoon.

Dehydrated Gifts

In This Chapter

- Creating great dried gifts
- DIY flower drying
- Perfect potpourri and pomander balls
- Pointers for packaging your gifts

Now that you're an expert at dehydrating, it's time to share some of the (dried) fruits of your labor. Dehydrated fruits, vegetables, and even camping dishes make fabulous, fun gifts.

This chapter is all about creating gifts from your dehydrated bounty. I offer tips on what dehydrated foods and combinations work best as gifts and also show you how to dry flowers and create potpourri and pomander balls. And for the prettiest presentation, I give you ideas for how to best package your gifts to maximize the delight of your recipients.

Gifting the Fruits of Your Labor

After you've been dehydrating for a while, chances are, some of your dried foods have made people swoon. The day my stepmother-in-law popped a meringue kiss into her mouth, for example, I knew what I was making her for her birthday. And the fruit leathers I took to a La Leche League meeting? They were getting wrapped up as a Christmas grab bag gift for moms.

The best way to start thinking about creating gifts from your dehydrated goods is to think about your recipients and their likes and dislikes. My sister Karen is an adventurous cook, so she'd appreciate a gift of crème fraîche, packaged in a dainty glass jar wrapped with ribbon. But my sister Julie is more into really healthy eating, so a bag of raw crackers is perfect for her. If your aunt loves cabbage, give her some dried cabbage. If your brother loves apples, wrap up some dried apples. And anyone who loves pineapple will pine for your dried pineapple slices. Think about how you can customize your gifts to really make the recipient feel special.

> **DRYING TIP**
>
> One nice thing about dried gifts is that it doesn't take a lot of extra work. If you're already drying apples, pears, potatoes, or whatever for yourself, you only have to dry a little more to give as gifts.

The Best Food Gifts

Home-dried gifts are so well received. They taste better than anything you can buy from the store, and the recipient will appreciate the thought and care you put into creating something just for them.

Dried fruits make fantastic gifts, especially when you dry local, in-season fruits. For a little something extra, sprinkle apples with cinnamon before drying for some warm and rich cinnamon apples. If you know a raisin fan, show them how much better homemade raisins taste than anything that comes in a box.

Another great gift idea is home-dried herbs or herb blends. My neighbor Terese has gifted me with dried savory from her garden many times, and I just adore it. I've dried sage and thyme, and given them as gifts just before Thanksgiving to friends and relatives who are hosting the holiday dinner. You can even combine dried herbs and dried fruits to create herbal teas, which make amazing gifts.

Dehydrated vegetables can be gifts, too, but they're generally not as exciting as some other dehydrated foods. To jazz them up a bit, package them with other foods or spices to create gift baskets. Combine a container of dehydrated corn, some Mexican seasonings, a jar of homemade salsa, and some tortillas for a Southwestern-themed basket. Dried tomatoes, some dried Italian herbs, a good-quality Italian olive oil, and a bag of pasta make an fun Italian-themed basket. Dehydrated soup mixes make an easy gift, especially for recipients (like your nephew in college) who don't cook much.

DRYING TIP

Picking a theme helps me when creating a gift. Dried pineapple, some macadamia nuts, and the first season of *Hawaii Five-0* makes a fun gift for someone who's a fan of either Hawaii or the TV series. Themes help you narrow your focus, and they help determine how you'll package the gift, too.

Other things you make in your dehydrator can also be phenomenal gifts. Dried fruit leathers make sweet gifts, as are dried crackers, homemade croutons, granola, meat jerkies, and even homemade yogurt or crème fraîche. (Although be sure to keep the latter two refrigerated.) Fruit and vegetable powders make great gifts for foodies. My sister Karen, for example, loves dehydrated mushroom powder.

Many of the recipes from Chapter 13 are perfect for gift-giving. Dried Onion Soup Mix, Salad Crunchies, Gorp, Trail Mix, and all the cookie recipes from Chapter 15 are always well received.

Drying Flowers

One of the best nonfood uses for your dehydrator is drying flowers. You can dry just about any kind of flower or flowering herb—roses, wild flowers, lavender, lilacs, lilies, mums, and even the flowery tops of chives.

Before you start snipping your garden's roses and posies, it helps to first decide on what you're going to do with the dried flowers. You can use your dried flowers to create dried floral arrangements, potpourri, sachets, and wreaths. Dried edible flowers can be sprinkled in dishes or dipped in egg whites and sprinkled with sugar to create beautiful candied flowers. Dried flowers make amazing gifts, too.

CHEF'S CHOICE

One of the nicest gifts I received after my wedding was my bouquet turned into a Christmas ornament. My neighbor Terese (whose then 7-year-old daughter Kate had caught my bouquet) dried the individual flowers and then glue-gunned them to a plastic heart, with my wedding invitation on the back. I still hang it up on my tree every year.

If you're planning on making a wreath from your dried flowers, you'll want to twist or braid them into a wreath shape before placing them in the dehydrator. You can use the stems themselves, but you can also use floral wire and floral tape. Both are available at most craft stores.

If you'd like to create a dried floral arrangement, you'll likely want to dry the flowers on their stems individually and keep them shapely as they dry so they don't look flat or mashed. You might need to remove a tray or two from your dehydrator so they fit in without being crushed.

If potpourri or fragrant sachets are what you're after, you can either dry the flowers whole or pull the petals off the stems before drying them.

You also should think about whether you're drying the flowers for color or fragrance or both. If you're just drying for color or for filler, the flowers don't have to be as fresh as if you're drying for fragrance. Also, decide which flowers and herbs will be the focal point of your wreaths or potpourri and which flowers and herbs will be "fillers."

It's generally best to dry flowers at their peak for color and fragrance. You still can dry flowers that are a little past their prime, especially if you're planning to use the petals as fillers.

The main rule when drying flowers is to dehydrate them at lower temperatures— about 90°F to 115°F. Depending on humidity, drying takes anywhere from a few hours to overnight.

Making Potpourri and Fragrance Sachets

Potpourri and fragrance sachets make lovely gifts. Your homemade versions will smell fresher than store-bought versions, and they won't have that artificial scent some potpourris do. Both are easy and inexpensive to make, provided you have a lot of flowers to dry.

DRYING TIP

If you have pollen allergies, you might want to set your dehydrator in the garage or the basement while you dry flowers. I love making potpourri, but my nose tends to run until the petals are completely dry.

Potpourri consists of three main ingredients: dried flowers or herbs, essential oils, and a fixative. Let's look at each in turn.

Flowers, Flowers, Flowers

When you dry your flowers, they'll shrink quite a bit. For example, if you start with 5 cups loosely packed rose petals, they'll dry down to 2 cups. Smaller buds like lavender and baby's breath shrink even more, with 1 cup shrinking to ¼ to ½ cup.

If you plan on making a large quantity of potpourri for gifts, you need to start with a lot more than what you plan to use in the final product. For 1 quart potpourri, you'll need anywhere from 2 to 3 quarts flower petals, leaves, or herbs.

Essential Essential Oils

As far as essential oils go, you need to add about 10 to 20 drops essential oil per potpourri mix. You can use a single type of oil, a blended fragrant oil, or more than one oil, depending on what scents you're looking for. Essential oils are available at craft stores, health food stores, some department stores, and online.

When I'm making a potpourri, I try to blend fragrant flowers, with their leaves, and I try to be sure I have two or three colors in the mix that really pop. I typically use one or two essential oils—scents that blend together and enhance the flowers' natural aromas.

> **DEHYDRATING DON'T**
>
> Don't use more than three essential oils max when making potpourri—it's best to use only one or two. Any more, and you'll end up with fragrance overload. Instead of providing a whiff of something sweet, your potpourri will smell overpowering.

Getting a Fix on Fixatives

A *fixative* is basically a fragrance purveyor—it's what keeps the potpourri smelling nice over a longer period of time than just the flowers themselves would. You can use a variety of fixatives, from coriander seeds to gum arabic to mint leaves, but the most popular and easy-to-use fixative is *orris root powder*, which I've found at several spice stores. You only need about 1 tablespoon orris root powder per 2 or 3 cups dried flowers.

> **DEFINITION**
>
> A **fixative** is a substance that keeps potpourri, sachets, and dried pomander balls fragrant and fresh smelling. It interacts with the essential oils and the dried flowers to help them release their fragrances more slowly. **Orris root powder** is made from the root of a specific type of iris. It's used alone to keep linens smelling sweet and fresh. Although it's not considered edible, it is nontoxic, as I discovered from calling Poison Control when my 2-year-old son decided to lick his fingers after mixing some pomander balls we were making for Christmas gifts!

Fragrance sachets are simply cloth or tight mesh bags filled with a tablespoon or two of potpourri. They're meant to be tossed in your clothing drawers to make your clothes smell sweet and fresh. If you're crafty, you can sew a bag together from muslin or linen, but you can also purchase ready-made bags at craft stores, too.

Lavender Rose Potpourri

This simple potpourri is fragrant without being overpowering. Plus, it's beautiful to look at.

Yield:	Prep time:	Dry time:
6 cups	10 minutes	4 to 12 hours

5 cups fresh rose petals

8 cups fresh lavender petals and leaves still on the stems (about 4 large bouquets)

2 TB. orris root powder

20 drops lavender essential oil

1. Set the dehydrator to 90°F to 115°F. Evenly arrange rose petals and lavender stems on the dehydrator trays, leaving some space between them.

2. Dehydrate for 4 to 12 hours (more if it's especially humid). Rose petals will shrink to half their size and be fragile and papery. Lavender is dry when petals and leaves crumble off stems easily.

3. In a large bowl, preferably glass, place orris root powder. Add lavender essential oil on top, followed by dried rose and lavender flower petals (2 cups dried rose petals and 4 cups dried lavender buds and leaves). Mix well using your fingers or a wooden spoon.

4. Store in an air-sealed or zipper-lock plastic bag. Potpourri should stay fragrant for about 3 months if in an open bowl and up to 6 months if stored in a closed container.

Making Pomander Balls

Pomander balls are fragrant, spice-studded dried fruit. The first pomander balls were made in the Middle Ages, when they were decorative balls filled with ambergris, musk, and other spices worn to simultaneously ward off diseases and combat the aromatic result of a lack of regular bathing. The word *pomander* comes from the French word, *pomme d'ambre*, or "apple of amber."

You can make pomander balls from apples, oranges, limes, or lemons. They generally contain three or four ingredients: the fruit, whole cloves, spices, and/or orris root powder. They're also typically tied with festive ribbons and hung on walls or Christmas trees. You can wrap them in muslin or linen bags to scent your dresser drawers, too.

Pomander balls are easy to make, they smell fabulous, and they make outstanding gifts. What's not to love?

Basic Pomander Balls

These festive dried fruit balls smell just like the holidays. They're fun holiday craft projects to do with your children.

Yield:	Prep time:	Dry time:
4 pomander balls	20 minutes	7 to 10 days

4 medium apples, oranges, lemons, or limes	1 cup spices
	2 TB. orris root powder
¼ to ½ cup whole cloves	1 tsp. vanilla extract

1. Using a toothpick, clean meat thermometer, knitting needle, or another sharp object, poke holes all over apple. Stick 1 whole clove in each hole. You can stud fruit as much or as little as you'd like, but it's nice to do designs.

2. In a medium bowl, preferably glass, combine spices and set aside.

3. In a large bowl, place orris root powder. Pour in vanilla extract, and whisk in spices. Add clove-studded fruits, and stir to cover fruit with.

4. Transfer fruit and orris root powder[nd]spice mixture to a large (gallon-size) zipper-lock plastic bag. Seal the bag, and shake to fully cover fruit with spices. Unseal the bag a bit, and let the fruit sit for 3 to 7 days, shaking at least once a day to refresh and recover fruit with spices. It's important that the bag be left open or fruit left out in the open to better air-dry. The longer you let fruit dry in the air before placing them in the dehydrator, the less time it will take for them to finish in the dehydrator.

5. After the 3rd to 7th day, set the dehydrator to 115°F to 135°F. (The longer you air-dry fruit, the lower the temperature should be.)

6. Remove fruit from spice mixture, and discard spice mixture. Evenly arrange fruit on the dehydrator trays, leaving space between them.

7. Dehydrate for 24 to 36 hours. Fruits will be hard.

8. Tie with festive ribbons, package in tissue paper if giving as a gift, or hang. Pomander balls should stay fragrant from 6 months to 1 year.

> **CHEF'S CHOICE**
>
> Your 1 cup spice blend can consist of whatever you like, but try this mixture: ½ cup ground cinnamon, ¼ cup ground nutmeg, and ¼ cup pumpkin pie spice blend. You also can use allspice, ground cloves, ginger, mace, etc. Whatever you like!

If you're planning on hanging your pomander balls from a tree, insert a metal paper clip into the top of each ball when you're adding the cloves. Unfold the paper clip, and jab in each end, pushing them in at angles so they "hook" the fruit. Then attach ornament holders on top when the balls are dry, and voilà! You have a lovely Christmas ornament.

Creating Pretty Packages for Your Dried Gifts

I used to fret about packaging my dehydrated gifts. I can present the prettiest platters of foods, plate desserts almost as good as a professionally trained pastry chef, and whip up the most fantastically decorated cakes, but when it comes to packaging, I'm no Martha Stewart. Wrapping and packaging gifts used to give me the biggest cases of anxiety. I could make a darn good-lookin' gift, but the package surrounding it often looked like something a third-grader wrapped.

Then my friend (and co-author of *The Complete Idiot's Guide to Wine and Food Pairing*) Jaclyn Stuart introduced me to decorative plastic bags. They don't require much cutting or measuring, you don't need a bunch of exotic craft supplies you'll never use again, and you don't need to own a glue gun. These bags are the easiest way to package your home-dried foods as gifts. The bags also work well for dog treats, especially if the bags have paw prints on them, and you can use them for pomander balls and small portions of potpourri, too. Most craft stores like Michaels carry a variety of sizes, colors, and even holiday-themed bags and ribbons to match. Just pop in your dried goodies, tie a bow, and you're set.

Another way to contain your home-dried gifts is to use canning jars. Cover the lid with a brightly colored square of fabric, and tie with a ribbon. Canning jars are particularly good when packaging things like soup mixes. Add a tag—either premade or cut out from construction paper—and you have a great gift ready to give. If you're packaging soup, tea, or dried mixes, include cooking or baking instructions so your recipients know how to enjoy your gifts.

Decorative tins and boxes lined with tissue paper work well for cookies, dried fruits, and fruit leathers. A box of three different kinds of fruit leathers, including apple spice, makes a great teacher's gift. Craft stores often have a great selection of tins and boxes. You often can find them at garage sales, too.

The decorative tins and boxes also work well for potpourris and dried flower gifts. Or package potpourri in pretty cloth bags tied with string.

You also can package your dried fruits or vegetables in sealed plastic bags and then place the bags in decorative, colored Chinese food take-out boxes. Craft stores sell them, and they're fun gift wrappers!

 DRYING TIP

If you'd like to experiment with more advanced packaging techniques, I highly recommend *Gourmet Gifts: 100 Delicious Recipes for Every Occasion to Make Yourself and Wrap with Style* by Dinah Corley. Corley's book includes some amazing packaging ideas, and even if you're not good at wrapping (like me), her instructions are easy to follow and understand.

The Least You Need to Know

- Almost anything you dry can become a gift.
- Always dry flowers at lower temperatures than what you use for drying foods.
- It takes a lot of petals to create a potpourri, so start with more than you'll need.
- Potpourri and pomander balls make fun, festive, and fragrant gifts.
- Decorative plastic bags are the easiest way to package your gifts.

Glossary

artisan   Food that's handcrafted in small batches. Also a person who handcrafts food.

ascorbic acid   Another name for vitamin C.

blanch   To cook vegetables by plunging them into a pot of boiling water. *See also* refresh.

buckwheat groats   A nutty-tasting, whole grain often used in raw food cooking. *See also* raw food.

citric acid   A natural preservative; an acid found in citrus fruits.

cold water bath   A technique in which you stop the cooking process of fruits or vegetables by plunging them into a bowl filled with cold water and ice cubes.

crack   To soften or tenderize the skin of a fruit so moisture can more easily evaporate when the fruit is drying.

dehydrate   To remove moisture from foods using heat.

dice   To chop finely.

dry   To remove moisture. Can be used interchangeably with *dehydrate*.

E. coli   *Escherichia coli* is a type of bacteria that can cause severe food poisoning.

enzymes   Molecules, mostly protein, that perform many of cells' chemical reactions.

fixative   A substance that keeps potpourri, sachets, and dried pomander balls fragrant and smelling fresh.

food dehydrator   A kitchen appliance that produces heat to dry foods, similar to an oven, but the heat it produces isn't as hot as an oven's. Most high-quality dehydrators also have a fan to circulate the air flow for evaporation.

food grade A minimum standard of quality for products or substances the U.S. Department of Agriculture determines are okay for handling food safely.

freeze-dry To quickly freeze food and then use a strong vacuum to remove the moisture.

freezer burn When air trapped inside or surrounding a frozen container destroys the food inside.

jerky gun A piping tool for making beef jerky. It looks like a cookie dough shooter or a pastry gun, but it's used for meat.

kasha Another name for buckwheat groats.

kosher salt Salt that comes in larger-size granules than table salt and most sea salts. It has been blessed by a rabbi. Does not contain iodine.

local Food grown, raised, or produced close by, usually within a 100-mile radius, but that distance can be expanded to a region of one or two states.

locavore Someone who embraces and tries to eat local foods, often grown within a 100-mile radius of his or her home.

mandoline A cooking utensil used for slicing, with two parallel working surfaces, which can be adjusted in size for the width of cuts.

mise-en-place A French term that means "everything in its place."

nitrate A naturally occurring chemical that contains nitrogen (hence the name) and is added to cured and smoked jerkies and sausages to prevent botulism. Nitrates become nitrites during the curing process.

nitrite Another type of naturally occurring chemical that contains nitrogen (hence the name) and is added to cured and smoked jerkies to prevent botulism.

organic A practice of farming that uses lower amounts of pesticides, fertilizers, and other chemicals.

orris root powder The best fixative to make potpourri, sachets, and dried pomander balls. It's made from the root of a specific type of iris and used by itself to keep linens smelling sweet and fresh.

oxidation When fruits and vegetables turn brown as a result of being exposed to oxygen.

pan-fry To cook large pieces of food, with a little fat, over medium to medium-high heat, occasionally stirring or flipping.

pemmican A mixture of venison or buffalo meat, fat, berries, and herbs packed into containers made of animal hides.

raw food A diet in which people try to eat foods as close to their natural state as possible. Dehydrators are often used to dry foods instead of cooking them.

refresh To put vegetables in a bowl of ice-cold water to stop the cooking process after they've been blanched. *See also* blanch.

rehydrate To add water to dried foods.

salmonella A type of bacteria that can cause severe food poisoning.

sauté To cook small pieces of food quickly, using a small amount of oil, over very high heat, stirring or jerking the pan so all the ingredients heat together evenly. It's not the same technique as pan-frying.

Scoville scale The scale used to measure the amount of heat in a hot pepper.

sea salt Salt that's harvested from the sea. Usually does not contain iodine, unless indicated on package.

sodium metabisulfite A chemical compound recommended for home drying instead of sulfur dioxide.

solar food dehydrator A contraption that helps accelerate sun-drying of foods.

steam To cook using moist heat or steam.

steel A rod that sharpens your knife when you rub the blade edge against it.

sulfur A chemical element added to dried foods to prevent oxidation.

sulfur dioxide A chemical compound used in many commercially dried fruits. It's not recommended for home use because it's a toxic gas.

sun-dry To dry foods in the sun.

table salt Finely ground salt or sodium chloride. Often called iodized salt, but it does not necessarily contain iodine.

umami The fifth taste, a savory flavor that doesn't fall into the sweet, salty, sour, or bitter categories.

vacuum sealer An appliance that removes air from food-storage bags or jars.

vegan Food that contains no dairy, meat, or eggs. Also a lifestyle where these ingredients, and all animal products, are avoided.

Resources

In this appendix, I've gathered several great resources to further your dehydrating journey. Check these sites for supplies and equipment, recipes, safety and preservation tips, and so much more.

Backpacking Chef
backpackingchef.com

Canning Pantry
canningpantry.com/dehydration-of-food.html

Choosing Raw
choosingraw.com

Colorado State University Extension
www.ext.colostate.edu

Dehydrate2Store
dehydrate2store.com

The Dry Store
drystore.com

Excalibur
excaliburdehydrator.com

Fooducate
fooducate.com/blog

Jerky Gun
jerkygun.com

LocalHarvest
localharvest.com

National Center for Home Food Preservation
nchfp.uga.edu

Nielsen-Massey Vanillas
nielsenmassey.com

Penzeys Spices
penzeys.com

The Sausage Maker, Inc.
sausagemaker.com

The Spice House
thespicehouse.com

University of Wisconsin-Extension
uwex.edu

Troubleshooting

In this appendix, I've assembled some of the most common questions new dehydrating enthusiasts might have.

Why aren't my tomatoes/peaches/leather drying fast enough?

If your foods aren't drying fast enough, keep reading. One of the following questions might hold the answer.

What happens if I crowd the food on my dehydrator trays?

If you fit in every last onion or crowd on extra banana slices or pour in just a dollop more of fruit purée, it might take longer to dry.

There's a reason you're instructed to evenly place food pieces on your dehydrator trays—foods dry more quickly when air can circulate freely around them. When you crowd food pieces too closely together, the air doesn't circulate as well, so moisture takes longer to evaporate from foods.

To remedy this, simply remove the trays from the dehydrator and remove some of the food to give the remaining food pieces more space. Then, when the first trays are done, you can add the not-finished pieces back to finish drying.

Or at the very least, stir the food pieces around on the trays and move the trays around in the dehydrator to get the air circulating around the food a bit better.

Your food should be just one layer per tray. Don't crowd or stack food on a tray.

Do I have to "crack" the skin on the fruits?

If you chose not to boil the cherries or figs or another thick-skinned fruit, the fruit won't dry evenly, and it will take at least—*at least*—6 to 8 additional hours to dry.

If you forgot to crack the skin—or you didn't let them boil long enough—try poking the skin of the fruit pieces with a fork or a toothpick. That might eliminate some of the extra drying time, but it's not as good as actually cracking the skin on the fruits.

Do I have to blanch or pretreat the vegetables?

If you choose not to pretreat the vegetables, they will take longer to dry.

Why do I have to slice the vegetables or fruits so thin?

If you don't slice the vegetables or fruits thin enough, they will take longer to dry. Whole garlic—not pretreated and not sliced—won't properly dry at all. Thick tomatoes will take at least 12 hours longer to dry.

Tomatoes and most fruits should be about ¼ inch thick or thinner. If you slice them to ½ inch thickness, it may take them an extra 4 hours to try. Anything above ½ inch thickness will take an exceptionally long time to dry.

If you find this is a problem, remove the vegetables from the dehydrator, slice them thin enough, and put them back in the dehydrator to see if they'll dry more quickly.

What happens if I pour too much fruit purée on the sheet for my fruit leather?

The thicker you smooth the purée on the sheet, the longer it takes to dry.

Why do I have to flip over the crackers?

Flipping the crackers over during the dehydration period makes them dry more evenly and more quickly.

What if I don't slice the jerky thin enough?

Thicker jerky slices take longer to dry. Because you can't re-slice them thinner without re-marinating them, just remember to slice them thinner the next time.

How do I know if I'm drying this fruit/vegetable/jerky at the right temperature?

Always follow the recipe. If you dry foods at a different temperature than what the recipe calls for, the cooking time will vary accordingly.

What if I don't have a temperature gauge on my dehydrator?

Use a meat thermometer to check to see what your dehydrator's temperature is set at. Many dehydrators without a temperature gauge have a temperature of about 130°F. So except for vegetables, herbs, and raw foods, your drying temperature will be different from what many recipes call for. You'll need to take note of how long it takes for *you* to dry certain foods. That means you'll dry your veggies and herbs for a shorter period of time, and technically, your raw foods will not be raw.

What if I don't have a convection fan in my dehydrator?

If you don't have a convection fan your food will take longer to dry, even if they're drying at the correct temperature. A convection fan circulates the air through the dehydrator so all the food pieces dry more evenly. To compensate, you may have to flip the food pieces or move the trays around as the foods dry.

I have a temperature gauge and a convection fan, but my foods still are taking longer to dry. What's up?

Test your dehydrator using a meat thermometer to see if it's actually drying foods at the temperatures it's supposed to be drying foods. If it's not heating up properly, you may have to fix your dehydrator, or you might just need to turn up the heat a little bit.

The temperature is working on my dehydrator, and my foods are still taking longer to dry.

How humid is it, right now, in your kitchen? More humidity equals greater drying times. Less humidity equals quicker drying times.

In my kitchen, I find it's much quicker and easier to dry foods in the fall than in the summer when it's hot and humid. If I lived in Arizona, I'd be drying foods more quickly all year long, but if I lived in Georgia, I'd be drying foods more slowly all year long. It just depends on where you live.

My peaches have flattened to an undesirable shape as they are drying. Is there any way to fix that?

Sometimes, overripe fruit just does that. It just happens. The dehydrated food will taste just as good, even if it looks kind of smooshed.

These leeks/cucumbers/whatever have dried up to almost nothing. Are they still nutritionally sound?

Yes. Dehydrated fruits and vegetables—even though they take up, in some cases, less than half of the space they took up when they were fresh—are just as nutritious as their fresh versions. They just don't have any water in them.

And because you removed the water at a lower temperature than cooking would, you actually preserved more of the nutrients in the food. That's why raw food enthusiasts love the dehydrator—it "cooks" without changing the enzymes or nutrients in foods.

Why does part of my fruit leather dry fast, but there are still sticky spots in the middle?

If you don't spread the fruit purée evenly across your sheet, there may be wet bumps in the middle. If it seems exceptionally lumpy, spread part of it onto another sheet instead of trying to spread all the purée onto one tray.

To correct a bump, just simply pull or cut away the leather that's already cooked. That will get the air circulating closer to what needs to be dried while not overdrying the rest of the leather.

Why does my leather crack sometimes?

Sometimes, leather cracks when you overdry it. If one particular recipe regularly cracks, you might also try adding 1 or 2 teaspoons pectin or adding $\frac{1}{2}$ cup applesauce to the recipe to correct the situation. Fruits lower in pectin crack more in leather form.

My leather is stuck to the wax paper. What do I do?

Throw it away. Wax paper, while fine to wrap your leathers after they're cooked, is *not* good to line your trays because the fruit purée bonds to the wax. Don't use wax paper.

I've heard that some people spray their wax paper with oil first, and that works, but I'd rather just use dehydrator tray sheets made of silicone and sometimes called Teflex sheets. They're an expense up front, but they're worth every penny.

If you don't have such sheets, silicone baking sheets are a good substitute. If you don't have those kind of baking sheets, line your trays with parchment paper. Parchment paper, unlike wax paper, does not stick to fruit leather.

If you don't have parchment paper, try plastic wrap. Although plastic wrap works, sometimes the ends fold over, which makes drying the ends of your leather problematic, resulting in gummy, not-quite-dried ends.

Why do the nuts I add to the pudding and fruit leathers I make always seem to fall off after the leathers are dried?

You need to gently press the nuts into the leathers. If you just sprinkle them on top, the leathers will dry without binding to the nuts so the nuts will fall off.

Index

W-X-Y-Z

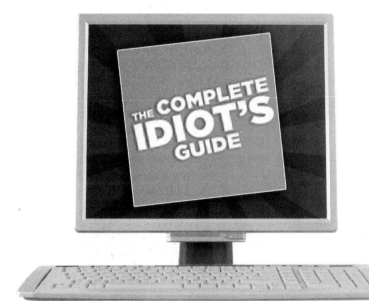